I0011891

Early Praise for *Kotlin Coroutine Confidence*

The first tech book I could not put down. Sam has created something truly special; it is brilliantly structured, effortlessly engaging, and full of moments that make complex ideas click. If you are an engineer who loves a well-told technical story, then you will get a lot from this book, maybe even a new appreciation for Kotlin.

➤ **Rob Chapman**
  Author of Observability with Grafana

A compelling journey through the intricacies of Kotlin coroutines, this book delivers a perfect cocktail of practical wisdom and best practices. It's a fun and fruitful read whether you're new to coroutines or looking to deepen your expertise.

➤ **Joffrey Bion**
  Senior Developer

Sam's writing is fantastic; he has the ability to reframe knowledge often taken for granted, not only to aid with the matter at hand but to take away as a solid ground for teaching peers. Reading his work makes me a better engineer!

➤ **Amy Jo Turner**
  Software Engineer

This book is essential reading for folks coming to Kotlin's approach to concurrency from other languages—whether from Java, JavaScript, C#, or something else. It covers the similarities as well as the important differences. I will be encouraging my employer to buy some copies and make this required reading for folks working in Kotlin.

➤ **Martin Sandiford**
Senior Engineering Manager

Sam has distilled this complex but highly valuable topic into an easily understandable format so we can quickly learn and readily apply it to create high-performance asynchronous applications.

➤ **Venkat Subramaniam**
Award-winning author and Founder, Agile Developer, Inc.

Kotlin Coroutine Confidence

Untangle Your Async, Ship Safety at Speed

Sam Cooper

The Pragmatic Bookshelf

Dallas, Texas

Pragmatic
Bookshelf

See our complete catalog of hands-on, practical,
and Pragmatic content for software developers:
https://pragprog.com

Sales, volume licensing, and support:
support@pragprog.com

Derivative works, AI training and testing,
international translations, and other rights:
rights@pragprog.com

The team that produced this book includes:

Publisher:	Dave Thomas
COO:	Janet Furlow
Executive Editor:	Susannah Davidson
Development Editor:	Michael Swaine
Copy Editor:	Karen Galle
Indexing:	Potomac Indexing, LLC
Layout:	Gilson Graphics

Copyright © 2025 The Pragmatic Programmers, LLC.

All rights reserved. No part of this publication may be reproduced by any means, nor may any derivative works be made from this publication, nor may this content be used to train or test an artificial intelligence system, without the prior consent of the publisher.

When we are aware that a term used in this book is claimed as a trademark, the designation is printed with an initial capital letter or in all capitals.

The Pragmatic Starter Kit, The Pragmatic Programmer, Pragmatic Programming, Pragmatic Bookshelf, PragProg, and the linking *g* device are trademarks of The Pragmatic Programmers, LLC.

Every precaution was taken in the preparation of this book. However, the publisher assumes no responsibility for errors or omissions or for damages that may result from the use of information (including program listings) contained herein.

ISBN-13: 979-8-88865-155-1
Book version: P1.0—August 2025

Contents

Part II — Better Together

Acknowledgments

One of the things I love most about creating software, and especially about working with Kotlin, is being surrounded by a community of smart, creative, and endlessly helpful people who love what they do. This book only exists because it has just such a group behind it.

First and foremost, I must thank my developmental editor, Michael Swaine, for guiding me tirelessly through the process of publishing my first full-length book. I couldn't have asked for a more knowledgeable and experienced mentor on this journey. I also want to thank Sandra Williams, who patiently coached me through countless early drafts of the opening chapters.

The book has benefited immensely from thorough technical reviews by software engineers and fellow authors whose opinions I deeply value and respect. Thank you to Rob Chapman, Venkat Subramaniam, Joffrey Bion, Martin Sandiford, James Baker, and Amy Jo Turner for your time, your support, and your valuable suggestions. In addition to those reviewers, I'm grateful to everyone who read the beta version of the book and took the time to point out opportunities to improve the final release. The entire text has also been meticulously checked and polished by my copy editor, Karen Galle, who has my sincere appreciation.

I'm particularly indebted to the legendary Dave Thomas for his insightful feedback, which made this a better book and me a better writer. I also thank Susannah Davidson, Janet Furlow, Dave Rankin, and everyone else at The Pragmatic Programmers who has contributed to making this book the best it can be.

Among that group is Margaret Eldridge, whom I thank for her help with everything from the initial proposal to the book's presence on forums and social media. Margaret first approached me about writing a book for The Pragmatic Bookshelf in 2023. Here, I also thank Anupam Chugh, along with his team at *Better Programming*, who welcomed me so warmly into the world of tech authorship and helped me publish the early stories and articles that caught Margaret's eye.

Next, I'm hugely thankful to everyone who's worked or corresponded with me throughout my Kotlin coroutine career. I've learned an immeasurable amount from colleagues, online strangers, and the amazing Kotlin community. Thank you to the team at JetBrains for creating the Kotlin language, and especially to coroutine mastermind Roman Elizarov.

Finally, I'm grateful to you for joining me on this journey. Thank you, and enjoy!

Introduction

For as long as I've been writing code, programming has been a tale of two styles.

One is the undisputed heavyweight champion—the original programming paradigm we all know and love. It's sequential. It's synchronous. It's structured. It lays out its statements in a clear and logical parade of loops, function calls, and conditionals.

In the other corner is the lightweight challenger. Zipping from thread to thread with freedom and agility, the callbacks and continuations of asynchronous code weave a dancing web that juggles inputs, outputs, and user interactions with unmatched efficiency.

Asynchronous programming has long held the advantage when it comes to responsive user interfaces and high throughput. But its stilted, stitched-together style often falls far short of the ergonomic control flow, resource management, and error handling that have earned synchronous programming its unassailable spot at the top.

So, for years, the two have been locked in a stalemate.

Today, old-fashioned synchronous programming styles are staging a comeback. More and more languages have begun introducing features and frameworks that bridge the gap, letting us write clear and sequential programs that execute with the speed and efficiency of asynchronous code.

Kotlin's coroutines are part of this renaissance. And with structured concurrency, they have a secret weapon that could turn the tide and solve some of asynchronous programming's greatest flaws.

Who Is This Book For?

If you write Kotlin code, this book is for you.

Coroutines have something to offer for almost every program. Whether you build mobile apps, web pages, back-end servers, or something else altogether, you can use the tools and techniques in this book to improve your code and enhance your development experience.

For those new to coroutines, the book will take you on a step-by-step journey. We'll jump right in with a real-world example of an asynchronous program, and we'll gradually build on that foundation with a new topic in each chapter. You'll learn how coroutines can upgrade your asynchronous code and how they compare with other tools you might have used, both in Kotlin and in other languages.

Perhaps you've already started using coroutines, and you're here to learn more about them. Yes, we'll answer all those frustrating questions. Why can't I launch a coroutine there? Why does that function work that way? And what's this exception doing here? You'll learn about the unique challenges that come with asynchronous programming and concurrency and understand how each tool in your coroutine toolbox has been carefully designed to help solve these problems.

Online Resources

You'll find a dedicated page[1] for this book on the Pragmatic Bookshelf website. From there, you can download the complete source code for all the examples you'll be working with. If you're reading the book in digital form, you'll also find a handy link above each code snippet that'll bring you directly to the source file.

Got feedback or questions? Follow the links on the book's webpage to find the DevTalk forum, where you can report a mistake, make a suggestion, or discuss what you've learned with other readers.

What You'll Need

Before you start, you should already be familiar with the Kotlin programming language. We will be looking closely at how coroutines work with common control-flow structures—things like functions, loops, and try–catch–finally blocks—so it'll help if you have a clear understanding of how those basics work in everyday code.

As we introduce each topic, we'll work through a code example where we use coroutines to solve a real-life problem. If you'd like to follow along with the

---

1. http://pragprog.com/titles/sckotlin

code examples in the book, you'll also need to be comfortable using an IDE like IntelliJ IDEA or Android Studio, setting up and executing a simple project, and adding dependencies. If you'd rather read the code without running it, that's fine, too!

For simplicity, we'll run our code examples in a desktop Java environment. They've been written and tested using Kotlin 2.1 and Java 21, but they should work fine on any recent version. We won't include any code examples for other targets, aside from one or two illustrative Android snippets, but when there are changes required to translate the code from platform to platform, we'll talk about what those are.

What's in This Book?

We'll begin our journey with a simple program that uses coroutines to wait for outside events without blocking its thread. To do so, we'll introduce suspending functions, which are the building blocks that give coroutines their power. We'll compare them to ordinary functions and to other kinds of asynchronous programming. Why use suspending functions instead of callbacks or blocked threads? We'll build a photo gallery app that demonstrates how coroutines can give us the best of both worlds, keeping our single-threaded user interface code clean and responsive.

But why do suspending functions come with extra rules and syntax—restrictions that don't seem to apply to other solutions like callbacks and futures? As we continue to improve our photo gallery app, we'll add a coroutine scope and use its coroutine builder functions to add new coroutines to an existing application. We'll compare this to the ways we might make an asynchronous call in other languages or frameworks, and we'll see how Kotlin's approach is protecting us from a memory leak minefield.

Coroutines aren't just for user interface code, and we'll use them to harness the multitasking power of any asynchronous operation. As we do so, we'll also learn about the rules that link our tasks together into a safe, structured hierarchy. We'll make sure errors don't go missing, and we'll use cooperative cancellation to stop our coroutines becoming resource-stealing zombies.

Next, we'll stage a contest to pit our coroutines against old-fashioned threads. You'll learn why coroutines are sometimes called *lightweight threads*, and we'll use a new coroutine dispatcher to give our coroutines an even bigger speed boost with parallel execution.

Coroutines can interoperate with almost any other asynchronous programming style you can think of. They can even call blocking functions if you use the right dispatcher. You'll learn some built-in functions and facilities to convert between threads, coroutines, callbacks, and futures, and we'll even try our hand at creating our own suspension point from scratch. As we near the end of our journey, we'll introduce flows, using them to encapsulate asynchronous procedures and integrate with Reactive Streams.

Since no software is complete without tests, we'll wrap up with some handy tools and techniques for testing the coroutines we've written.

Ready to get started?

Let's dive into the world of coroutines and write our first suspending function!

Part I

Best of Both Worlds

Familiar sequential control flow, or responsive user interfaces? Powerful parallel processing, or low-cost lightweight execution? Safe, predictable outcomes, or efficient asynchronous multitasking? It's a world full of compromises—but it doesn't have to be.

In the first part of this book, you'll learn to speak the language of coroutines. We'll unpick all of those difficult choices, and you'll assemble the coroutine tools and techniques to make them each a thing of the past.

CHAPTER 1

Wait Without Worrying

Today's apps and servers are constantly interacting with the world—through networks, user inputs, sensors, and more. All those things take time, and so computer programs spend a lot of their time simply waiting for things outside their own control.

In Kotlin, coroutines are there to make all that waiting as efficient as possible.

This chapter is where you'll write and execute your first coroutine. Using a suspending function, you'll pause your new coroutine without blocking its thread. Finally, you'll apply that knowledge to fix an unresponsive program that's stuck waiting for a timer.

What Is a Coroutine?

Before we jump in and start writing that coroutine, let's take a look at the problem we'll be using it to solve. You'll see what can go wrong when an important thread gets blocked, and you'll begin to understand how Kotlin's coroutines can change the rules.

Our journey begins with a puzzling story.

Puzzling Problems

Theo loves jigsaw puzzles. He's never happier than when he's sitting at the kitchen table, lost among the colorful pieces of a half-finished picture.

It's a great table, by the way—wide, sturdy, and flat. Everything you could want a table to be. It takes up half the room, and it's the center of family life. Or at least, it should be.

The problems start when it's time for dinner. The family would normally sit at the table to eat their meal, but now the table is unavailable. Theo's puzzle is nearly finished, but not quite—and it's not in a state where it can be moved. Try to clear it off the table, and the puzzle pieces would fall apart, undoing all of Theo's hard work. Instead, the family meal takes place in an uncomfortable huddle on the sofa while the huge table sits unused.

Theo's table represents a thread in a computer program, and his jigsaw puzzle is a function that's running on it. A running function lives on a thread and doesn't leave until it's finished. So, when the code in the function takes a break, the thread is blocked. Inactive but unavailable.

Our story has a happy ending, though. One day, Cory comes home with a big grin on his face.

"I've got it!"

He produces a great big wooden tray, laying it flat on the table.

"Next time, do your jigsaw puzzle on this tray. Then, when it's time for dinner, we'll move the tray, and the table will be free!"

Cory's puzzle tray represents a coroutine. It's an activity that can be paused and resumed, occupying a thread only when it's in use. When a function that's running in a coroutine needs to take a break, the coroutine *suspends*, vacating the thread so other tasks can use it.

Coroutines in Other Languages

 In Kotlin, a coroutine is a thread-like activity that can pause and resume its execution. In other programming languages, the word *coroutine* might mean something slightly different. We'll talk a little more about this in Chapter 10, Go with the Flow, on page 161.

Pick Your Thread

One place where thread management can be particularly important is in a graphical user interface. Let's apply Theo's story to a real programming challenge. We'll start with a faulty UI that's not managing its threads correctly and then learn how we can fix it with a coroutine.

For simplicity, we'll be using the Swing toolkit that comes with Java—but the techniques and concepts you learn in this chapter will apply equally to many other programs, including Android apps.

To write safe user interface code in Swing, we'll need to start with a call to SwingUtilities.invokeLater():

timers/v1/src/main/kotlin/com/example/timers/TimerApplication.kt
```kotlin
fun main() = SwingUtilities.invokeLater {
  // TODO: UI code goes here
}
```

This is Java's equivalent of Android's runOnUiThread() function, and you'll recognize it if you've worked with Swing before. It sends our code to run on the framework's main UI thread, where we can safely create and update user interface components. Remember this because it's central to the first problem we'll be using coroutines to solve.

Build a User Interface

With our starting thread selected, we're ready to display some UI components. For now, our app has no coroutines—we'll add those later:

timers/v2/src/main/kotlin/com/example/timers/TimerApplication.kt
```kotlin
fun main() = SwingUtilities.invokeLater {
  val window = JFrame("Timer")
  window.defaultCloseOperation = JFrame.DISPOSE_ON_CLOSE
  window.size = Dimension(400, 300)
  window.isVisible = true

  val message = "Please wait for ten seconds…"
  val label = window.add(JLabel(message, JLabel.CENTER)) as JLabel

  Thread.sleep(10_000)
  label.text = "Done!"
}
```

Even if you're not familiar with Swing, it's easy enough to get a rough idea of what this code's supposed to do. It displays a message, waits for 10 seconds, and then announces that it's done. Or at least, it should.

Blocked Threads

Go ahead and run the code, and you'll simply see a blank window, at least until the 10 seconds are up, as shown in the figure on page 6.

There's no sign of the text that the program was supposed to display. But that's not even the worst of its issues.

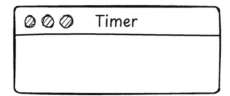

Notice what happens when you try to resize the window, or even close it, while the Thread.sleep() function is pausing the thread's activity. The UI won't react to any inputs, and your cursor will most likely change to a waiting indicator to let you know that the application isn't responding.

Like Theo's unfinished jigsaw puzzle hogging the kitchen table, our timer program is tied to the thread where it started executing. So, when it wants to stop and wait, its thread has to wait, too. A thread that's forced to do nothing like this is referred to as *blocked*.

Not Just Any Thread

Using a single *main thread* is how Swing, Android, and other graphical app frameworks make sure things can only happen one at a time. Their UI toolkits are built for speed and simplicity and aren't meant to handle simultaneous updates from different threads in different parts of the application.

But the UI thread isn't just the place where we have to set up our components. It's also the nerve center of the user interface, handling every incoming user interaction and every change to what's displayed on-screen. For the app to remain responsive, this thread must always be available to react quickly to incoming events. Block the thread, and the UI will be completely frozen, unable to update its visual state or process new inputs.

In our program, we've called Thread.sleep() right in the middle of a code block that's running on the main UI thread. While the thread is busy inside that function, it can't handle any new inputs, and that's why our application is unresponsive.

Our simple desktop app will probably recover from its ordeal, but mobile apps can be more impatient. Android will reward you with a nasty error message if your code is unresponsive for too long. Have you ever seen this in an app you've built or used?

> Application isn't responding
>
> ✕   Close app
>
> 🕐   Wait

Blocked threads can increase resource usage or impede important tasks in any program, but in user interface code, they're an absolute no-go. You need to be able to wait for data and inputs without relying on thread-blocking functions that could freeze your app and ruin the user experience.

Cory solved Theo's problem by finding a way to move the half-finished jigsaw puzzle out of the way, leaving the table free for other activities. In the rest of this chapter, you'll apply the same idea to fix this timer code with coroutines.

Suspend Your First Function

You've seen how things can go wrong when an important thread gets blocked, and you've learned what kind of solution coroutines might offer. It's time to introduce the tools we'll be using to swap our sleeping thread for a suspended coroutine.

In this section, we're going to put the UI code to one side for a while, and you'll learn the coroutine basics on their own. Once you know how to create, suspend, and resume a coroutine, you'll be ready to put it all back together and fix that unresponsive application.

Suspend, Don't Block

The Thread.sleep() function is like a car that's parked in the middle of the street. While it's stopped, the road is blocked. No other traffic can get by, which is why our user interface stops responding to all our instructions and inputs.

There's more than one way to solve this problem, and we'll start comparing some other approaches in Chapter 2, Escape From Callback Hell, on page 17. For now, we'll jump right in with our first coroutine. We'll be replacing that Thread.sleep() function with a different instruction—one that tells the code to pull up somewhere safely out of the way, leaving the thread clear for other traffic.

In Kotlin, a function that can pause its execution without blocking its thread is called a *suspending function*. Suspending functions are the key building blocks of coroutines.

Blocked Threads, Suspended Coroutines

- A thread that's waiting for something is *blocked*. It can't do anything else.

- A waiting coroutine is *suspended*. The underlying thread is free to run other code.

An Important Dependency

Kotlin's suspending equivalent of the Thread.sleep() function is called delay(), and it's part of the core kotlinx.coroutines library. Let's add that package to our dependencies so we can start using the delay() function in our code:

timers/v3/build.gradle.kts
```
dependencies {
    implementation("org.jetbrains.kotlinx:kotlinx-coroutines-core:1.10.1")
}
```

This library is packed with general-purpose tools for working with coroutines and suspending functions, and we'll be using it as a starting point for pretty much everything we do in this book.

With the dependency in place, we've got access to the delay() function that we want to use. But if you try calling it, even in the simplest of programs, you're going to run into a problem:

timers/v3/src/main/kotlin/com/example/timers/TimerApplication.kt
```
import kotlinx.coroutines.*

fun main() {
    println("Waiting for ten seconds…")
    delay(10_000) // oops!
    println("Done!")
}
```

The code doesn't compile, and the build fails:

```
> Task :compileKotlin FAILED
```

```
Suspend function 'delay(…)' should be called only from a coroutine
  or another suspend function.
```

Suspension Restrictions

What is it that stops us from calling delay() in ordinary code?

Take a look at its documentation[1] or source code, and you'll see that it starts its signature with the word suspend:

```
suspend fun delay(timeMillis: Long)
```

This new suspend keyword is a function modifier like private, override, inline, and so on. It's what marks delay() as a suspending function, letting Kotlin know that it contains instructions that will suspend its coroutine.

An instruction that suspends a coroutine is called a *suspension point*. These special instructions are easy to spot because a function containing a suspension point will always have the suspend modifier. Remember this because it'll be the key to solving our problem.

Now, to use a suspension point, your code must be running in a coroutine. Calling delay() with no coroutine would be like trying to move Theo's jigsaw puzzle off the table without ever having put it on the movable tray in the first place. Cory's solution only works if Theo remembers to put the tray down on the table before starting work on the puzzle.

We didn't do anything special when we started our program, so it's running directly on a thread. Kotlin isn't going to let us call functions that have the suspend modifier because those contain suspension points that aren't applicable to our non-coroutine program.

Coroutine Inception

Clearly, we're going to need a coroutine. So, how do we get one? The answer is simpler than you might think. We need to let Kotlin know that the program contains suspension points, and it'll take care of the rest. Read on to learn how.

You've learned that the delay() function contains a suspension point—an instruction that will suspend its coroutine. We'll be taking a look at these special coroutine-suspending instructions much later in Chapter 9, Upgrade

---

1.   https://kotlinlang.org/api/kotlinx.coroutines/kotlinx-coroutines-core/kotlinx.coroutines/delay.html

Every Callback, on page 145. But those are just the nuts and bolts that other suspension points are built on top of.

Calling a function means executing the instructions it contains, and that means an instruction to call a suspending function such as delay() is itself an instruction that will suspend its caller's coroutine. Since a suspending function contains suspension points, every call to a suspending function is itself a suspension point.

Instructions Inside Instructions

 There are two types of suspension points:

1. The special instruction that suspends the coroutine.
2. Any instruction that includes another suspension point as part of its execution.

Do you remember how Kotlin keeps track of which functions contain suspension points? That's right—a function containing a suspension point must always have the suspend modifier.

In other words, to invoke a suspending function, the caller must also be a suspending function. This is the foundational rule of coroutines in Kotlin, and it's one you're going to become familiar with as you continue your coroutine journey.

Create a Coroutine

The main() function of the program we just wrote isn't a suspending function, so it's not allowed to call delay().

Lucky for us, that's easy to fix. All we need to do is add the suspend modifier to our own code. You'll add the suspend keyword any time you write a function that uses suspension points to wait for things:

timers/v4/src/main/kotlin/com/example/timers/TimerApplication.kt
```kotlin
suspend fun main() {
  println("Waiting for ten seconds…")
  delay(10_000)
  println("Done!")
}
```

Now that our main() function is a suspending function, it's free to include suspension points. That means it can call other suspending functions such as delay(). The program compiles and even runs without any problems:

```
Waiting for ten seconds…
Done!
```

If you're using IntelliJ IDEA or Android Studio, notice the suspension point icon in the left-hand margin of the code, next to the delay() function. It looks like an arrow that's been split in two by a wavy line crossing through it.

$$\text{-}\!\rightsquigarrow\!\rightarrow \mid delay(...)$$

You'll see this icon any time you call a suspending function.

Coroutines and Threads

When you fire up a program with a regular, plain old main() function, it starts running directly on a thread. Add the suspend modifier, as we just did, and now Kotlin knows that this code needs to be wrapped up in a coroutine. That means our entire program can suspend and resume without blocking its thread. In jigsaw puzzle terms, we've told our program to place the tray down on the table before it starts work.

So, by running this program, you've just run your first coroutine. Congratulations! How does it feel?

When suspending functions execute, they execute as coroutines. To remember the relationship, think of the suspending function like the script for a play and a coroutine as the performance. It can also be helpful to think of coroutines as Kotlin's suspending equivalent of threads—though, as you've already learned, there's still a thread underneath.

Keep the Main Thread Clear

Now you know how to create a coroutine and how to pause its execution without blocking the thread it's running on. In the final section of this chapter, you'll put those skills to use in fixing the broken timer app.

But there's still one piece of the puzzle missing. To combine suspending functions with user interface code, you'll need to learn how to choose which thread your coroutine runs on.

Close, But Not Quite

You might have suspended your first coroutine, but you haven't yet had a chance to see it do anything particularly useful. A program's main() function always has its own thread and won't normally have to worry about sharing it. With no other tasks vying for time on the thread, we were never going to gain much from using suspending functions to keep the thread clear.

But in our timer app, things are different. Since it's creating user interface components, the code needs to run on Swing's main UI thread. We're sharing that thread with the rest of Swing's inner workings, and we need to let go of it when we're not using it. That's exactly where the suspending delay() function can help us.

Let's try putting our new tools to use in the timer app.

Just like we did before, we'll add the suspend modifier to our main() function. Next, we'll swap the thread-blocking Thread.sleep() function for Kotlin's suspending delay() alternative:

timers/v5/src/main/kotlin/com/example/timers/TimerApplication.kt
```kotlin
➤ suspend fun main() = SwingUtilities.invokeLater {
    val window = JFrame("Timer")
    window.defaultCloseOperation = JFrame.DISPOSE_ON_CLOSE
    window.size = Dimension(400, 300)
    window.isVisible = true

    val message = "Please wait for ten seconds…"
    val label = window.add(JLabel(message, JLabel.CENTER)) as JLabel

➤  delay(10_000) // oops!
    label.text = "Done!"
}
```

Functions in Functions

Alas! This code doesn't compile. Instead, we get an error like the one we saw when we first tried to use delay() in a non-suspending function:

```
> Task :compileKotlin FAILED

Suspend function 'delay(…)' should be called only from a coroutine
  or another suspend function.
```

What did we do wrong?

We've given our main() function the ability to call suspending functions, but, in fact, that's not the function where our code is running. Instead, everything's being passed to Swing's invokeLater() function. That's important because it lets Swing run our code on its own thread, where we can safely create and update those user interface components.

Now, the code block accepted by invokeLater() is a separate function—and it's a plain old Java function that doesn't know anything about suspension points or coroutines.

To solve this problem, we need a replacement for invokeLater(). We still want to submit a block of code for execution on Swing's UI thread since we'll be working with user interface components. But now, we also want our submitted code to run as a coroutine so it can benefit from suspending functions, such as delay().

Let's make it happen.

Coroutine Dispatchers

Since a coroutine's progress isn't tied directly to a thread, it's free to choose which thread it wants to run on. As you'll find out in Chapter 8, Call Blocking Functions Safely, on page 129, it can even move from one thread to another in the middle of its execution! Just imagine Theo picking up his jigsaw puzzle tray and taking the whole thing to a friend's house or setting it down on a picnic table in the park to do some puzzling in the sunshine.

A coroutine is executed by its *coroutine dispatcher*, and the dispatcher is responsible for choosing the underlying thread. When you want a coroutine to run on a different thread, you need to select a different dispatcher.

To run our coroutines on the UI thread, we'll be using Dispatchers.Main. This is one of a few dispatchers that come with the kotlinx.coroutines library. It can be configured to work with various user interface toolkits, making it a useful tool for writing reusable multiplatform code. It gets its name from platforms such as Android, where the UI thread is often referred to as the *main thread*.

To wire our new coroutine dispatcher up to the UI thread of our Swing application, we just need to add an extra dependency:

```
timers/v6/build.gradle.kts
dependencies {
  implementation("org.jetbrains.kotlinx:kotlinx-coroutines-core:1.10.1")
  runtimeOnly("org.jetbrains.kotlinx:kotlinx-coroutines-swing:1.10.1")
}
```

When you're working on Android, you'll still use Dispatchers.Main—swap kotlinx-coroutines-swing for kotlinx-coroutines-android to change which framework's thread it's hooked up to. We'll be talking much more about how to use coroutines within existing frameworks such as Android in Chapter 3, Start It, Scope It, Stop It, on page 39.

Coroutine Context

A coroutine's dispatcher forms part of its *coroutine context*—a set of options and customizations that live alongside the coroutine and affect how it runs. To update our coroutine context and choose our dispatcher, we'll use the withContext() function. You'll discover more coroutine context elements, including some other dispatchers, in the coming chapters.

```
timers/v6/src/main/kotlin/com/example/timers/TimerApplication.kt
suspend fun main() = withContext(Dispatchers.Main) {
    val window = JFrame("Timer")
    window.defaultCloseOperation = JFrame.DISPOSE_ON_CLOSE
    window.size = Dimension(400, 300)
    window.isVisible = true

    val message = "Please wait for ten seconds…"
    val label = window.add(JLabel(message, JLabel.CENTER)) as JLabel

    delay(10_000)
    label.text = "Done!"
}
```

Perfect! Our compiler error is gone since we replaced invokeLater() with a coroutine-capable equivalent. The code block passed to withContext() is a suspending function, and when it reaches the suspension point inside the delay() function, it can leave the UI thread free to work on other things. When the 10 seconds are up, the dispatcher will take care of resuming the coroutine on the correct thread.

That means we've finally fixed the broken timer code. Run the program, and you'll see it behaving correctly.

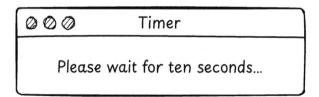

The window updates promptly to show each new message and stays responsive and resizable even while the delay() function is waiting for the seconds to tick down.

What Have You Learned?

In this chapter, you wrote a suspending function, ran it as a coroutine, and used it to fix an unresponsive application. Along the way, you learned about coroutine context and selected the right dispatcher for running user interface code.

But coroutines aren't the only way to free up your blocked threads. In the next chapter, we'll pit suspending functions against asynchronous callbacks when we build two competing versions of the same photo gallery code.

Key Concepts

Suspending function

This is a function that has the suspend modifier and can pause its execution to wait for events outside its own control.

Coroutine

This holds the state of a running suspending function, letting it vacate the underlying thread when its code is paused. If suspending functions are the script, coroutines are the performance.

Suspension point

This is an instruction that can suspend the current coroutine. Suspension points can only appear inside suspending functions. Calling another suspending function counts as a suspension point.

Coroutine context

These are options that live alongside a coroutine and influence its execution. Use withContext() to run a code block and set its coroutine context.

Dispatcher

This is part of the coroutine context. It chooses which thread a coroutine runs its code on. Use Dispatchers.Main to run code on the app's main UI thread.

CHAPTER 2

Escape From Callback Hell

Suspending functions aren't the only way to wait without blocking a thread. Long before Kotlin's coroutines came on the scene, apps of all kinds were using asynchronous callbacks to handle their inputs, outputs, and UI events.

So, why do we need a new solution at all?

In this chapter, we'll compare coroutines with callbacks. You'll see how callbacks conflict with common control-flow keywords, and you'll use suspending functions to bring loops and try–catch blocks back to your asynchronous programs. Finally, you'll put your skills to use in building a photo viewer application, where you'll combine the best of two programming styles to fetch data right on the main thread.

Plot Your Program's Path

You've written two different versions of a timer program—first with a blocked thread and then with a suspended coroutine. To kick off our conversation about callbacks, we'll write a third version of the same program. You'll see how an asynchronous callback can provide the same functionality as a coroutine, and you'll explore the callback challenges that coroutines are designed to fix.

But first, what does the word *asynchronous* mean, and what does it have to do with our callbacks and coroutines?

Asynchronous Programming

You're taking your car for a routine oil change and tire check. But it seems like everyone had the same idea today, and the service center is busy.

"It might be a while," apologizes the mechanic. "Make yourself comfortable in the waiting room—there's magazines and coffee."

If you think of your day's to-do list like the lines of code in a single-threaded computer program, then this is what it feels like for your thread to be blocked. You're stuck waiting for the car to be ready, and you can't move on to the rest of your tasks.

But you've got a better idea.

"I have some errands to run nearby. If I leave my phone number, can you give me a call when the car's ready?"

Now you'll be able to do something productive while the car's in the shop.

You can apply the same concept to a computer program. When you need some results or input from another task, thread, or system, you don't always have to write code that just sits around and waits for it. Instead, you can leave the outside operation to take care of its own execution and ask it to call you back when it's done.

That's the principle behind *asynchronous programming*.

The word *asynchronous* roughly means *not at the same time*—the *chrono* part is the same Greek root that gives us other time-related words such as *chronological*. In programming, it refers to events that happen outside the program's current flow of control. Those might be user inputs, network traffic, sensor data, background tasks, or something as simple as a timer.

What Is a Callback?

Asynchronous programming is based on *callbacks*. What's a callback? It's the follow-up code that's triggered by one of those asynchronous outside events. Think of it like the phone call the mechanic makes to let you know your car's ready and the actions you take in response.

Callbacks crop up all over the place, so there's a good chance you already know what they look like. Let's remind ourselves what we're dealing with. Just as we did in the last chapter, we'll create a window and use it to display a message after 10 seconds. But this time, we won't be putting a 10-second pause directly in the middle of our code. Instead, we'll use Java's Timer class to schedule a follow-up task:

```kotlin
timers/v7/src/main/kotlin/com/example/timers/TimerApplication.kt
fun main() = SwingUtilities.invokeLater {
  val window = JFrame("Timer")
  window.defaultCloseOperation = JFrame.DISPOSE_ON_CLOSE
  window.size = Dimension(400, 300)
  window.isVisible = true

  val message = "Please wait for ten seconds…"
```

```
val label = window.add(JLabel(message, JLabel.CENTER)) as JLabel
val timer = java.util.Timer()
timer.schedule(10_000) {
    SwingUtilities.invokeLater { label.text = "Done!" }
    timer.cancel()
  }
}
```

You can spot callbacks by the characteristic indentation they introduce in the left margin. See that extra set of braces around the last few lines of code, where we set the new label text and cancel the timer? That's our callback. It's a separate function, passed as an argument to schedule(), and it'll run when the 10 seconds are up.

Save a Thread, Use a Callback

From the point of view of the UI thread, this is a great arrangement. The schedule() function itself just needs to set the timer running, and then it can return control to its caller. The main thread isn't blocked, and the user interface remains responsive.

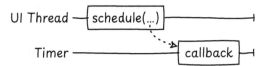

One of the potential pitfalls of callbacks is already visible here, though. When our timer callback runs, it's going to be on the timer's own separate thread. That's no good because we want to continue interacting with our user interface components. To do so safely, we need one last call to invokeLater(), moving us back onto the correct thread with what's essentially another callback.

By splitting our code into separate callbacks, we've written a program that can jump on and off the UI thread. It's the same trick we pulled in the last chapter with coroutines—but this time, there's not a single suspending function or coroutine in sight.

Callbacks or Coroutines?

Callbacks and coroutines both confront the same problem. An ordinary function can't leave its thread until it's finished, so it can't wait for outside events without blocking the thread.

Now, a callback offers a neat way to sidestep the problem altogether. Instead of trying to pause the execution of a single function, it simply splits the work into two separate functions—a *before* and an *after*. You can easily see the two distinct blocks in the code we wrote, separated by those curly-bracket boundaries.

Remember this two-part split because it has some far-reaching implications, both in this chapter and beyond.

So, how do coroutines do the seemingly impossible and move code freely between threads without splitting it across more than one function? Behind the scenes, it turns out they're using the same two-part trick as a callback. Before your program is executed, the Kotlin compiler rewrites your suspending functions in a different form. You might write a single function with a suspension point in the middle, but the thread that's executing your code sees two separate chunks, like the disjoint code blocks of an asynchronous callback. In Chapter 9, Upgrade Every Callback, on page 145, we'll dive deeper into how this works.

Suspending functions are Kotlin's way of gluing the two halves of an asynchronous operation back together, using some new syntax and a little compiler magic.

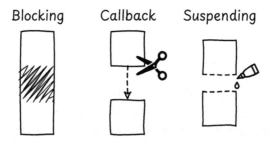

Are Two Tasks Better Than One?

- Callbacks split a task into two parts, so it doesn't need to stay on a single thread.

- Suspending functions join the two parts back together as a coroutine, so it looks like one code block again.

Does That Look Asynchronous to You?

Since callbacks and coroutines use the same underlying trick to solve the same blocked-thread problem, you'll hear coroutines described as an asynchronous programming style. Even in this book, we'll often use the word *asynchronous* to refer to those off-thread operations and events that our suspending functions are waiting for.

But when it comes to style and appearance, a suspending delay() has far more in common with the thread-blocking sleep() function than it does with schedule() and its asynchronous callback.

Coroutines combine the visuals of synchronous code with the efficiency of an asynchronous call, and trying to reduce them to one style or the other would be an oversimplification. So, don't get too hung up on this terminology! As we continue our journey, we'll introduce other, more useful distinctions—such as what it means to block a thread or which operations introduce diverging background tasks.

No Restrictions

You can think of coroutines as a fresh coat of paint for your asynchronous code. It makes the code look new and shiny, sure—but is it worth it? We wrote our callback-powered timer program without needing to worry about things such as suspend modifiers and coroutine context. By contrast, coroutines seem like a lot of extra trouble. If callbacks can already keep those important threads unblocked, then why go to the trouble of repainting the whole house with suspending functions?

That might be the most important question we need to answer in this book. Callbacks are good enough for simple programs such as the one we just wrote, but if you've ever had to rely on them in a more complex program, you'll know that all those nested, disconnected code blocks come with some serious drawbacks of their own.

It's those problems that coroutines have been carefully designed to solve.

Two-Part Timer

Think about the way you read and write a computer program. It's a list of instructions, where the computer executes each one before moving on to the next one.

Callbacks undermine that programming principle, and in doing so, they completely change the way you have to think about assembling your functions. To see how, let's make some changes to our timer code. We'll ditch the user interface and just set up some simple callbacks.

Before we start, we'll also write a simple log() function that'll help us see what's going on:

timers/v8/src/main/kotlin/com/example/timers/Logger.kt

```kotlin
val start = TimeSource.Monotonic.markNow()

fun log(message: String) {
  println("[t=${start.elapsedNow().inWholeSeconds}s] $message")
}
```

Each time we log a message, the output will include the number of seconds that have passed since the program started running. Now, let's use it in a program. We'll take the same 10-second wait that we used in some of our earlier programs, but this time, we'll split it into two parts:

timers/v8/src/main/kotlin/com/example/timers/TimerApplication.kt

```kotlin
fun main() {
  waitFiveSeconds()
  waitFiveSeconds()
}

fun waitFiveSeconds() {
  val timer = java.util.Timer()
  log("Waiting for five seconds…")
  timer.schedule(5_000) {
    log("Done waiting")
    timer.cancel()
  }
}
```

We've added a function called waitFiveSeconds(), and we're simply calling it twice. What output are you expecting to see from this program? How long do you think it will take to run?

```
[t=0s] Waiting for five seconds…
[t=0s] Waiting for five seconds…
[t=5s] Done waiting
[t=5s] Done waiting
```

As you know, the schedule() function doesn't do any waiting of its own. That's handled by the separate timer callback. So, as soon as the first timer has started, the first call to waitFiveSeconds() returns, and the program moves on to the second one. Both timers start running at the same time, and after five seconds have elapsed, they're both done.

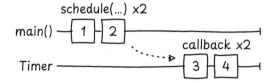

Cancel the Timer

If waitFiveSeconds() returns immediately, and there's no UI, why doesn't this program exit right away? The answer is the Timer's extra thread, which keeps the app running until we cancel() it.

Callbacks can hide inside ordinary functions, making it hard to predict how a program's going to behave. The waitFiveSeconds() doesn't give any outward clues of its asynchronous contents. But despite the way the code in the main() function looks, this program is no longer a sequential list of instructions. Instead, it's made up of several interacting tasks, each contributing their own instructions to the program at different times. This has some seriously interesting consequences, and we'll be talking much more about it when we reach Chapter 4, Split Up to Speed Up, on page 59.

No, After You

If you've worked with callbacks before, you might have an idea of how we could fix that code. We'd need to put each subsequent operation inside the previous one's callback. We'll come back to that later, but for now, let's see what happens to this program when we upgrade those callbacks to suspending functions. We'll add the suspend modifier to the main() function and swap our timer calls for the suspending delay() function:

timers/v9/src/main/kotlin/com/example/timers/TimerApplication.kt
```kotlin
suspend fun main() {
  waitFiveSeconds()
  waitFiveSeconds()
}

suspend fun waitFiveSeconds() {
  log("Waiting for five seconds…")
  delay(5_000)
  log("Done waiting")
}
```

Run the program, and you'll see a single, ordered sequence of steps. The program runs in the order we wrote it, and it finishes each step before moving on to the next one:

```
[t=0s] Waiting for five seconds…
[t=5s] Done waiting
[t=5s] Waiting for five seconds…
[t=10s] Done waiting
```

Is that what you were expecting, or does it seem surprising?

A suspending function always finishes all its work and all its waiting before it returns to its caller and lets the rest of the program continue. That's exactly what you would expect from any ordinary function, but it can be unintuitive if you're comparing suspending functions to the other asynchronous programming styles you might be used to. Take a moment to make sure you're comfortable with this behavior before we continue.

Suspending is Sequential

 Just like an ordinary function, a suspending function executes its contents in order, one line at a time. This is the key difference between suspending functions and callbacks and one of the main reasons for suspending functions to exist.

Reclaim Control-Flow Keywords

As you've just seen, callbacks can undermine the most basic principles of a computer program's sequential execution, making for code that's hard to follow.

In this section, you'll see that the implications go further than readability. Callbacks are incompatible with some of the control-flow tools you're used to using in your programs. Good news, though—upgrading to coroutines can remove those limitations.

Can You Repeat That?

With the help of suspending functions, we've broken down our waiting time into two almost identical steps. Any time a program does the same thing twice, it's a sign we could simplify things with a loop. We'll use Kotlin's repeat() function to do just that:

```
timers/v10/src/main/kotlin/com/example/timers/TimerApplication.kt
suspend fun main() {
  repeat(2) {
    waitFiveSeconds()
  }
}

suspend fun waitFiveSeconds() {
  log("Waiting for five seconds…")
  delay(5_000)
  log("Done waiting")
}
```

We've removed some repetition, and the program works the same as before. Suspending functions work just fine in loops, allowing the loop to pause and resume its execution along with the coroutine that it's running in:

```
[t=0s] Waiting for five seconds…
[t=5s] Done waiting
[t=5s] Waiting for five seconds…
[t=10s] Done waiting
```

Out of the Loop

Try to make the same improvement to the callback version and things aren't so straightforward. Remember how our two-callback program ended up running both of its five-second timers at the same time? Well, exactly the same thing happens when the two calls are arranged in a loop:

timers/v11/src/main/kotlin/com/example/timers/TimerApplication.kt

```
fun main() {
  repeat(2) {
    waitFiveSeconds()
  }
}

fun waitFiveSeconds() {
  val timer = java.util.Timer()
  log("Waiting for five seconds…")
  timer.schedule(5_000) {
    log("Done waiting")
    timer.cancel()
  }
}
```

It's not too difficult to understand why this doesn't work. A repeat() block might be more concise than writing out the function name several times, but it amounts to the same thing when we run it. So, when we use it to repeat the same callback-based waitFiveSeconds() function that we tried before, it's going to have exactly the same behavior and exactly the same problems. As soon as the schedule() function returns, the loop reaches the end of its code block and moves on to its second iteration.

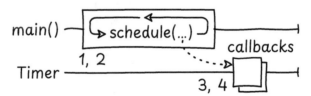

You'll see the same problem with any other loop, including for and while. In fact, no matter what you try, you'll find that callbacks and loops aren't compatible.

To repeat an asynchronous operation such as this one, you'll need to trigger each iteration by hand from inside the previous one's callback.

It's Finally Time

Loops aren't the only control-flow concept that conflicts with callbacks. Can you think of another? If you guessed anything to do with exceptions, error handling, or resource management, you're on the right track.

To see the problem, let's start with another simple function that uses a timer callback:

timers/v12/src/main/kotlin/com/example/timers/TimerApplication.kt
```kotlin
fun drive() {
  log("Driving in the car…")
  val timer = java.util.Timer()
  timer.schedule(5_000) {
    log("You have reached your destination.")
    timer.cancel()
  }
}
```

When we call the function, we'll add a try–finally block:

timers/v12/src/main/kotlin/com/example/timers/TimerApplication.kt
```kotlin
fun main() {
  try {
    drive()
  } finally {
    log("Looks like we're done driving, let's shut down the engine.")
  }
}
```

What are you expecting to see when you run the program?

```
[t=0s] Driving in the car…
[t=0s] Looks like we're done driving, let's shut down the engine.
[t=5s] You have reached your destination.
```

Did you predict the problem? The drive() function returns immediately since it does all its waiting via outside callbacks. As a result, the try block doesn't know that there's anything to wait for, and the finally block runs too soon.

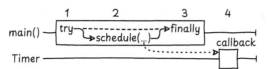

This is a cruel blow for callbacks because it makes them significantly worse at one of the main things they're designed to be used for. A finally block is your purpose-built tool for ensuring that files and network connections are always safely cleaned up, no matter what. But working with files and network connections is exactly when you're most likely to want an asynchronous callback to avoid blocking your thread while you wait for your data. Try to use a finally block with an asynchronous file operation, and your file will be closed before you're done using it. Oops!

Kotlin's use() function is based on the same try–finally machinery, so it has the same problem with asynchronous calls.

Catch Me if You Can

As you've probably guessed, we can fix this with a suspending function. But while we're here, let's keep looking at this problem. We can't talk about the try and finally keywords without also mentioning catch.

Let's rewrite our function to fail with an error instead of completing normally:

timers/v13/src/main/kotlin/com/example/timers/TimerApplication.kt
```kotlin
fun drive() {
  log("Driving in the car…")
  val timer = java.util.Timer()
  timer.schedule(5_000) {
    log("No more gas, can't drive any further!")
    throw Exception("The car is out of gas")
  }
}
```

Now, we'll add a catch block:

timers/v13/src/main/kotlin/com/example/timers/TimerApplication.kt
```kotlin
fun main() {
  try {
    drive()
  } catch (exception: Throwable) {
    log("Caught an exception: $exception")
  } finally {
    log("Looks like we're done driving, let's shut down the engine.")
  }
}
```

Unless you know what's going on inside drive(), this looks like a real program, right? But, of course, we're not going to end up catching our error. Just like before, the drive() function returns as soon as it's queued up its callback. Our catch block never executes at all, and there's no sign of its output:

```
[t=0s] Driving in the car…
[t=0s] Looks like we're done driving, let's shut down the engine.
[t=5s] No more gas, can't drive any further!
Exception in thread "Timer-0" java.lang.Exception: The car is out of gas
  …
Process finished with exit code 0
```

Even though we fail to catch the error, we still finish with a zero exit code, indicating successful completion. The stack trace does show up in the console, but it's not coming from our own code. Instead, it comes from the timer's background thread, which has crashed due to our unhandled error. The main() function itself doesn't have a clue that anything went wrong and would happily carry on running more code.

When you think about working with exceptions in Kotlin, you probably think of the throw and catch keywords. But it's no use writing throw inside a callback or trying to use catch to handle asynchronous failures. And that's a problem for two reasons.

First, it's inconvenient. You'll need to come up with a new way to structure your asynchronous code and handle its errors. Second, it leaves traps in your code. If you look at a function such as the one we just wrote, it's not always going to be obvious from the outside that it contains asynchronous operations with callbacks. Without knowing what's inside the function, you might add a try–catch block and think that you've handled all its outcomes. Meanwhile, important errors go uncaught or even unnoticed in background threads and callbacks.

Remember this because it'll play an important role in Chapter 5, Plan for Any Outcome, on page 75.

Structured Programming

Structures such as loops and try–catch–finally blocks work by wrapping around some other operation. You can see this in the code by the braces surrounding the region of code that's going to be affected. Depending on the control structure you're using, it might add some extra instructions that run before the wrapped operation starts, after it finishes, or both. This is a principle called *structured programming*, and it's pretty fundamental to the way all modern code is written.

Now, remember the way callbacks change a program's shape. To break away from their starting thread, they split a single operation into separate *before* and *after* functions. It's this two-part structure that causes the control-flow problems we've seen in this chapter.

If the *before* and *after* aren't in the same function, there's no way a single code block can wrap around both. Just try writing a loop that has its opening brace in one function and its closing brace in another, and you'll understand why callbacks and structured control flow are never going to see eye-to-eye.

Control structures such as loops and catch blocks are fundamental features of the Kotlin programming language, and losing the ability to use them can make callbacks a difficult pill to swallow. Luckily, with suspending functions, we can have the best of both worlds. But that doesn't mean we've solved all our structured programming problems. Far from it! Keep an eye out for the same two-way control-flow split in Chapter 5, Plan for Any Outcome, on page 75, where we introduce the idea of structured concurrency.

Suspending Functions to the Rescue!

Suspending functions don't cause any problems for structured programming because they keep your code in a single function, even while it's waiting for outside operations. And if the code stays inside the same function, it can stay inside the loops, try–catch–finally blocks, and other structures that the function contains.

Let's use a coroutine to fix that timer program:

timers/v14/src/main/kotlin/com/example/timers/TimerApplication.kt
```
suspend fun drive() {
  log("Driving in the car…")
  delay(5_000)
  log("No more gas, can't drive any further!")
  throw Exception("The car is out of gas")
}
```

Now that our drive() function suspends until all its work is finished, you can use the control-flow keywords you're used to:

timers/v14/src/main/kotlin/com/example/timers/TimerApplication.kt
```
suspend fun main() {
  try {
    drive()
  } catch (exception: Throwable) {
    log("Caught an exception: $exception")
  } finally {
    log("Looks like we're done driving, let's shut down the engine.")
  }
}
```

This time, the output looks like what you'd expect from any other program:

```
[t=0s] Driving in the car…
[t=5s] No more gas, can't drive any further!
[t=5s] Caught an exception: java.lang.Exception: The car is out of gas
[t=5s] Looks like we're done driving, let's shut down the engine.
```

Notice how we no longer have to look at the drive() function's implementation to figure out how this program's going to behave. When you see the suspend keyword or the suspension-point icon, you can always assume that the work happens inside the function. Errors and results will arrive back at the original call site, and the program won't move on to run finally blocks or subsequent instructions until all the work is finished.

So, coroutines are much more than a cosmetic upgrade for your callbacks. A suspending function doesn't just look like an ordinary function—it also behaves like one. That means you can rely on the tools and concepts you are already used to for all your control-flow, error-handling, and resource-management needs.

Excavate the Indentation Pyramid

Now that we've completed our exploration of asynchronous callbacks, you've seen three different ways to write programs that wait. To finish off this chapter, let's see how those three techniques translate to other kinds of waiting. We'll build a photo viewer to showcase some striking space photography.

Downloading a photo is an outside operation that our code will need to wait for as it needed to wait for our 10-second timer in the last program. As we build out the app, we'll explore the three different ways of waiting for those network calls—first, with blocked threads, then with callbacks, and finally, with suspending functions. You'll recap what you've learned about callbacks and coroutines, and you'll discover how to do more with suspending functions than just count down the seconds.

Astronomy for Beginners

Since 1995, the United States National Aeronautics and Space Administration (NASA) has used their *Astronomy Picture of the Day* site[1] to share a daily photo. It's an awe-inspiring collection, with subjects ranging from black holes and supernovas to scientists and space shuttle launches.

Alongside the site, there's an API we can use to fetch information about the available pictures. We're going to use Retrofit, an open source HTTP client, to connect to the API and retrieve some photos. We'll start with our dependencies:

astronomy/v1/build.gradle.kts
```
dependencies {
  implementation("org.jetbrains.kotlinx:kotlinx-coroutines-core:1.10.1")
  implementation("com.squareup.retrofit2:retrofit:2.9.0")
  implementation("com.squareup.retrofit2:converter-moshi:2.9.0")
  runtimeOnly("org.jetbrains.kotlinx:kotlinx-coroutines-swing:1.10.1")
}
```

1. https://apod.nasa.gov

Retrofit works by generating an implementation for an ordinary Kotlin or Java interface. This code will be the same for all three versions of our program, and we'll group it together in its own file:

astronomy/v1/src/main/kotlin/com/example/astronomy/AstronomyService.kt
```
const val apiKey = "DEMO_KEY"

interface AstronomyService {
  @GET("apod")
  fun getPictures(
    @Query("count") count: Int,
    @Query("api_key") apiKey: String,
  ): Call<List<PictureInfo>>

  @GET
  fun downloadImage(@Url imageUrl: String): Call<ResponseBody>
}

data class PictureInfo(val title: String, val url: String)

private val executor = Executors.newCachedThreadPool { task ->
  Thread(task).apply { isDaemon = true }
}

private fun createHttpClient() = OkHttpClient.Builder()
  .protocols(listOf(Protocol.HTTP_1_1)).dispatcher(Dispatcher(executor))

val astronomyService = Retrofit.Builder()
  .client(createHttpClient().build())
  .baseUrl("https://api.nasa.gov/planetary/")
  .addConverterFactory(MoshiConverterFactory.create())
  .build().create<AstronomyService>()
```

Make sure not to skip any of the HTTP-client configuration here. Selecting the right executor and protocol ensures we won't have any persistent background threads, so our example programs will exit properly when we're done making requests. That's useful for this simple example program, but it'll become even more important later on in the book.

You'll also notice the demo API key in this file, which will give you a fixed number of requests each day. It's free to get your own key from the website[2] if you want to play around with the API some more.

Before we start fetching pictures, let's also set up two helper functions for our user interface. These will help us create and update our window, and once again, they'll be the same for all three versions of our app:

astronomy/v1/src/main/kotlin/com/example/astronomy/Helpers.kt
```
fun createImageViewerWindow() = JFrame("Image Viewer").apply {
  defaultCloseOperation = JFrame.DISPOSE_ON_CLOSE
```

---

2. https://api.nasa.gov

```kotlin
    size = Dimension(400, 300)
    add(JLabel("Loading your image…", JLabel.CENTER))
    isVisible = true
}

fun JFrame.displayImage(data: ByteArray) {
  contentPane.removeAll()
  add(JLabel(ImageIcon(data)))
  pack()
}
```

The first function creates our window and populates it with some loading text. Once we've downloaded our data, the second function will update the window to display the photo.

Ready for Lift-Off

Finally, let's put all those pieces together with a function that will download our photo and display it in a window.

Each of the functions in our AstronomyService interface is going to return a Call object to represent the request. To get hold of our photo, we need to execute those requests and retrieve the responses.

One easy way to do that is with the request's execute() function:

astronomy/v1/src/main/kotlin/com/example/astronomy/AstronomyApplication.kt
```kotlin
fun loadImage(window: JFrame) {
  val infoRequest = astronomyService.getPictures(count = 1, apiKey)
➤ val infoResponse = infoRequest.execute()
  val imageUrl = infoResponse.body()!!.single().url
  val imageRequest = astronomyService.downloadImage(imageUrl)
➤ val imageResponse = imageRequest.execute()

  window.displayImage(imageResponse.body()!!.bytes())
}
```

We're making two requests. The first one will fetch a JSON object containing our image URL. The second one uses that URL to download the contents of the photo itself. Remember this two-stage download process because it's something our upcoming callbacks will struggle to handle neatly.

With a single, clear list of instructions, it's easy to figure out what this code is going to do and what order it's going to do it in.

Let's put it to use in a program. For good measure, we'll also add a try–catch block to deal with any connectivity issues:

Failing on Purpose

If you want to test the program's error-handling capabilities, just try disconnecting your network cable or turning off your Wi-Fi! You can also swap the base URL in AstronomyService.kt for a dummy address such as https://example.invalid.

astronomy/v1/src/main/kotlin/com/example/astronomy/AstronomyApplication.kt

```kotlin
fun main() = SwingUtilities.invokeLater {
  val window = createImageViewerWindow()

  try {
    loadImage(window)
  } catch (error: Throwable) {
    window.contentPane.removeAll()
    window.add(JLabel("Sorry, something went wrong", JLabel.CENTER))
    window.revalidate()
  }
}
```

At first glance, everything's looking good! Our program waits for a couple of seconds while the image is downloading, and then we get to see our first space photo.

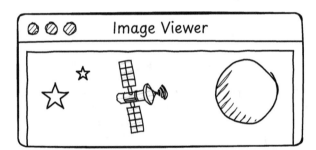

But take a closer look, and you'll see the same problems we had in the first chapter when we blocked our UI thread with a call to Thread.sleep(). The loading text is missing, and the window is frozen while the download is in progress.

Our network responses come from outside the program, and when the execute() function needs to wait for them, it's going to block its thread. In modern apps with smooth touchscreen scrolling and sleek animations, even a couple of hundred milliseconds of waiting is long enough to cause a noticeable stutter—and with a large file or a slow network connection, the waiting time might be much longer.

We can rule out using execute() in our user interface code or in any program that wants to avoid blocking its threads.

Join the Queue

In Retrofit, we can swap execute() for enqueue() to trigger a callback when our request is complete.

Like the schedule() function we've been using in our timer examples, enqueue() takes its follow-up code as an extra argument. A Retrofit callback can handle more than one possible outcome, so it takes the form of an object containing a couple of functions.

We're going to start out with a simple ImageViewerCallback interface containing the functions we need:

astronomy/v2/src/main/kotlin/com/example/astronomy/AstronomyApplication.kt
```kotlin
fun interface ImageViewerCallback<T> : Callback<T> {
  override fun onResponse(call: Call<T>, response: Response<T>)
  override fun onFailure(call: Call<T>, t: Throwable) = t.printStackTrace()
}
```

Our new interface isn't too different from the base Callback interface that comes with Retrofit. We've added the fun modifier and filled in a placeholder implementation for the onFailure() function. That'll let us create a simple callback object by providing just the onResponse() implementation—we'll worry about failures another time.

Let's give it a try in the loadImage() function:

astronomy/v2/src/main/kotlin/com/example/astronomy/AstronomyApplication.kt
```kotlin
fun loadImage(window: JFrame) {
  val infoRequest = astronomyService.getPictures(count = 1, apiKey)
  infoRequest.enqueue(ImageViewerCallback { _, infoResponse ->
    val imageUrl = infoResponse.body()!!.single().url
    val imageRequest = astronomyService.downloadImage(imageUrl)
    imageRequest.enqueue(ImageViewerCallback { _, imageResponse ->
      SwingUtilities.invokeLater {
        window.displayImage(imageResponse.body()!!.bytes())
      }
    })
  })
}
```

When you run this code, things are looking much better. The enqueue() function doesn't need to wait and return a response to its caller, so it doesn't block the caller's thread. The loading text shows up properly, and the window remains responsive and interactive while the photo is downloading.

Out Of Sight, Out Of Mind

 Retrofit can still use its own threads to work on our request in the background. The important thing is not to block the caller's thread. Later, we'll see some asynchronous calls that save even more resources by doing without blocked threads altogether.

Callbacks All the Way Down

This new callback code has some extra indentation that wasn't there in its earlier thread-blocking incarnation. If you follow the data as it flows from one part of the program to the next, it's easy to see why these nested code blocks are such an inevitable part of asynchronous programming.

Remember, the response from our first request contains the URL for our image download. We can't start building and executing our second network call until we have that URL—which means the second request has to start inside the first one's callback.

Jumping back onto the UI thread with a final call to invokeLater() makes things worse. The growing pyramid of whitespace in the left margin, with its cascade of closing brackets at the end, is the characteristic sign of what's become known as *callback hell*.

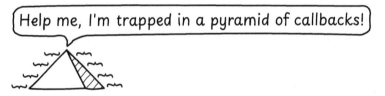

Nobody really wants to read or write code that looks like this. Our program should be a single sequence of instructions, with each task happening one after the other. That's how it looked when we blocked a thread with execute(). But with callbacks, we can't write it that way. Instead, the staircase of nested calls makes it look as though each new operation is somehow included as part of the previous request.

Network Failure

Our code might not look so tidy, but at least the problems are contained inside the loadImage() function. Or are they? The function's signature looks the same as before, but now that we've converted it to use callbacks, it's no longer compatible with that try–catch block we added earlier:

astronomy/v2/src/main/kotlin/com/example/astronomy/AstronomyApplication.kt
```kotlin
fun main() = SwingUtilities.invokeLater {
  val window = createImageViewerWindow()

  try {
    loadImage(window)
  } catch (error: Throwable) { // oops, that won't work!
    window.contentPane.removeAll()
    window.add(JLabel("Sorry, something went wrong", JLabel.CENTER))
    window.revalidate()
  }
}
```

What do you think will happen to this program if it runs into a connection problem? Once again, you can give it a try by disconnecting from the Internet or swapping to an invalid URL.

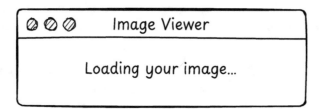

The loading screen shows up, but the window never updates to show our error message. Instead, the exception ends up inside our callback object's onFailure() function, where it simply gets swallowed up. It's easy to see how the same mistake could cause important errors to go uncaught or even unnoticed in a real program.

Suspending Functions to the Rescue

Adding proper error handling to this program would mean more code, more callbacks, and more complexity. On the other hand, if we can upgrade our program from callbacks to coroutines instead, we won't need to change anything at all. Our try–catch block will simply start working again.

So, how do we convert this program to use suspending functions? Later in this book, you'll learn techniques for upgrading both callbacks and blocked threads into coroutine suspension points. Many libraries and frameworks will also offer coroutine support as an extra add-on dependency, and some, such as the first-party Ktor[3] web framework, are even written with coroutines from the ground up.

---

3. https://ktor.io/

But for now, we don't need to worry about any of that because Retrofit comes with suspending functions built right in. We can simply swap enqueue() or execute() for the suspending awaitResponse() function:

astronomy/v3/src/main/kotlin/com/example/astronomy/AstronomyApplication.kt
```kotlin
suspend fun loadImage(window: JFrame) {
  val infoRequest = astronomyService.getPictures(count = 1, apiKey)
➤ val infoResponse = infoRequest.awaitResponse()
  val imageUrl = infoResponse.body()!!.single().url
  val imageRequest = astronomyService.downloadImage(imageUrl)
➤ val imageResponse = imageRequest.awaitResponse()

  window.displayImage(imageResponse.body()!!.bytes())
}
```

Best of Both Worlds

Great! Without those extra indents and brackets, this code looks like the first version you wrote with execute(). It's when you compare awaitResponse() and execute() in IntelliJ IDEA or Android Studio that you'll see the key difference. Only awaitResponse() has the distinctive suspension-point icon, showing it'll suspend a coroutine where execute() would have blocked the whole thread. With the main thread unblocked, this new code should behave like the asynchronous enqueue() version.

Using coroutines, we've combined the best of both worlds.

Now, just as we did with our timer program in the first chapter, we will use the withContext() block to select our dispatcher and move our coroutine onto the main UI thread, replacing the invokeLater() function we were using before. The dispatcher applies to the whole coroutine, so once it's in place, we don't need to switch threads again, no matter how many times we vacate the thread with an asynchronous suspending operation:

astronomy/v3/src/main/kotlin/com/example/astronomy/AstronomyApplication.kt
```kotlin
suspend fun main(): Unit = withContext(Dispatchers.Main) {
  val window = createImageViewerWindow()

  try {
    loadImage(window)
  } catch (error: Throwable) {
    window.contentPane.removeAll()
    window.add(JLabel("Sorry, something went wrong", JLabel.CENTER))
    window.revalidate()
  }
}
```

Our suspending awaitResponse() function doesn't block its thread, so you won't see any sign of unresponsive UI components. But now, we don't have to make any control-flow compromises. That try–catch block is working again. In the next chapter, we'll even add a loop to periodically refresh our photo.

Suspending functions let you have your cake and eat it, too, combining the efficiency of asynchronous callbacks with the control-flow capabilities of a joined-up sequential operation.

	Blocking	Callbacks	Suspending
Resource-efficient, and safe for UI code		✓	✓
Uncluttered code that's easy to follow	✓		✓
Works with try–catch–finally blocks and loops	✓		✓
Starts and finishes on the correct thread	✓		✓

What Have You Learned?

In the course of this chapter, you've used suspending functions to write asynchronous operations that look and behave like any other code. You've seen how structured programming fundamentals such as loops and exceptions just don't work with callbacks, and you've used suspending functions to bring those familiar control-flow keywords back to your asynchronous code.

Coroutines offer the efficiency of asynchronous execution without the control-flow compromises of a callback. But not every program can easily have the suspend modifier added to its main() function. So, how do we get the benefits of coroutines in an existing codebase?

You'll find the answer in the next chapter when you learn a new way to start coroutines that'll work in your mobile apps and more.

Key Concepts

Asynchronous programming
> This is a code style that avoids blocked threads and instead triggers follow-up tasks in response to background tasks and outside events.

Callback
> This is a function that's passed as input to an asynchronous operation to be executed when the task is complete.

CHAPTER 3

Start It, Scope It, Stop It

We've been using a suspending main() function to start our photo viewer app in its own coroutine.

But not every project has a main() function you can modify. In this chapter, let's change up our code so that it doesn't rely on that suspending entry point. You'll find out more about why ordinary functions can't use suspension points, and you'll introduce a coroutine scope to keep your asynchronous code safe from memory leaks.

By the end of the chapter, you'll know how to start a new coroutine as part of an existing program. Not only will you pick up the tools to call suspending functions on Android, but you'll also learn how to identify suitable classes and components where you can do the same in any other codebase.

Access Suspending Functions Anywhere

In our first chapter, you learned an important rule of suspending functions. To call a suspending function, you have to suspend your own code, too. The result? Only a suspending function can call another suspending function.

When you're writing simple standalone programs such as the examples we've been working on so far, that's not a problem. You can add the suspend modifier to your main() function to start the whole thing in a coroutine. But when you're working on real applications, things aren't always quite so easy. You'll often find yourself needing to add new features to an existing class or function without the option of adding suspend modifiers all over the place.

To see the problem, let's make some changes to the structure of our last chapter's image viewer code—after a quick detour via the world of mobile applications.

Android Activities

If you've ever written an Android app, you know that you don't start by writing a main() function. Instead, you create an Activity:

```
android/v1/src/main/kotlin/com/example/astronomy/MainActivity.kt
class MainActivity : ComponentActivity() {
  override fun onCreate(savedInstanceState: Bundle?) {
    super.onCreate(savedInstanceState)
    // TODO: download and display an image
  }
}
```

Plenty of other frameworks take a similar approach, giving you a class or interface that acts as a template for you to fill in.

How do we start using suspending functions here? As you're about to see, it's not as simple as adding the suspend modifier. Instead, you'll need to learn a new tool.

But writing an Android app sounds like hard work, and it's not what this book is about. To keep our code examples easy, we won't be introducing any new frameworks, Android or otherwise. All the same, we can still master the tools and techniques that allow any framework or library to integrate with coroutines. To get started, all we need to do is update our Swing code to look a little more like an Android app. When we're done, we'll take a quick look at a real Android version of the same code. As you continue through the chapter, think about how you'd apply the same principles to a component in the other frameworks and architectures you might have used.

I Can't Believe It's Not Android

We're going to put our window code inside a new ImageViewer class. We'll start by extending from WindowAdapter, a base class that implements Swing's WindowListener interface:

```
astronomy/v4/src/main/kotlin/com/example/astronomy/AstronomyApplication.kt
class ImageViewer : WindowAdapter() {
  override fun windowOpened(e: WindowEvent) {
    val window = e.window as JFrame
    // TODO: download and display an image
  }
}
```

Notice how our code is already starting to look similar to the simple Android activity we just saw. You can think of this windowOpened() function like Android's onCreate() function. Once you learn how to use suspending functions in this program, you'll be able to use the same technique in your Android apps and other frameworks.

If we were writing a real Android app, the system would set up and execute each Activity for us. For our program, we'll make a createWindow() function that does the same:

astronomy/v4/src/main/kotlin/com/example/astronomy/Helpers.kt
```kotlin
fun createWindow(title: String, listener: WindowListener) {
  SwingUtilities.invokeLater {
    val window = JFrame(title)
    window.defaultCloseOperation = JFrame.DISPOSE_ON_CLOSE
    window.size = Dimension(400, 300)
    window.add(JLabel("Loading your image…", JLabel.CENTER))
    window.addWindowListener(listener)
    window.isVisible = true
  }
}
```

This function should look a little familiar since it's mostly the same as the createImageViewerWindow() function from the code on page 31. But there are a couple of important differences this time. First, this function doesn't return our new JFrame. Instead, the whole function runs in the background on the UI thread, where it can't return anything back to its caller. To update the window once it's been created, we pass in an instance of the listener class we've already created:

astronomy/v4/src/main/kotlin/com/example/astronomy/AstronomyApplication.kt
```kotlin
fun main() = createWindow("Image Viewer", ImageViewer())
```

Swing makes sure to run its listeners on the correct thread, so our main() function won't need to worry about thread choices at all. Run the code, and you'll see the placeholder message in a small window, just like last time.

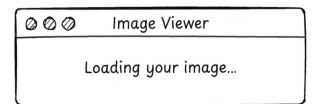

Suspension Restrictions

Okay, let's use this new starting point to implement our photo viewer. You'll need the AstronomyService from the code on page 31, along with all of its dependencies. With that in place, we just need to fill in the code to download and display a photo.

Just like last time, we'll need to make sure we do this asynchronously. Swing makes sure the windowOpened() event happens on the UI thread, and Android does the same for its Activity lifecycle events. If we start making blocking calls that wait for data to download, we'll end up with a frozen and unresponsive app.

Based on everything we've learned so far, suspending functions should be a perfect solution for that! We can use the loadImage() function that we wrote in the last chapter, along with its displayImage() helper function:

astronomy/v5/src/main/kotlin/com/example/astronomy/AstronomyApplication.kt
```kotlin
suspend fun loadImage(window: JFrame) {
  val infoRequest = astronomyService.getPictures(count = 1, apiKey)
  val infoResponse = infoRequest.awaitResponse()

  val imageUrl = infoResponse.body()!!.single().url
  val imageRequest = astronomyService.downloadImage(imageUrl)
  val imageResponse = imageRequest.awaitResponse()

  window.displayImage(imageResponse.body()!!.bytes())
}
```

astronomy/v5/src/main/kotlin/com/example/astronomy/Helpers.kt
```kotlin
fun JFrame.displayImage(data: ByteArray) {
  contentPane.removeAll()
  add(JLabel(ImageIcon(data)))
  pack()
}
```

But when we try to call loadImage() from our new activity-style code, we'll run into a familiar problem:

astronomy/v5/src/main/kotlin/com/example/astronomy/AstronomyApplication.kt
```kotlin
class ImageViewer : WindowAdapter() {
  override fun windowOpened(e: WindowEvent) {
    val window = e.window as JFrame
    loadImage(window) // error!
  }
}

fun main() = createWindow("Image Viewer", ImageViewer())
```

This code won't compile because the windowOpened() function doesn't have the suspend modifier. Without it, our activity code doesn't have a way to pause its execution and wait for the network response from the AstronomyService:

```
> Task :compileKotlin FAILED

Suspend function 'displayImage(…)' should be called only from a coroutine
  or another suspend function.
```

You Can't Teach an Old Function New Tricks

Is there a way to fix that? Can we add the suspend keyword and upgrade windowOpened() to a suspending function? Well, let's try it and see what happens:

astronomy/v6/src/main/kotlin/com/example/astronomy/AstronomyApplication.kt
```kotlin
class ImageViewer : WindowAdapter() {
  override suspend fun windowOpened(e: WindowEvent) { // error!
```

No luck—now we just have a different error telling us that this function signature doesn't match the one we're trying to override:

```
> Task :compileKotlin FAILED

'windowOpened' overrides nothing.
```

We're providing an implementation for an existing function—one that was declared for us by Swing in its WindowListener interface. That class and all its callers will be expecting the regular windowOpened() function without the suspend modifier.

To make windowOpened() into a suspending function, we'd need to modify its original declaration in the WindowListener superclass, as well as every other place it's overridden—and then make sure all its callers were suspending functions as well. That's something we just can't do because we don't declare or call the windowOpened() function from our own code. Instead, Swing invokes it for us as the user navigates around our app. The story's exactly the same for functions such as onCreate() in an Android activity.

Frameworks such as Swing and Android come with their own interfaces and expectations, many of them originating in Java. Much of the time, you'll find yourself adding code to pre-existing functions that are called from elsewhere and have signatures we can't change. That means you're stuck with two different types of functions with different capabilities—suspending functions, which can pause to wait for asynchronous calls, and ordinary old-fashioned functions, which can't.

Check Your Framework

 Some frameworks, including Spring, Quarkus, and Micronaut, have special support for coroutines and let you add the suspend modifier directly to your controller methods. Check the documentation for your chosen tool to see what options you have.

Can't Wait, Won't Wait

So, is that it? If we can never suspend existing functions such as onCreate() and windowOpened(), does this mean we can't use coroutines in our Android apps?

Well, a function with a name like onCreate() or windowOpened() is just a starting point. The window or Activity will still exist and will still be able to display our image for us after that function has finished running. There's no way to make the onCreate() or windowOpened() function wait, but there's no real need to, either.

The answer is to move our code into a new background task of its own. The windowOpened() function will kick the new task off, but after that, the two pieces of code will go their own separate ways. The new task will be able to suspend and resume its own execution, but the windowOpened() function won't need to hang around and wait for it.

A task that runs suspending functions is a coroutine. So when we say we want to start a new background task to call our loadImage() function, what we're talking about is starting a new coroutine.

Prepare for Launch

So far, we've only written programs that use a single coroutine, which we got Kotlin to create for us by adding the suspend modifier to our main() function. But, just as we can start new threads besides the main one our code starts out with, we can also start new coroutines. Starting extra tasks to run asynchronous code is exactly what coroutines are all about, and we're going to need more than one coroutine for most of the things we do in the rest of this book. How do we make new ones?

First, we'll need to gather a couple of new tools. Our code is about to embark on a journey out of the safety of our windowOpened() listener function and into the great unknown. And, as we're going to learn, it's important that we don't lose track of this new task after we've created it.

To add new coroutines to an existing program and start running suspending functions as background tasks, we need a *coroutine scope*. Like a teacher looking after a classroom full of kids, our coroutine scope will be responsible for keeping track of our background tasks, making sure they don't wander off into the distance, and picking up the pieces when things go wrong.

A coroutine scope links each coroutine back to the part of the app where it was created. So, one program might have several different coroutine scopes, each representing a different group of related tasks.

Many of the components in an Android app come with a built-in coroutine scope, and we'll take a quick look at those later on. In our Swing application, we're not so lucky, and we'll need to create our own scope.

Create a Custom Coroutine Scope

To create a coroutine scope for our image viewer window, we'll use Kotlin's MainScope() function:

astronomy/v7/src/main/kotlin/com/example/astronomy/AstronomyApplication.kt
```kotlin
class ImageViewer : WindowAdapter() {
  val coroutineScope = MainScope()

  override fun windowOpened(e: WindowEvent) {
```

Next, we need to use the scope's launch() function to create a new coroutine. Inside the coroutine, we'll be free to call the suspending loadImage() function that we've already prepared:

astronomy/v7/src/main/kotlin/com/example/astronomy/AstronomyApplication.kt
```kotlin
class ImageViewer : WindowAdapter() {
  val coroutineScope = MainScope()

  override fun windowOpened(e: WindowEvent) {
    val window = e.window as JFrame
    coroutineScope.launch {
      loadImage(window)
    }
  }
}

fun main() = createWindow("Image Viewer", ImageViewer())
```

Great! Our app's working. It'll show our placeholder text and then use its new coroutine to fetch and display our image without blocking the UI thread.

This is looking good—but be careful! Our coroutine scope is still missing one crucial piece and isn't safe to use in a real application. As we continue building out our application, see if you can spot the point where our oversight causes a memory leak.

Coroutine Builders

The launch() function is our first *coroutine builder*. When we call it, we pass a block of code. That's the code that will form the basis of our new background task.

Since the launch() function returns right away, the windowOpened() function doesn't need to wait for it or suspend its own execution. But the code we're passing to the launch() block is defined as a suspending lambda function, and inside it, we can call all the suspending functions we like. When we do that, we'll be suspending not an existing function but the new background coroutine that we just created.

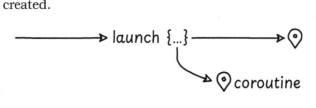

That means we've achieved exactly what we were looking for. Our asynchronous code, including the loadImage() function, can benefit from all the features of suspending functions. But the windowOpened() function, which doesn't have the ability to suspend, won't need to worry about waiting.

So, what role does our coroutine scope play in all this?

Anatomy of a Coroutine Scope

A coroutine scope provides the initial coroutine context for its coroutines. That's obvious if you take a quick peek at the kotlinx.coroutines source code, where you'll find the CoroutineScope interface. With only three lines of code, it's about as simple as it gets:

```
interface CoroutineScope {
  val coroutineContext: CoroutineContext
}
```

We briefly introduced coroutine context in Chapter 1, Wait Without Worrying, on page 3. It's the set of options and attributes that live alongside a coroutine and control how it runs. Coroutine builders such as launch() are extension functions—they take the scope as their receiver parameter and use its coroutine context to build their new coroutines.

The MainScope() gets its name from the fact that it comes with Dispatchers.Main in its coroutine context. That means our window will automatically run all its coroutines on the right thread without any extra withContext() blocks or additional setup. Easy!

But, our Dispatcher is just one of the important things our coroutine scope needs to take care of. In the next section, let's find out what's missing from the scope we just made.

Fix a Scope to Plug a Memory Leak

You've used a coroutine scope along with its launch() coroutine builder function to start a new coroutine and call a suspending function without waiting for it to finish. That's your key to unlocking the benefits of coroutines from anywhere, even in regular functions that are bound to their thread and don't know anything about Kotlin's suspension point capabilities.

But starting a coroutine is only half the story—what goes up must come down. Once our new coroutine is running, when does it stop?

When Will It End?

We're using NASA's API to fetch a random photo. But we're only doing that once, when the window first opens. Once it's downloaded, that's it. There's no way to pick a new photo without forcing the whole app to quit and restart. To change that, let's make one more upgrade to our app.

As you learned in Chapter 2, Escape From Callback Hell, on page 17, suspending functions let you include loops and other control structures in your asynchronous code. This is a great opportunity to try that out. With our new coroutine, it'll be easy to update our code so that it keeps on refreshing to display a new photo.

We'll start by adding a while loop, with a delay() to determine how often we want our download to repeat:

```
astronomy/v8/src/main/kotlin/com/example/astronomy/AstronomyApplication.kt
class ImageViewer : WindowAdapter() {
  val coroutineScope = MainScope()

  override fun windowOpened(e: WindowEvent) {
    val window = e.window as JFrame
    coroutineScope.launch {
      while (true) {
        loadImage(window)
        delay(15.seconds)
      }
    }
  }
}

fun main() = createWindow("Image Viewer", ImageViewer())
```

Great! We're now grabbing a new random photo every few seconds so our users won't get bored looking at the same old picture.

I Think It's Leaking

Did you spot the leak?

A memory leak happens when a program claims a chunk of memory and then fails to release it again when it's no longer needed. An app with a memory leak will gradually run out of memory and slow down or crash. Thankfully, memory leaks are rare in Kotlin since the garbage collector automatically cleans up objects that are no longer in use. But one thing the garbage collector won't do is clean up an object that's referenced by a running task. As long as a coroutine is still running, its data remains in memory, even if the task and its results are never referenced or used again by the rest of the application!

By writing while (true) in our code, we've created a loop that runs forever. Even after you close the window, it'll keep right on downloading more pictures that you'll never see. In our simple program, you can solve this with the *stop* button in your IDE or by exiting the process some other way. But real apps don't end after one window or activity. Imagine a version of this program where the user can come back to look at the photo several times, closing and reopening the window between each viewing session. Each time the windowOpened() function runs, it'll start a new coroutine that downloads a fresh photo and holds it permanently in memory.

An abandoned coroutine that's holding data and resources that will never be used or cleaned up is called a *coroutine leak* or a *task leak*. And it's not just memory we need to worry about—all those leaked coroutines will also be competing for CPU time, network bandwidth, and more.

Even without any infinite loops, a coroutine can easily run—or suspend—for long enough to outlive the class or component that created it. The sooner we can clean up an unneeded task, the faster we can release its memory and resources back to the rest of the system, and the better our app's overall performance will be.

That's why Kotlin is so careful to link every coroutine to a coroutine scope.

Turn the Lights Out When You Leave

How do we stop those unwanted coroutines? Easy! When we're done with our coroutine scope, we need to call its cancel() function.

We'll talk more about how this cancellation mechanism works in Chapter 6, Cooperate with Cancellation, on page 91. For now, it's enough to know that once the coroutine has been canceled, it'll stop running any more code. That means the garbage collector will finally be free to come in and release any memory that the task was using.

So, where should we call this cancel() function? Well, our window listener's windowOpened() function is matched by a corresponding windowClosed() function. It's a similar story on Android, where onCreate() is mirrored by onDestroy(), giving us a chance to clean up resources associated with the activity and make sure that we haven't left anything behind.

Let's set it up in our Swing application:

astronomy/v9/src/main/kotlin/com/example/astronomy/AstronomyApplication.kt
```kotlin
class ImageViewer : WindowAdapter() {
  val coroutineScope = MainScope()

  override fun windowOpened(e: WindowEvent) {
    val window = e.window as JFrame
    coroutineScope.launch {
      while (true) {
        loadImage(window)
        delay(15.seconds)
      }
    }
  }

  override fun windowClosed(e: WindowEvent) {
    coroutineScope.cancel()
  }
}

fun main() = createWindow("Image Viewer", ImageViewer())
```

When the program's running, try closing the window. Only a second or two after you do so, the application terminates. All its coroutines have been properly canceled, and the memory leak is fixed.

What Goes Up Must Come Down

Any time you create a coroutine scope, you'll need to think about which component your background tasks belong to. Perhaps you're dealing with a window or dialog box in a desktop application. Maybe you're writing a web server that launches coroutines associated with each request or user session. Or, maybe you're running code that's attached to a particular level, character, or entity in a game engine. Each background task is going to be associated with a different part of the program's job, and each background task needs an appropriate coroutine scope that can make sure it gives up its memory and resources promptly when that job is complete.

So, every coroutine scope you create will have two symmetrical parts—creation and cancellation—representing two points in time during the life of your application. These two points represent the boundaries for the background tasks belonging to that part of the app.

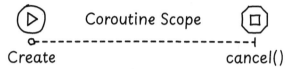

Sometimes, it's easy to figure out where to cancel a coroutine scope if the component you're building already implements an interface such as Android's LifecycleOwner or Java's Closeable. Other times, it might require some more thought or even some changes to the application's design. Later on, we'll explore some different strategies for organizing tasks and sending data between them.

Lifecycles Aren't Optional

If you're struggling to figure out the right lifecycle, it might be tempting to create a scope that skips the cancellation step. But, in fact, that's not something that would ever be useful. Why not? Well, setting a lifecycle for your coroutines is the only reason to create a custom coroutine scope in the first place. If you don't want to cancel your coroutines, you probably don't want a custom scope at all.

In Chapter 4, Split Up to Speed Up, on page 59, we'll introduce another way to get hold of a coroutine scope for coroutines that live not in a class or component but inside a suspending function. If you're totally sure that you want a scope that never gets canceled, then the built-in GlobalScope already has you covered. It's there for those rare coroutines that answer to no one and last for the whole lifetime of the application. You'll have to acknowledge a warning each time you use it because it comes without any protection against accidental coroutine leaks.

Same App, Different Platform

Now that you know how to create and cancel your own coroutine scope, let's see the same program on Android. Building and running an Android app could be a whole tutorial of its own, so there's no need to try running this one unless you happen to have an Android development environment already set up.

We can use the same AstronomyService, but we'll need a new version of that loadImage() function:

android/v2/src/main/kotlin/com/example/astronomy/MainActivity.kt

```kotlin
suspend fun Activity.loadImage() {
  val infoRequest = astronomyService.getPictures(count = 1, apiKey)
  val info = infoRequest.awaitResponse().body()!!.single()
  val imageRequest = astronomyService.downloadImage(info.url)
  val image = imageRequest.awaitResponse().body()!!.bytes()

  val bitmap = BitmapFactory.decodeStream(image.inputStream())
  setContentView(ImageView(this).apply { setImageBitmap(bitmap) })
}
```

Now, we can fill in our activity code using exactly the same coroutine scope recipe you just learned:

android/v2/src/main/kotlin/com/example/astronomy/MainActivity.kt

```kotlin
class MainActivity : ComponentActivity() {
  val coroutineScope = MainScope()

  override fun onCreate(savedInstanceState: Bundle?) {
    super.onCreate(savedInstanceState)
    setContentView(TextView(this).apply { text = "Loading your image…" })
    coroutineScope.launch {
      while (true) {
        loadImage()
        delay(15.seconds)
      }
    }
  }

  override fun onDestroy() {
    super.onDestroy()
    coroutineScope.cancel()
  }
}
```

Compare this code against the Swing version. The scaffolding might be different, but our coroutine and its coroutine scope look the same. Even the MainScope() function is unchanged, though you'll need to adjust your dependencies to swap kotlinx-coroutines-swing for kotlinx-coroutines-android.

Here's One They Made Earlier

With the simple recipe you've just learned, it's easy to add a coroutine scope to any Android activity. But in fact, you might not even need to do that. As long as you have Android's Lifecycle KTX[1] module among your app's dependencies, you'll be able to use the lifecycleScope that's already built into your Activity:

---

1. https://developer.android.com/kotlin/ktx

```
android/v3/src/main/kotlin/com/example/astronomy/MainActivity.kt
class MainActivity : ComponentActivity() {
  override fun onCreate(savedInstanceState: Bundle?) {
    super.onCreate(savedInstanceState)
    setContentView(TextView(this).apply { text = "Loading your image…" })
    lifecycleScope.launch {
      while (true) {
        loadImage()
        delay(15.seconds)
      }
    }
  }
}
```

This lifecycleScope is like the custom scope we made earlier, and you can use it in the same way. It's available for any Android component that has a Lifecycle, including activities, fragments, and dialogs. It uses the component's lifecycle to determine when the scope should be canceled, so there's no need to add your own onDestroy() function.

There's also a separate ViewModel KTX extension module, providing a viewModelScope that'll cancel its coroutines when the view model is cleared.

Both of those scopes will take care of setting the right dispatcher, too, along with some other things you'll learn about later on. Pre-built scopes such as these can come with ready-made configurations for coroutines in a particular type of application or component so that you don't need to worry about setting up each new coroutine from scratch. Easy!

No Scope?

If we need a scope to provide the starting context for every new coroutine, why are we only hearing about them now? Haven't we been using coroutines for more than a chapter already?

When you use a coroutine builder, such as launch(), you're sending some code to run in a background task. Coroutine scopes keep track of these background tasks, and you need one any time you want to add a new coroutine as a background task to an existing application.

But in our first chapter, we didn't do that—we had Kotlin create a single coroutine to run our suspending main() function. Even when the main() function runs in a coroutine, it's still the program's main task. It doesn't run in the background, so it doesn't need a coroutine scope.

Get Rid of Unwanted Tasks

You've learned how to move a suspending function into a background task—a new coroutine of its own—so that you can call it from a non-suspending function that doesn't have the ability to wait for it. To do that, you used a coroutine scope along with its launch() coroutine builder function.

These new functions and concepts might seem unfamiliar if you're used to other asynchronous programming styles. Why does Kotlin need background tasks and coroutine machinery just to call an asynchronous function?

In the last section of this chapter, we'll explore why Kotlin does things differently. We'll unmask the background task that's hiding in every asynchronous call, and you'll learn how suspending functions let you choose whether you really want it.

Hiding in Plain Sight

Asynchronous callbacks are a simple enough idea, but they do something interesting and unexpected to the control flow of a program. Their two-part structure creates a foundational problem—one which suspending functions have been carefully designed to solve.

To see what's going on, let's go back and look at some simple timer callbacks like the ones we wrote in the last chapter:

timers/v15/src/main/kotlin/com/example/timers/TimerApplication.kt
```
fun main() {
  val timer = java.util.Timer()

  timer.schedule(1000) {
    println("Callback started after 1 second.")
    timer.cancel()
  }
}
```

As you already know, this asynchronous schedule() function will return right away. It isn't going to wait for its callback to run, meaning this is a simple way to add a delay without blocking our starting thread.

```
Callback started after 1 second.
```

But it's worth pausing for a moment to consider the implications of this. If the starting thread doesn't need to wait around for our callback code, it can move right on and start doing other things. The result? Our code is diverging in two different directions:

timers/v16/src/main/kotlin/com/example/timers/TimerApplication.kt

```kotlin
fun main() {
  val timer = java.util.Timer()

  timer.schedule(1000) {
    println("Now I'm running too!")
    timer.cancel()
  }

  println("I'm still running…")
}
```

```
I'm still running…
Now I'm running too!
```

You might be familiar with this concept if you've worked with JavaScript, where the similar setTimeout() function is the easiest way to introduce multitasking. But this trick isn't unique to timer-style functions such as JavaScript's setTimeout() or Java's Timer. Every asynchronous event—whether it's a network response, a user interaction, or a simple timed delay such as the one we're using here—has the potential to act as a trigger that starts a new piece of code regardless of what the program is already doing. Any time we fire a callback in response to an outside event, we're creating a new background task, whether we like it or not.

Look familiar? It's not too far from what we're doing when we call our coroutine scope's launch() function.

Like coroutine builders, callbacks begin executing a piece of code without waiting for that code's execution to finish. When you think about it, that's another way of saying they create background tasks. There's a background task concealed inside every asynchronous call, no matter what programming style you're using. So, when you launch a coroutine, Kotlin isn't pulling a background task out of thin air. The task's creation was already an important component of the asynchronous operation, and Kotlin's coroutine builder functions serve to make it more visible.

Background tasks can open the door to some nasty bugs, such as the memory leak we fixed earlier, so making them visible is a good thing. Now that we've got a background task, we've also got the potential for a task leak. If we're not careful, code that we put inside our callback could continue running indefinitely, holding onto valuable resources long after the program has moved on to do other things.

Rewrite the Rules

Now, take a look at how this program changes when we swap our Timer for the suspending delay() function:

```
timers/v17/src/main/kotlin/com/example/timers/TimerApplication.kt
suspend fun main() {
  delay(1000)
  println("Continuing the function after 1 second.")
}
```

With the callback, there were three different places we could have added code to the program—before the call to schedule(), after the call to schedule(), or inside the callback itself.

But now, one of those paths has disappeared. There are only two places we could put new code here—before the delay() or after it. That means there's nowhere for any background tasks to hide. We're back to a single, sequential control flow, and what used to be a branching intersection has now become another step on a single direct route.

When you replace a callback with a suspending function, you're getting rid of an extra background task. Remember this because it explains many of the differences between coroutines and other asynchronous styles.

To Wait, or Not to Wait?

Cleaning up unwanted background tasks makes asynchronous code safer and easier to use, solving many of the problems we saw in the last chapter. So, it shouldn't come as a surprise that Kotlin isn't the first language to try it. JavaScript, C#, Python, Swift, and many others can convert asynchronous calls into sequential style with their async and await keywords.

But that C#-style async modifier still isn't doing the same thing as Kotlin's suspend keyword. For one thing, if you've used async functions in other languages, you'll know that they seem to manage without any of Kotlin's coroutine scopes and coroutine builders.

Why does Kotlin need all the extra baggage?

It all comes down to one key design difference between the two approaches.

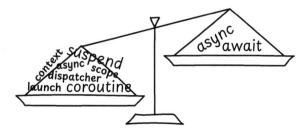

Call a suspending function, and it always waits for all of its work to finish. You learned this in Chapter 2, Escape From Callback Hell, on page 17. This single-track sequential waiting is Kotlin's default behavior, and background tasks are an opt-in extra that you can enable via the launch() function.

Well, with async functions in other languages, it's the other way around. Multitasking is the default, and you'll need to opt out if you don't want it. That means when you first call an async function, it'll return immediately—as if it was using a callback—while the asynchronous operation continues in the background. To get the sequential behavior of Kotlin's suspending functions when you're writing JavaScript or C#, you add the extra await keyword.

Would You Like Multitasking With That?

An async function in a language such as JavaScript can be called from anywhere. If you don't have the ability to wait for it, you don't have to. That sounds handy—so why does Kotlin flip the background-task-creation script and go for a waiting-first approach that ends up feeling more restrictive?

There are two main reasons that Kotlin makes you ask for all your background tasks explicitly.

First, it means nobody's going to get a background task they weren't expecting. You've learned that callbacks and their background tasks can lead to resource leaks and missing errors. So, if starting a coroutine to call a suspending function feels like more steps than queueing up a callback, that's absolutely by design. By making asynchronous background tasks as visible as possible, Kotlin is making sure bugs have fewer places to hide.

Second, it moves the responsibility for creating and configuring background tasks away from the individual asynchronous operations and onto the caller. Whether you're using coroutines or callbacks, you always need to think about what thread your code will end up running on or how it will handle its errors and resources. So, a coroutine scope, with its dispatcher and other coroutine context elements, isn't adding anything that callbacks and async functions didn't already need to do. It's making it easier for you to configure it all in one place and making it more difficult to forget.

What Have You Learned?

You can't always give an existing function the ability to pause its execution, so you've learned how to launch() your suspending functions in a background task instead.

But, with background tasks come task leaks, and to fix that, your new coroutine needs a lifecycle. You learned an easy recipe to create and cancel a custom coroutine scope for any component, and you discovered some pre-built implementations of the same recipe in Android.

Now that you can use coroutine builder functions to make new coroutines, why stop at one? Next, you'll speed up an asynchronous operation by dividing it into multiple subtasks.

Key Concepts

Coroutine builder

    This starts a new coroutine as a background task within a coroutine scope. The launch() function is a coroutine builder.

Coroutine scope

    This sets the lifecycle for a new coroutine and provides it with its starting coroutine context. The MainScope() function creates a scope for UI coroutines.

Cancellation

    This stops a coroutine, preventing task leaks. Making sure this happens is one of the coroutine scope's key responsibilities.

CHAPTER 4

Split Up to Speed Up

Even on its own, a coroutine is useful for keeping long-running tasks clear of important threads. But it's when multiple coroutines are running together that they start to show their real power.

We're going to upgrade our photo viewer to display more than one photo at a time, and we'll give the whole thing a speed boost by using a new coroutine for each download.

By the end of the chapter, you'll have a reusable multitasking template that you can use to speed up any suspending function without even changing the function's signature.

Write Code That Can Multitask

So far, we've been focusing on the bad things about background tasks, such as resource leaks and errors that vanish into dead-end callbacks. But by cleaning up all our background tasks, we've also removed our code's ability to work on more than one thing at once.

Background tasks aren't all bad, and with coroutine builders, you've got the tools to use them in a safe and controlled way. In this section, you'll learn how.

Concurrency

Ever found yourself thinking you could be so much more productive if only you could be in two places at once?

Whenever you start a new background task, whether that's by launching a coroutine, queueing up a callback, or even starting a whole new thread, you're introducing *concurrency* into your program.

The word *concurrent* means *running together*, and it describes a situation where a program is following more than one path through the code at the same time.

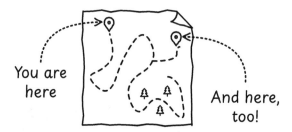

To understand more about concurrency, let's look at a way we might make use of some multitasking in everyday life. After you learn the ropes through this made-up scenario, you'll apply the same principles to some network calls with Retrofit.

Get Ready to Party

Imagine you're preparing for a party. First, you'd like to clean and dry your favorite outfit. Next, you need to bake and decorate the cake.

We can write out the tasks as a simple Kotlin program with a named function for each task:

party/v1/src/main/kotlin/com/example/party/PartyPlanningApplication.kt
```
suspend fun doTasks() {
  doLaundry()
  bakeCake()
}

suspend fun main() {
  doTasks()
  println("All done!")
}
```

Both tasks are a good fit for asynchronous suspending functions because they each involve some waiting. The clothes will sit in the washer without any intervention from you, and the cake will need some time to bake in the hot oven.

Let's implement the functions for the two tasks so we can run the program.

We'll use the suspending delay() function to simulate the time you'd spend waiting for the real task to complete. To show what each task is doing, we'll also include some println() calls:

`party/v1/src/main/kotlin/com/example/party/PartyPlanningApplication.kt`

```kotlin
suspend fun doLaundry() {
  println("[Wash1] Putting the clothes in the washer")
  delay(1.seconds)
  println("[Wash2] Moving the clothes to the dryer")
  delay(1.seconds)
  println("[Wash3] Laundry's ready")
}

suspend fun bakeCake() {
  println("[Cake1] Putting the cake in the oven")
  delay(1.seconds)
  println("[Cake2] Waiting for the cake to cool")
  delay(1.seconds)
  println("[Cake3] Decorating the cake")
}
```

When you run the program, notice how it works through the instructions one by one, completing each function before moving on to the next. It won't start to work on the cake until the laundry is clean and dry. You can read through the output in exactly the same order as you read through the program's code:

```
[Wash1] Putting the clothes in the washer
[Wash2] Moving the clothes to the dryer
[Wash3] Laundry's ready
[Cake1] Putting the cake in the oven
[Cake2] Waiting for the cake to cool
[Cake3] Decorating the cake
All done!
```

As you learned in Chapter 2, Escape From Callback Hell, on page 17, a suspending function executes its contents in order—one line at a time like an ordinary function.

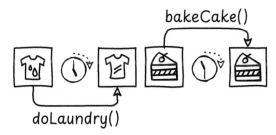

Unlike the callbacks they replace, suspending functions don't create their own background tasks. But is that really what we want? If you were doing these jobs around the house, you wouldn't separate them out sequentially. Instead, you'd multitask, working on both jobs concurrently.

Once the clothes are in the washer, there's no need to sit and wait for them. You can start on the cake recipe while the washing machine carries on doing its thing. Later, while you wait for the cake to cool, you can come back and move the clothes to the dryer.

By switching between the tasks, you'll finish the work quicker without getting help from anyone else or working any harder.

Start Your Coroutines!

A suspending function frees up its thread while it's waiting—but that's only useful if there are other things that thread can do during the gaps. This program has one task with its own dedicated thread, so our code doesn't yet have any opportunities for multitasking.

Let's fix that and let our program know that it doesn't need to wait for the first task to complete before starting work on the second. All we need to do is launch() each function in its own coroutine.

To make new coroutines, we'll need a coroutine scope, just as we did in the last chapter. But this time, we're doing everything from within a suspending function that's perfectly capable of waiting for things. That gives us a whole new way to manage our background tasks. If we use a suspension point to wait for all our coroutines to finish, none of them will ever outlive the function that created them, and there won't be any risk of task leaks. Clever, right?

That's exactly the job of the coroutineScope() function, which is part of the kotlinx.coroutines core library.

Be careful not to confuse this with the capitalized CoroutineScope() constructor function, which is a more customizable version of the MainScope() function we've used before. While MainScope() and CoroutineScope() both create and return a CoroutineScope object, the lowercase coroutineScope() function does things differently. It takes your code as an argument, including any coroutines you want to launch, and runs everything in its own in-house coroutine scope. It's also a suspending function, and it'll wait for all the code and tasks inside its scope to finish before it returns.

Let's put it to use in our doTasks() function and break our code into separate coroutines:

party/v2/src/main/kotlin/com/example/party/PartyPlanningApplication.kt
```
suspend fun doTasks() = coroutineScope {
  launch { doLaundry() }
  launch { bakeCake() }
}
```

```
suspend fun main() {
  doTasks()
  println("All done!")
}
```

Ready to Receive

The coroutineScope() function's code block can access its coroutine scope as an implicit receiver. In the last chapter, we had to write out coroutineScope.launch() with its explicit receiver in full. This time, we're free to write launch() on its own. Nice!

You'll notice two things that are different when we run the program this time.

First, the lines of output are in a different order:

```
[Wash1] Putting the clothes in the washer
[Cake1] Putting the cake in the oven
[Wash2] Moving the clothes to the dryer
[Cake2] Waiting for the cake to cool
[Wash3] Laundry's ready
[Cake3] Decorating the cake
All done!
```

After the first task starts, the second task kicks off right away. Within each individual task, the normal rules of ordering still apply—so you'll never see the cake being decorated before it's baked, for example. But the program's free to switch back and forth between the two tasks, just like we wanted.

Out of Order

Whenever a program's output appears in a different order from the lines of code in the actual program, it's a clue that there's some concurrency going on.

Second, the program finished faster! We included two seconds of simulated delay in each task, so running them sequentially would have taken a total of four seconds. But this time, the program finished in closer to two seconds.

Fill in The Blanks

How did adding more code make our program go faster?

You learned right at the start of our journey that suspending functions are all about waiting. Each suspension point, whether it's a timed delay(), a network call, or some other outside event, leaves a gap where its thread is no longer busy running code. Using those gaps to make progress on other tasks is a big part of how coroutines help make our programs more efficient.

That means coroutines aren't just for user interface code. As you'll learn in Chapter 7, Unlock Parallel Processing, on page 109, new threads don't come for free. The more we can make use of the threads we already have, the more we can save resources and improve performance, no matter what kind of work we're doing.

By launching more coroutines, we've provided more options to keep our thread busy. When one coroutine is held up, the program can simply pick one of the others to make progress on instead.

In our upgraded doTasks() function, we're creating two coroutines—one for each of our two tasks. When the doLaundry() task reaches its first call to delay(), that coroutine is going to be suspended for a while. It's during that waiting time that the program can switch its attention and make a start on the bakeCake() function in coroutine number two.

Each task still took the same amount of time, but we took advantage of the gaps in each task to make progress on the other at the same time.

This kind of concurrency is also called *cooperative multitasking* because the tasks are cooperating with each other by giving up their thread at each suspension point. Since we're making more efficient use of the resources we already have, cooperative multitasking lets us complete asynchronous tasks faster without any need for extra threads, processor cores, or other resources. Who says there's no such thing as a free lunch?

Breaking It Down

When we use the coroutineScope() function, we're dividing a single suspending function into a number of concurrent subtasks. Inside the new scope, those subtasks can execute concurrently, but the coroutineScope() function acts as a boundary that stops that concurrency from leaking into the outside world.

This is sometimes called *concurrent decomposition* because we're *decomposing* a task into several smaller tasks.

Regardless of whether we're doing things sequentially or concurrently, our function isn't finished until all its subtasks are complete. Since our upgraded doTasks() function doesn't return until all its background tasks are finished, nobody calling the function ever needs to know it contains any concurrency at all. From the outside, it'll look and behave the same as any other suspending function.

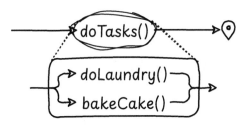

Two Types of Scope

Let's recap the difference between this new coroutineScope() function and the MainScope() we set up in the last chapter:

- The coroutineScope() function makes coroutines within a suspending function. It waits for all the coroutines to complete so they don't leak outside the function. Use a scope like this when you want to multitask within a function.

- A custom scope such as MainScope() attaches coroutines to a class or component in our application. It doesn't do any waiting of its own. Instead, the coroutines are cleaned up when the component reaches the end of its lifecycle so they don't leak outside the component. Use a scope like this when you want to start a new task in the background of a particular part of the app.

When your starting point is a function that has the ability to suspend, the coroutineScope() function is almost always the right choice. A suspending function should always wait for the coroutines it starts—more on that in Chapter 8, Call Blocking Functions Safely, on page 129.

Download Two Things at Once

Now that you're an expert in concurrent decomposition with coroutines, let's put those skills to use in our NASA photo viewer app.

So far, we've downloaded and displayed one picture at a time. In this section, you'll use your concurrency knowledge to download a handful of photos and display them in a scrollable gallery.

Once more, you will be using the coroutineScope() function to decompose the task into independent coroutines. But this time, the launch() function doesn't do what we need, so we'll need to introduce a second coroutine builder function.

If One Is Good, Two Must Be Better

You'll need the full AstronomyService.kt file from the code on page 31, along with all of its dependencies.

We've been using the NASA API to download a single random photo. Let's make it a bit more interesting. Our AstronomyService accepts a count parameter, and we can increase that number to get a larger selection of pictures.

If we're going to be displaying more than one picture, we're going to need to upgrade our displayImage() function. So, let's start by making a new function, displayImageGallery(), which will accept a whole list of pictures:

astronomy/v10/src/main/kotlin/com/example/astronomy/Helpers.kt
```kotlin
fun displayImageGallery(window: JFrame, images: List<ByteArray>) {
  val panel = JPanel(GridLayout(0, 1))

  for (image in images) {
    panel.add(JLabel(ImageIcon(image)))
  }

  window.contentPane.removeAll()
  window.add(JScrollPane(panel))
  window.pack()
}
```

We'll use Swing's GridLayout to arrange the photos in a vertical column and add a JScrollPane so we can navigate through the list.

Abstract Base Class

When we last worked on the image viewer app, we'd just finished installing a custom coroutine scope, complete with cancellation. We'll be keeping most of the code, but the part where we download and display the photo will need to change. To make things easy, let's turn our ImageViewer into an abstract class that contains the pieces we want to keep:

astronomy/v10/src/main/kotlin/com/example/astronomy/ImageViewer.kt
```kotlin
abstract class ImageViewer : WindowAdapter() {
  val coroutineScope = MainScope()

  override fun windowOpened(e: WindowEvent) {
    val window = e.window as JFrame
    coroutineScope.launch {
      update(window)
    }
  }
```

```
protected abstract suspend fun update(window: JFrame)

override fun windowClosed(e: WindowEvent) {
  coroutineScope.cancel()
}
}
```

This class will act as a template that we can use to try out a few different programs. When we want to try a new way of loading and displaying our images, we need to extend this class and implement that update() function.

Scrolling Through Space

Okay, we're ready to start downloading these photos! Let's first try fetching a pair of photos one after the other without any concurrency:

astronomy/v10/src/main/kotlin/com/example/astronomy/AstronomyApplication.kt
```
class ImageGallery : ImageViewer() {
  override suspend fun update(window: JFrame) {
    val infoRequest = astronomyService.getPictures(count = 2, apiKey)
    val (info1, info2) = infoRequest.awaitResponse().body()!!

    val image1 = downloadImage(info1.url)
    val image2 = downloadImage(info2.url)

    displayImageGallery(window, listOf(image1, image2))
  }

  private suspend fun downloadImage(url: String): ByteArray =
    astronomyService.downloadImage(url).awaitResponse().body()!!.bytes()
}
```

Run the app with the same createWindow() function we used last time. You can find the code on page 41:

astronomy/v10/src/main/kotlin/com/example/astronomy/AstronomyApplication.kt
```
fun main() = createWindow("Image Viewer", ImageGallery())
```

Since the API we're using returns a random selection of results, you'll see a different pair of photos each time you run the code.

This works fine, but we can make it more efficient using our new concurrency knowledge. Right now, the program pauses as soon as the first download starts. It won't start work on the second request until the first one is complete.

Criteria for Concurrency

Did you spot some similarities between these tasks and the party planning example we used earlier? Just like the bakeCake() and doLaundry() functions, our image file downloads have two key properties that make them suitable for concurrency:

- We don't need them to execute in a specific order. Right now, our program has no choice but to run the code in the order we wrote it. But if we swapped the order of those two lines, we'd still get the same result.

- They're suspending functions that involve some waiting. Each asynchronous network request will need to run a bit of code and then wait for data to travel over the Internet. When the first request suspends to wait for its result, that'll create a gap where we could start working on the second request.

When tasks in a program fit these two criteria, it's a sign that we can use concurrency to make them more efficient. The asynchronous gaps in the tasks are wasted time, and a sequential program like this one has no way to fill those gaps with useful work.

We can use our concurrent decomposition recipe to fix that. But first, let's pause to talk about some other programming languages.

Async and Await

At the end of Chapter 3, Start It, Scope It, Stop It, on page 39, we talked about the async and await keywords found in many other programming languages, such as JavaScript, C#, Swift, and Python. Let's focus on JavaScript for a moment and see how its approach compares to Kotlin's.

An async function in JavaScript starts its work in the background and immediately returns a Promise—more on those in Chapter 9, Upgrade Every Callback, on page 145. The Promise is a placeholder for the actual result, which might not even have been computed yet. To wait for the background operation to finish and the result to be available, you use the separate await operation.

JavaScript's async functions have two important capabilities. When combined with await, they join asynchronous callbacks back into a sequential style, so you can use them in loops, try–catch blocks, and so on—like suspending functions in Kotlin. But leave out the await keyword, and you also get multitasking thrown into the deal. Just call several async functions in a row, and they'll all start running concurrently in the background. When you want to get the results from all your concurrent tasks, that's when you reintroduce the await operation.

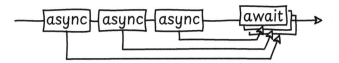

Wait for a Coroutine

Suspending functions always include their waiting, so they don't have this extra multitasking capability. That's the key difference between Kotlin's suspend modifier and the async keyword found in other languages.

You learned how to solve this problem when you used the launch() function to start a coroutine in the code on page 62. Expressing the party planning tasks as separate coroutines allowed the program to multitask between them instead of running them in a fixed sequence.

But with those tasks, we didn't need to get hold of any output from the coroutine's code. This time, we're going to need each coroutine to return its photo to us so we can display it in our gallery. To do that, Kotlin has its own take on *async* and *await*—and this time, they're functions, not keywords.

In fact, async() is going to be our second coroutine builder function. Just like launch(), async() starts a new task and returns immediately. That's how it introduces concurrency.

The difference between the two coroutine builder functions is in their return types:

- launch() is for coroutines that don't produce anything, like the way a Unit function doesn't have a return value.

- async() is for coroutines that deliver some output. It returns a Deferred result—Kotlin's version of a Promise or Future.

Keywords or Functions?

Suspension points enable several control-flow tricks, and async isn't the only common keyword that Kotlin swaps for a coroutine-powered function. In Chapter 10, Go with the Flow, on page 161, you'll see another.

Once again, we can rely on the coroutineScope() function's task-grouping suspension point to wait for our image-fetching operations and prevent any task leaks:

astronomy/v11/src/main/kotlin/com/example/astronomy/AstronomyApplication.kt

```
class ImageGallery : ImageViewer() {
  override suspend fun update(window: JFrame) = coroutineScope {
    val infoRequest = astronomyService.getPictures(count = 2, apiKey)
    val (info1, info2) = infoRequest.awaitResponse().body()!!

    val image1: Deferred<ByteArray> = async { downloadImage(info1.url) }
    val image2: Deferred<ByteArray> = async { downloadImage(info2.url) }

    displayImageGallery(window, listOf(image1.await(), image2.await()))
  }

  private suspend fun downloadImage(url: String): ByteArray =
    astronomyService.downloadImage(url).awaitResponse().body()!!.bytes()
}

fun main() = createWindow("Image Viewer", ImageGallery())
```

Chef's Choice

Okay, so this program should run twice as fast, right?

Well, maybe. Downloading a file is a whole lot more complicated than the simple timed delays we were using in our party planning example. So, the speed increase we see here will depend on all kinds of factors. For example, if all the photos in our gallery are coming from the same place, we might be limited by the remote server as much as by our own code.

Creating two coroutines doesn't necessarily mean we'll be able to download our files at double the speed. In fact, it might not make things any quicker at all. So why bother?

Concurrency is all about creating options. A program with no concurrency will always run the same sequence of instructions in the same strict order. But when we add coroutines, we're removing those constraints and giving the system more freedom. Now, it can pick and choose pieces from different tasks, depending on what resources are available at the time.

That means our concurrent program can execute in a different way every time we run it. Maybe it'll jump right into both tasks, saving time by creating and using two network connections at once. Or, maybe it only has the resources to run them one by one in exactly the same sequence as the non-concurrent version.

Compared to the network requests we're making, a coroutine uses barely any resources. So, we haven't lost much by giving the system more options, even if it doesn't end up using them.

Download a List of Photos

Let's make our new code a little more versatile. We'll write a getImages() function that accepts a count parameter. That way, we can populate our photo gallery with any number of images we want.

Just like we did with the two-photo version, we'll start out by writing the function without any coroutines. The AstronomyService will give us a list of images. We just need to use Kotlin's built-in map() function to transform the list one element at a time:

astronomy/v12/src/main/kotlin/com/example/astronomy/AstronomyApplication.kt

```
suspend fun getImages(count: Int): List<ByteArray> {
  val infoRequest = astronomyService.getPictures(count, apiKey)
  val imageInfo = infoRequest.awaitResponse().body()!!

  return imageInfo.map { downloadImage(it.url) }
}

private suspend fun downloadImage(url: String): ByteArray =
  astronomyService.downloadImage(url).awaitResponse().body()!!.bytes()
```

The map() function works like a regular loop, completing each task before moving on to the next one. How do we make this program run concurrently instead?

Wait for a List of Coroutines

Instead of doing the work directly inside our map() function, let's have it start a coroutine for each item in the list:

astronomy/v13/src/main/kotlin/com/example/astronomy/AstronomyApplication.kt

```
suspend fun getImages(count: Int): List<ByteArray> = coroutineScope {
  val infoRequest = astronomyService.getPictures(count, apiKey)
  val imageInfo = infoRequest.awaitResponse().body()!!

  val images: List<Deferred<ByteArray>> = imageInfo.map {
    async { downloadImage(it.url) }
  }

  images.awaitAll()
}

private suspend fun downloadImage(url: String): ByteArray =
  astronomyService.downloadImage(url).awaitResponse().body()!!.bytes()
```

Now that we've added our new coroutines, the work is no longer happening inside the map() function. Instead, that line of code sets all the coroutines running. The program doesn't stop and wait for any of the results until it reaches the awaitAll() function in the next line.

By starting a separate coroutine for each item, we let the system know that the items can be processed concurrently rather than in strict order. No, that doesn't mean the order of the results will be different from the order of the inputs! Keeping the Deferred results in a list means we never lose track of the actual order of the items. What it does mean is that the list can be processed more efficiently by starting work on more than one item at the same time. You can use the same pattern any time you need to execute a list of tasks that meet the criteria for concurrency.

Kotlin's async() coroutines almost always travel in groups or lists like this, making awaitAll() a handy helper. In other languages, you might be used to seeing a single *async* operation paired with an immediate *await*—that's how you'd wait for the task's result. But in Kotlin, suspending functions already have asynchronous waiting covered, and the launch() or async() functions are only needed when you also want to start a background task. Following async() with an immediate await() would be like asking someone to run an errand for you, then jumping in their car to ride along with them anyway. The only reason to start a background task is if you're going to do something else in the foreground, such as starting some additional coroutines before you call await().

The new getImages() function slots in easily to our program, and now we can adjust the number of images in the gallery to any value we want.

Let's fetch six:

astronomy/v13/src/main/kotlin/com/example/astronomy/AstronomyApplication.kt
```kotlin
class ImageGallery : ImageViewer() {
  override suspend fun update(window: JFrame) {
    val images = getImages(6)
    displayImageGallery(window, images)
  }
}

fun main() = createWindow("Image Viewer", ImageGallery())
```

Matching Signatures

Notice how both the implementations we wrote for getImages()—the one with coroutines and the one without—have the same signature, with the same suspend modifier and the same List<ByteArray> return type. That means we can swap one for the other without changing anything in the ImageGallery's update() function.

Whichever implementation we use, it'll still perform all the same tasks and return the results when they're all complete. By adding coroutines, all we've done is remove some inefficiency that was built into our previous code.

Coroutines provide a language that lets you break down an operation into one or more independent subtasks. Giving the program more accurate information about how these tasks relate to one another—or don't—allows it to be more efficient when executing them. With the help of the coroutineScope() function, you can add concurrency to any suspending function without affecting its callers in any way.

What Have You Learned?

In this chapter, you sped up a suspending function by breaking it up into async() coroutine subtasks, then using awaitAll() to gather the results.

Thanks to the coroutineScope() surrounding the whole thing, there's no sign of concurrency or task leaks from outside. That's because the scope waits for all its coroutines to complete.

Both awaitAll() and coroutineScope() are suspending functions, and both offer a way to suspend and wait for a group of coroutines. Isn't that just two different ways of doing the same thing? The two ways of waiting are connected by a parent–child hierarchy, which is what we'll cover next.

Key Concepts

Concurrency
> This is the ability to have more than one task in progress at the same time. Add coroutines to create concurrency and let suspending functions multitask.

Decomposition
> This is a way to create concurrency by breaking a single task up into coroutine subtasks. Create a coroutineScope() and then use async() to create tasks and await()/awaitAll() to collect their results.

CHAPTER 5

Plan for Any Outcome

Multitasking might mean more speed, but it also means more tasks and results to keep track of.

In this chapter, you'll learn how Kotlin carefully links each task to its subtasks, and you'll use the Three Rules of Jobs to figure out how a success or failure in one coroutine will affect the rest of the program.

There'll be no more guessing where an exception is going to end up or how long a task will take to finish. Once you read this chapter, you'll be back in control of your code's destiny, with the tools to organize and customize your coroutines to fit the structure of your program.

Build a Hierarchy of Tasks and Subtasks

In our last chapter, we introduced the coroutineScope() function, which lets us start new coroutines within an existing suspending function. When all the subtasks are finished, the code returns to a single path, as if the concurrency was never there in the first place.

How does the coroutineScope() function monitor its coroutines and know which ones to wait for? Let's kick off this chapter with a look at the machinery that powers the coroutine scopes we've been using. You'll learn how you can use the same tools to customize coroutine behavior in your own code.

A Job for Every Coroutine

You've earned a break, so for our code examples in this chapter, let's make some coffee.

We'll start with a simple suspending makeCoffee() function. Brewing up a steaming cup of joe will take a few seconds, so we'll include a delay() as a placeholder for our implementation:

coffee/v1/src/main/kotlin/com/example/coffee/CoffeeApplication.kt
```kotlin
suspend fun makeCoffee() {
  println("Brewing your coffee…")
  delay(5.seconds)
  println("Coffee's ready!")
}
```

Next, we'll kick off our function in a new background coroutine. Now, one of the key characteristics of a background task is that it won't necessarily run for the whole lifetime of the program. Instead, the task has its own distinct beginning and end. That might sound obvious, but it's an important concept for working with coroutines. A typical coroutine starts when we call launch() or async() and ends when all the coroutine's work is complete. We can call this the coroutine's *lifecycle*.

To keep track of its progress, every coroutine has an associated Job object. The Job is part of the coroutine context, so it lives alongside the coroutine and follows it on its journey. This is the second coroutine context element we've introduced after the Dispatcher:

coffee/v1/src/main/kotlin/com/example/coffee/CoffeeApplication.kt
```kotlin
suspend fun main() = coroutineScope {
  val coffeeJob: Job = launch {
    makeCoffee()
  }
}
```

See the Job? It's the value being returned by the launch() function when we start our coroutine. We're assigning it to a variable, coffeeJob, so we can hold onto it and see what it's up to.

Active or Inactive?

It's easy to get a peek behind the scenes at how the Job is monitoring our coroutine's lifecycle. We need to look at its isActive property, which is true when the job is running and false when it's in a completed, failed, or canceled state:

coffee/v2/src/main/kotlin/com/example/coffee/CoffeeApplication.kt
```kotlin
suspend fun main() = coroutineScope {
  val coffeeJob: Job = launch {
    makeCoffee()
  }

  println("isActive: " + coffeeJob.isActive)
  println("Waiting for six seconds…")
```

```
    delay(6.seconds)
    println("isActive: " + coffeeJob.isActive)
}
```

The launch() function starts its coroutine right away, so this Job is active as soon as it's been created. Six seconds is long enough for the coroutine to finish all its work, so after our delay(), the Job has finished, and isActive has changed to false:

```
Brewing your coffee…
isActive: true
Waiting for six seconds…
Coffee's ready!
isActive: false
```

One-Way Trip

 A coroutine job's lifecycle is a one-way journey. Once completed, a coroutine can't start running again—so, after that isActive property has changed from true to false, it's not changing back.

A Deferred Result Is a Type of Job

You've seen some coroutine jobs in the previous chapter.

When we introduced the async() function, you learned that it returns a Deferred object. It's this object that provides the await() and awaitAll() functions.

Well, the Deferred object returned by async() is a lot like the Job object returned by launch(). A Deferred has a couple of extra functions since it needs to give us access to the async() coroutine's result value. When you look at the documentation or source code, you'll see that Deferred is a subtype of Job.

launch {…} ⟶ Job

async {…} ⟶ Deferred

Keep It in the Family

Like a Deferred result, a Job can wait for its coroutine to finish. A coroutine created with launch() doesn't provide a result, so in place of the await() function, it provides a simpler suspending join() function that returns Unit.

It's rare that you'll need to use the join() function, though—or even interact with Job objects at all. That's because every job is already being automatically monitored for you.

Remember how we said that a coroutine's Job is part of its coroutine context? Well, as you learned in Chapter 3, Start It, Scope It, Stop It, on page 39, a coroutine scope contains a set of coroutine context elements, which it provides as starting context to the new coroutines it creates. That means a coroutine scope contains a Job.

But a new coroutine doesn't inherit the Job from its scope. Instead, each coroutine builder function creates a brand new Job and links it to the parent Job it received in its starting context.

Where does the parent Job come from? Well, the first thing a function such as coroutineScope() does is to create a Job of its own, like Sauron forging his master Ring of Power in the world of *The Lord of The Rings*. This Job will act as the parent of all the jobs that are launched inside the scope—and in the darkness bind them. Of course, that Job can have its own parent too, and so on up the chain ... but more on that later.

Once two coroutine jobs have been joined together as parent and child, their destinies are intertwined, and the outcome of each job will affect the other. This is the foundation of *structured concurrency*, and it's how a coroutine scope keeps track of all its coroutines.

What Is Structured Concurrency?

In Chapter 2, Escape From Callback Hell, on page 17, you saw that adding a background task creates an escape route where code, resources, and errors can break free from the control-flow blocks of structured programming.

You already know that suspending functions solve the problem by getting rid of unwanted background tasks. But that means no more multitasking. When you want to start on two things at once, you can't avoid the need for diverging control flow.

Structured concurrency aims to bring some of those missing structured programming features back to your coroutines so you can have the best of both worlds. In the same way that you'd rely on structured programming to wait for or clean up after an ordinary function, you can rely on structured concurrency to link each of your program's background tasks to an appropriate parent Job that will keep track of its errors and resources.

Waiting for Coroutines

To wait for its child coroutines to finish, all the coroutineScope() function needs to do is keep an eye on the status of its own Job. That's because of a rule governing the completion of all coroutine jobs. Let's call it the First Rule of

Jobs. The First Rule says that a job isn't complete until all its child jobs are complete.

The First Rule of Jobs

 Rule 1: A job isn't complete until all its child jobs are complete.

You've seen this rule in action every time you've used the coroutineScope() function, like when you downloaded a list of images in the last chapter.

The rule explains why the coroutineScope() function and the awaitAll() function seem like two different ways of waiting for the same group of coroutines. When you use awaitAll(), you're fetching results directly from several individual subtasks. But, all those subtasks also form part of a single larger parent task, and it's that parent task that the coroutineScope() function is waiting for.

Coroutines in Coroutines

As you've learned, each coroutine has its own accompanying coroutine context. That's where it keeps the Job object that tracks its progress from creation to completion, as well as other context elements such as its Dispatcher.

Now, you also know that a coroutine scope works by providing a set of coroutine context elements for its child coroutines, including their parent Job.

Have you guessed where this is heading?

Yes, coroutines themselves can also act as coroutine scopes. When you launch one coroutine inside another, the new coroutine becomes a child of the first and inherits the rest of its coroutine context.

Let's try it in our coffee-making code and start breaking things down into a couple of subtasks:

```kotlin
coffee/v3/src/main/kotlin/com/example/coffee/CoffeeApplication.kt
suspend fun grindBeans(): String {
  delay(5.seconds)
  return "freshly ground coffee"
}

suspend fun heatWater(): String {
  delay(5.seconds)
  return "piping hot water"
}
```

To start these tasks, we're going to call launch() right inside an existing coroutine:

```
coffee/v3/src/main/kotlin/com/example/coffee/CoffeeApplication.kt
suspend fun main() = coroutineScope {
  val coffeeJob: Job = launch {
    launch {
      val beans = grindBeans()
      println("Prepared some $beans")
    }

    launch {
      val water = heatWater()
      println("Prepared some $water")
    }

    // TODO: finish making the coffee
    println("Done launching two child jobs!")
  }

  while (coffeeJob.isActive) {
    println("[Loop] coffeeJob.isActive is: ${coffeeJob.isActive}")
    delay(2.seconds)
  }
  println("[End] coffeeJob.isActive is: ${coffeeJob.isActive}")
}
```

Just like the coroutineScope() function, the launch() and async() functions both provide their code block with a CoroutineScope receiver.

To keep track of what's going on, we'll monitor the progress of the Job with a loop. This isn't something you'd be likely to do in a real program—you can use await() or join() when you need to wait for a coroutine—but in our case, it'll be an informative way to see how our job's state is changing over the course of the program's execution:

```
Done launching two child jobs!
[Loop] coffeeJob.isActive is: true
[Loop] coffeeJob.isActive is: true
[Loop] coffeeJob.isActive is: true
Prepared some piping hot water
Prepared some freshly ground coffee
[End] coffeeJob.isActive is: false
```

Our first line of output shows us that we reached the end of the coffeeJob code block almost immediately. Remember, the launch() function always returns right away, so starting the two child jobs doesn't hold up our progress.

But even though we've executed each line of code and reached the end of the code block, we can see that our coffeeJob isn't complete. That's because it's now also acting as a parent job. By calling launch() inside the existing task, we've given it two child jobs of its own. The parent job's isActive property still shows true and will continue to do so until both of those child jobs have been completed as well.

So, now we can start to picture our application's coroutines as a linked hierarchy, where each task is a child of the task that created it.

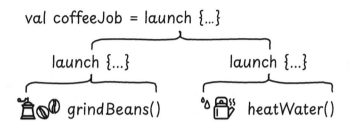

Keep Track of Every Exception

In the first part of this chapter, you learned how Kotlin organizes coroutines into a hierarchy of linked tasks and subtasks. As well as working on its own code, every task must also wait for its child tasks to finish their work.

But what happens when a task runs into a problem that stops it from completing its work at all?

As you've learned, a background task can't report back to its caller because the caller already moved on to do other things. In this section, we'll see how a failed coroutine reports its error to its parent Job instead.

Different Outcomes

We said that a coroutine's journey starts when it's created and ends when all its work is done. That's true for the lucky coroutines that make it to the end safely. But of course, there's another way that a piece of code can stop and that's by throwing an exception.

Let's see what happens when one of our coroutines fails. We'll add a new step to our coffee-making code so we can start making some fancy lattes and cappuccinos:

coffee/v4/src/main/kotlin/com/example/coffee/CoffeeApplication.kt
```kotlin
suspend fun frothMilk(): String = throw OutOfMilkException()

class OutOfMilkException() : RuntimeException("There's no milk!")
```

Oh no! We don't have any milk. This function is going to throw an error until we can sort out our supply chain and get that fridge restocked. It looks like we won't be having that latte after all.

What happens when we try to use this function in our code? Since we know it's not going to work, let's prepare for the worst with some error-handling code:

```
coffee/v4/src/main/kotlin/com/example/coffee/CoffeeApplication.kt
suspend fun main() {
  coroutineScope {
    try {
      launch { grindBeans() }
      launch { heatWater() }
      launch { frothMilk() }
    } catch (error: OutOfMilkException) {
      println("Your coffee is important to us! Please try again later.")
    }
  }
}
```

Before you run the code, see if you can guess what it will do. Are we going to catch the error? If not, where will it go?

```
Exception in thread "main" OutOfMilkException: There's no milk!
```

Instead of being caught and handled, the error crashes the program, and there's no sign of the output from our println() call. Why didn't our catch block work?

In Chapter 2, Escape From Callback Hell, on page 17, you saw how a background task, such as the one created by an asynchronous callback, can't throw exceptions back to its caller and won't participate in its caller's exception-handling catch blocks. In Chapter 3, Start It, Scope It, Stop It, on page 39, you learned that launching a coroutine creates exactly the same diverging structure with a task that's no longer contained within its creator's control flow. That means launch() has the same error-handling gotcha and won't be able to throw exceptions from its coroutine back to its caller. We're dealing with two separate tasks, and by the time the new coroutine succeeds or fails, the original function has already left the try–catch block and moved on somewhere else.

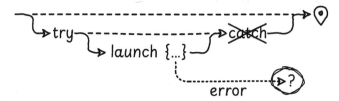

The simplest solution to this problem is often to handle your errors before they make it this far. Putting a try–catch block inside the call to launch() will work just fine. It's only when an exception hasn't been handled inside the coroutine that it needs to start looking for somewhere else to go.

Alternate Route

When a coroutine fails with an unhandled error, its Job will record that the coroutine has failed. The job's isActive property goes from true to false and then—here's the important part—the exception is passed on for handling by the parent Job. Let's call this the Second Rule of Jobs.

The Second Rule of Jobs

 Rule 2: When a child job fails with an exception, the exception is passed immediately to the parent job.

Without this backup route for exceptions to follow, errors in background tasks could simply sail off the edge of the map and disappear. If something goes wrong, you need to know about it so you can track down the problem and fix it! The Second Rule ensures that a failed background task sends its unhandled error upwards through the levels of the coroutine Job hierarchy—like the way a failed function throws an exception up the levels of the call stack.

That's how the error in our example makes it back to the main() function even after launch() has already returned. It takes a shortcut directly to the still-running coroutineScope() function, which, as you'll remember, is acting as the parent Job for all our coroutines.

A parent Job does have some say over how it responds to these propagated errors, as we'll see later on. Since the coroutineScope() function in our example is still suspended and waiting for its children to finish, it can simply throw the error to its own caller, the same as any other failed suspending function. That's what brings the exception out of the background task hierarchy and back into the program's main control flow.

This is a great example of how the coroutineScope() function encapsulates its concurrency by returning every task's outcome to the same suspended caller. Another way to safely catch errors from all these coroutines would be to wrap their parent coroutineScope() with a try–catch block of its own.

Customize Your Error Handling

Thanks to the first two Rules of Jobs, you know that a task's outcome depends on its subtasks. It won't finish until its child jobs are done—and if one of them fails, the parent job will fail too.

The third and final rule is about tying up loose ends. After the parent job fails, what happens to all its other child jobs? In this section, you'll learn about the automatic cancellation mechanism that cleans up abandoned tasks.

Once we've checked off the last of the three rules, we'll take a look at some scenarios where you might want to break them. Do you need to throw away all your hard work because one little thing went wrong, or can you be more selective with your error handling? You'll learn how to disable some of that automatic error propagation and the cancellation that comes with it, letting you catch errors from individual coroutines instead.

Unnecessary Effort

In our coffee-making example, we've now got three different coroutines preparing three different ingredients. When our milk-frothing function fails, what happens to the other two?

We already know that we're not going to be able to finish making the coffee because one of the required ingredients is missing. If we keep preparing the other ingredients anyway, that's a task leak! There's no point in continuing to waste time and resources getting the other ingredients ready for a drink that's never going to be made.

Remember, a task leak happens when a coroutine or other background task keeps on using memory or resources after it's no longer needed. When we first saw this problem in Chapter 3, Start It, Scope It, Stop It, on page 39, we fixed it by calling the scope's cancel() function. Cancellation is exactly what this code needs, too—but this time, the scope can identify the required action on its own. Did you notice that our coffee-making program stopped right away when the milk task failed? The other two functions still had work left to do, but they didn't bother completing it. Instead, they were automatically canceled, thanks to the Third Rule of Jobs.

The Third Rule of Jobs

 Rule 3: If a parent job fails or gets canceled, its remaining child jobs are also canceled.

We can see the Third Rule even more clearly if we write a coroutine with an infinite loop. Let's have one task display a message every two seconds so that we can see when it's running. Then, we'll launch another coroutine that fails after a few moments:

coffee/v5/src/main/kotlin/com/example/coffee/CoffeeApplication.kt
```kotlin
suspend fun main() {
  coroutineScope {
    launch {
      while (true) {
        delay(2.seconds)
        println("Making another cup of coffee…")
      }
    }

    launch {
      delay(10.seconds)
      throw RuntimeException("Sorry, it's closing time!")
    }
  }
}
```

As you run the program, notice how the loop inside the coffee-making coroutine stops running when the second task fails. The error is the last line of output we see before the program ends:

```
Making another cup of coffee…
Making another cup of coffee…
Making another cup of coffee…
Making another cup of coffee…
Exception in thread "main"
  java.lang.RuntimeException: Sorry, it's closing time!
```

When the second job throws an unhandled exception, its Job fails. That propagates up to the coroutineScope() function's Job, too, causing the scope to fail. And that, in turn, causes the scope's other jobs to be canceled.

Breaking the Rules

You've learned each of the Three Rules of Jobs and seen some examples of how they work and interact.

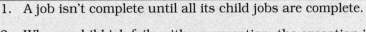

The Three Rules of Jobs

1. A job isn't complete until all its child jobs are complete.

2. When a child job fails with an exception, the exception is passed immediately to the parent job.

3. If a parent job fails or gets canceled, its remaining child jobs are also canceled.

Together, the three rules organize your coroutines into a structured hierarchy of work. Failures propagate up the hierarchy from a child task to its parent task so that a task can only be successful if all of its subtasks are also successful.

Cancellation propagates downwards so that you don't waste resources on the other subtasks of a job that you already know is going to fail.

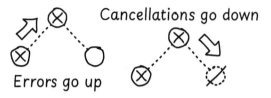

Waiting for Cancellation

 Cancellation isn't instantaneous, as you'll learn in the next chapter. While it's in progress, the First Rule still applies. For instance, a failed or canceled coroutineScope() won't exit until all its children have completed their entire cancellation process.

This strict arrangement of tasks and subtasks is Kotlin's default behavior, and it's the simplest way to keep your concurrent code clear of trouble. But not all tasks fit the same pattern—so let's see how the task hierarchy and its rules can be customized.

Failing Fast

In our coffee example, perhaps we can recover by refilling the milk mid-operation so that we don't need to waste the other ingredients. Or, maybe we can substitute something else for the milk while we wait for a delivery.

Using some async() coroutine builders, let's try and update our code so that we can catch the error and get that caffeine hit anyway.

You've already seen that you can't catch an exception directly from the launch() or async() coroutine builder functions. But you also know that you can use a Deferred result to retrieve the outcome of an async() coroutine. So, if we swap our launch() jobs for async() ones, maybe we can catch the exception from await() or awaitAll() instead?

It's a good start, but it won't solve the problem on its own. Let's see what happens when we try. We'll add a catch block that's supposed to fall back to making coffee without milk when it spots the OutOfMilkException:

coffee/v6/src/main/kotlin/com/example/coffee/CoffeeApplication.kt
```kotlin
suspend fun main() = coroutineScope {
  val beans = async { grindBeans() }
  val water = async { heatWater() }
  val milk = async { frothMilk() }

  val ingredients = try {
    awaitAll(beans, water, milk)
  } catch (error: OutOfMilkException) {
    println("Oops, looks like we're out of milk.")
    awaitAll(beans, water)
  }

  println("Brewing some delicious coffee with $ingredients")
}
```

Well, that didn't work. There's no sign of the output from our catch block, and
the program crashed without even trying to make any coffee:

```
Exception in thread "main" OutOfMilkException: There's no milk!
```

Remember the Rules

Why didn't the awaitAll() function throw an exception for us to catch? Kotlin's
documentation is clear that the await() and awaitAll() functions will throw an
exception if one of the corresponding Deferred jobs has failed. Is the documentation wrong?

Not exactly. It's just that the awaitAll() never makes it as far as throwing its
exception. That's because the Second Rule of Jobs kicks in first. Remember,
that's the rule that says a failed job passes an exception to its parent job. The
rule applies to all jobs—even the Deferred task belonging to an async() coroutine.

By default, the way errors propagate through this program is no different
from when we were using launch(). Our async() coroutine is a child of another
job, and if it fails, its parent job will be notified of the failure right away. When
that happens, the coroutineScope() function stops what it was doing and throws
an exception. And since the code in the coroutineScope() function is the thing
that was responsible for calling awaitAll(), that whole operation—along with its
try–catch block—stops in its tracks.

It's important to remember this default behavior because it can be a little
unexpected and unintuitive. Even if you're using other tools to wait for your
coroutines, errors always take the direct route and propagate from a failed
coroutine to its parent job.

So, how do we change that? To get our try–catch block working, we'd need to
let our parent job know that a failure in one of the child jobs is okay—that

we've got some error-handling code in place and that we'll be able to recover from the problem.

When we want more control over the outcome, we can customize the rules a little by using a *supervisor job*. This job has a more hands-off parenting style, and unlike a regular Job, it won't freak out when it sees one of its child coroutines fail.

Can I Speak to Your Supervisor?

You've learned that a coroutine scope starts out with its own set of coroutine context elements. Different scopes can provide a suitable starting context for different kinds of tasks and components.

You can't just create a replacement Job for your coroutines, though. Each new coroutine or withContext() block always creates its own Job, which you can't alter or replace. Passing a different Job in the starting context would only supplant the parent job—severing the job hierarchy and creating a task leak.

In our code, the parent job is being created for us by the coroutineScope() function. To replace the parent job, we need to replace that function. We'll swap it for a supervisorScope(), which comes with a built-in supervisor job:

```
coffee/v7/src/main/kotlin/com/example/coffee/CoffeeApplication.kt
suspend fun main() = supervisorScope {
  val beans = async { grindBeans() }
  val water = async { heatWater() }
  val milk = async { frothMilk() }

  val ingredients = try {
    awaitAll(beans, water, milk)
  } catch (error: OutOfMilkException) {
    println("Oops, looks like we're out of milk.")
    awaitAll(beans, water)
  }

  println("Brewing some delicious coffee with $ingredients")
}
```

Great! It's working the way we wanted, and our catch block is able to recover from the error:

```
Oops, looks like we're out of milk.
Brewing some delicious coffee with [freshly ground coffee,
  piping hot water]
```

Since the supervisorScope() allows its child jobs to fail independently, it won't give up as soon as anything goes wrong. With the parent job still running, the remaining child jobs can continue normally without being affected by the failure. That means we'll get results from two out of our three jobs instead of abandoning them all at the first sign of trouble.

Of course, the third job has still failed and won't be able to provide a result. So, when it's time to get the results, our awaitAll() function finally gets a chance to use its full functionality. The code in the supervisorScope() is still running, so awaitAll() can throw its exception—and we can catch it and recover from it. We'll see the output from our catch block, and we'll be able to extend this code to add some more detailed recovery procedures that separate the failed tasks from the successful ones.

Failing Faster

 Did you notice how our error output still appeared immediately? Just like a parent job, awaitAll() won't keep waiting for other jobs when one has already failed. If you're handling errors in-house like this, prefer awaitAll() over separate calls to await().

Supervisor jobs and scopes can be handy when you have some other way of handling failures—such as the Deferred results in this example—and don't want them to propagate via the ordinary job hierarchy. Don't forget about regular try–catch blocks, though! If you can catch an exception inside the coroutine and stop it from failing in the first place, that'll usually be easier than trying to handle errors using this kind of coroutine machinery.

Jobs All the Way Down

You've seen how coroutines and coroutines scopes work together to build a hierarchy of tasks and subtasks. Exceptions will always propagate back to the coroutine, function, or component that needs to know about them, and tasks won't keep using resources after they're no longer needed.

So, what's at the top of the hierarchy? Who creates the first Job from which all other jobs are descended?

Well, you've already seen two ways this question might be answered. One is when you use a suspending main() function, as we've been doing in many of our simple code examples. The main() function is right at the top of the application's call stack, letting it act as the starting point for all our coroutines. Using a function such as coroutineScope() in the main() function is structured concurrency in its purest and simplest form.

But an existing framework such as Android might not afford you that capability. The second option, and the one that might be more common in practice, is when you use a custom CoroutineScope that's linked to a class or component in your app—such as the one you created using the MainScope() function in Chapter 3, Start It, Scope It, Stop It, on page 39. Just like the coroutineScope() function, these custom scopes come with their own Job.

A top-level Job in a custom coroutine scope is still following the Three Rules of Jobs—it just doesn't run into them nearly so often. For one thing, it's acting only as a parent and doesn't have a coroutine of its own. With no coroutine to trigger its completion, it remains active indefinitely, no matter how many child coroutines it creates and completes. MainScope() also uses a supervisor job, so it won't react to child job failures. Some other custom scopes use a regular job and will cancel all their coroutines when a single child task fails, so keep an eye on what kind of scope you're using.

He's Dead, Jim

 A scope can't launch any new coroutines once its Job is inactive. The launch() and async() coroutine builders won't throw an exception—they'll do nothing.

What Have You Learned?

If an error isn't handled inside a coroutine's code, the coroutine's Job fails, triggering some important knock-on effects.

In this chapter, you've followed an exception on its journey up the coroutine hierarchy and seen the resulting automatic cancellation of the failed task's other children. Using the Three Rules of Jobs, we can plan how each task should affect the others or even change things up with a supervisor scope.

The coroutines in this chapter were easy enough to cancel, but some tasks can be trickier. In the next chapter, you'll fix some mistakes that can leave a canceled coroutine clinging to life as a resource-stealing zombie.

Key Concepts

Job

This is part of the coroutine context. It oversees a coroutine's lifecycle—running, completed, failed, or canceled.

Structured Concurrency

This is Kotlin's automatic hierarchy of linked coroutine tasks and subtasks. It ensures resources, outcomes, and errors don't go missing.

CHAPTER 6

Cooperate with Cancellation

Coroutine cancellation is something you're pretty familiar with by now. It's the mechanism that stops an unneeded task, releasing its resources back to the rest of the application.

Our experience of cancellation has been a smooth one so far—but in this chapter, that's going to change. We'll stumble into our first CancellationException, and we'll also find and fix some other cancellation snags.

By the end of this chapter, you'll understand the whole story behind coroutine cancellation, and you'll have a simple tool for dealing with its troublesome side effects. The next time you tell a coroutine to stop, you can be confident that's exactly what it's going to do.

Give a Task a Time Limit

New York's Metropolitan Museum of Art is the most visited museum in the United States and one of the largest art museums in the world.

Let's go for a visit!

In this chapter, we're going to connect to the museum's public API. We'll write a tour program that steps through the items in the museum's collection, displaying a short description of each one.

We'll be using coroutine cancellation to signal when it's time for our loop to terminate. We've done this a couple of times before. First, when we manually canceled a custom coroutine scope, and again, when we relied on structured concurrency to cancel a task after an error elsewhere. This time, you'll simply be canceling your code after a fixed amount of time, and you'll learn a new timeout function to help you do that more concisely. Next, we'll see how cancellation interacts with error handling, and you'll learn how to keep the two things cleanly separated.

A Day at the Museum

Let's start by assembling the tools we'll be using to fetch our data. We're using Retrofit again, so the setup should be familiar.

Our dependencies will be similar to the ones we've used in previous chapters, though we won't be adding a Swing UI this time:

museum/v1/build.gradle.kts
```
dependencies {
    implementation("org.jetbrains.kotlinx:kotlinx-coroutines-core:1.10.1")
    implementation("com.squareup.retrofit2:retrofit:2.9.0")
    implementation("com.squareup.retrofit2:converter-moshi:2.9.0")
}
```

Next, we'll create some classes to hold the data we'll be retrieving. Check the museum's online documentation[1] for full details of the available data:

museum/v1/src/main/kotlin/com/example/museum/MuseumService.kt
```
data class MuseumCatalog(val objectIDs: List<Int>, val total: Int)

data class MuseumObject(
    val title: String,
    val artistDisplayName: String,
    val objectName: String,
    val objectDate: String
)
```

The first data class, MuseumCatalog, will give us the list of exhibits that exist in the museum's collection. The second, MuseumObject, will hold the details of each individual artwork.

Finally, we'll need the MuseumService interface that we'll be calling in our code. It'll have two functions—one to fetch the list of objects and one to fetch the details of an individual item.

In our last Retrofit service, we had each function return a Call object, letting us test out three different ways of executing our requests. This time, we can take a shortcut and ask Retrofit to generate a single suspending function that executes and awaits the entire request:

Special Features

 As you've already learned, you can't add the suspend modifier to any old function and expect it to compile, let alone do anything useful. This trick only works because it's a feature that Retrofit intentionally provides.

---

1.   https://metmuseum.github.io/

`museum/v1/src/main/kotlin/com/example/museum/MuseumService.kt`

```kotlin
interface MuseumService {
  @GET("objects")
  suspend fun listObjects(): MuseumCatalog

  @GET("objects/{id}")
  suspend fun getObject(@Path("id") id: Int): MuseumObject
}

private val executor = Executors.newCachedThreadPool { task ->
  Thread(task).apply { isDaemon = true }
}

private fun createHttpClient() = OkHttpClient.Builder()
  .protocols(listOf(Protocol.HTTP_1_1)).dispatcher(Dispatcher(executor))

val museumService = Retrofit.Builder()
  .client(createHttpClient().build())
  .baseUrl("https://collectionapi.metmuseum.org/public/collection/v1/")
  .addConverterFactory(MoshiConverterFactory.create())
  .build().create<MuseumService>()
```

Great! We're ready to start planning the tour.

When You Hear the Buzzer, Stare at the Art

For our museum tour, we'll start with a function that will describe the artwork we're looking at:

`museum/v1/src/main/kotlin/com/example/museum/MuseumApplication.kt`

```kotlin
fun describe(exhibit: MuseumObject): String = buildString {
  append('"', exhibit.title, '"', " is a ", exhibit.objectName)
  exhibit.objectDate.let { if (it.isNotEmpty()) append(" from ", it) }
  exhibit.artistDisplayName.let { if (it.isNotEmpty()) append(" by ", it) }
}
```

After we fetch the list of exhibits, we'll enter a loop to explore the items. On each iteration of the loop, we'll fetch an item at random from the museum's collection and then pause to look at it for a couple of seconds:

`museum/v1/src/main/kotlin/com/example/museum/MuseumApplication.kt`

```kotlin
suspend fun main() {
  val catalog = museumService.listObjects()

  while (true) {
    lookAtArt(catalog.objectIDs.random())
  }
}

suspend fun lookAtArt(artworkId: Int) {
  val artwork = museumService.getObject(artworkId)
  println(describe(artwork))
  delay(2.seconds)
}
```

But like our auto-updating photo gallery in the first chapter, this loop is going to run forever. Run the code now, and your screen will slowly fill up with an endless stream of artwork until you intervene and stop the application:

```
"Head of a young girl" is a Print from 1645 by Wenceslaus Hollar
"Figure of a standing woman" is a Figure from 7th–8th century
"Dress Ornament Bead" is a Ornament, dress from ca. 1353–1336 B.C.
"Cap" is a Cap from 1830–50
"White Shadows" is a Print from 1935–43 by Theodore C. Polos
"Door Jamb of Rau" is a Door Jamb, Rau from ca. 1479–1425 B.C.
…
```

Closing Time

Mentally reinvigorating as it is, we can't keep staring at the art indefinitely. Let's use coroutine cancellation to end our loop and finish the tour.

In our ImageViewer class, we used the cancel() function to stop all the coroutines in a scope. Well, each individual coroutine also has its own cancel() function, accessed via the Job objects that we introduced in the last chapter. In fact, even when you cancel a whole scope, you're really canceling the scope's own Job—which automatically cancels all its child coroutines as well.

If we launch a new coroutine for our museum tour, we can monitor it via its Job, and cancel it when we're done. In a moment, you'll learn a more concise way to do this—but let's start with the tools we already know. We'll move our code into a new tourMuseum() function to keep things tidy, and we'll use launch() to start it in a separate task:

```
museum/v2/src/main/kotlin/com/example/museum/MuseumApplication.kt
suspend fun main() = coroutineScope {
    val tour: Job = launch {
        tourMuseum()
    }

    delay(15.seconds)
    println("The museum's closing, it's time to end the tour!")
    tour.cancel()
}

suspend fun tourMuseum() {
    val catalog = museumService.listObjects()
    while (true) {
        lookAtArt(catalog.objectIDs.random())
    }
}
```

With the tour running in its own coroutine, we can continue running other code while it's still going on. That gives us a way to jump in and cancel the tour when it's closing time. When you run the code now, you'll see a few exhibits, and then the loop will come to an end:

```
"Sleeve Band" is a Sleeve Band from early 18th century
"Dalmation" is a Hat from ca. 1955 by House of Dior
"Wedding Dress" is a Wedding Dress from ca. 1935 by Hattie Carnegie
"Dog" is a Crèche figure from second half 18th century
"Silent Wheels" is a Print from 1952 by Nicholas Hornyansky
The museum's closing, it's time to end the tour!
```

Normal Termination

Notice how our canceled coroutine doesn't crash the app or show any errors.

That's because cancellation is a normal outcome, not a failure. It might be triggered by a failure somewhere else in the application as you saw in our last chapter, but that doesn't mean the canceled coroutine itself has done anything wrong. You've also seen plenty of examples where cancellation doesn't involve any failed coroutines at all.

Many background tasks are designed to run for as long as a particular part of the application is in use, with cancellation as their normal—and only—way to exit. In the astronomy image viewer, you saw this in action when you launched a coroutine to periodically fetch a fresh photo. That background task needs to run for as long as the image viewer is in use, so like our museum tour, it's built around a loop. When the coroutine is canceled, the loop exits.

Business as Usual

Stopping a coroutine after a fixed amount of time is a common requirement, and there's a built-in function for it. Instead of launching our own separate timeout job, we can simplify our code with a call to the withTimeoutOrNull() function:

museum/v3/src/main/kotlin/com/example/museum/MuseumApplication.kt
```kotlin
suspend fun main() {
  withTimeoutOrNull(15.seconds) {
    tourMuseum()
  }
}
```

This new code is doing pretty much the same thing as the previous version. The withTimeoutOrNull() function wraps up the task monitoring and cancellation, so we don't have to write it all out. Under the hood, it's still starting a new Job and then canceling it when the time's up.

Why the wordy function name, with *or null* at the end? Well, withTimeoutOrNull() also works with code blocks that return a result, and it'll return that result value for you to use later. If the code doesn't complete within the timeout period, the result won't be available, and in that case, the withTimeoutOrNull() function will simply return null.

The other option is the withTimeout() function, which signals its timeouts by throwing an exception, sidestepping the need to return anything at all. But throwing an error would crash our program, and we want the tour to end successfully.

Our loop doesn't need to return a result at all, so a null value isn't a problem and is definitely preferable to an error. But don't forget about this choice because it's going to come back in a big way when we start to dive deeper into how the code inside a coroutine responds to its own cancellation.

When Is an Error Not an Error?

Our code's looking good. What can we do to polish up the program and make it even better?

One thing we might want to think about is error handling. When we're working with network requests and remote APIs, there's plenty that could go wrong. What if the museum's website goes down or our Internet connection drops out?

To make our application a bit more resilient, let's add a simple try–catch block. Since we don't know exactly what error we might run into, we'll cast a wide net and catch all types of Throwable.

Our try section doesn't contain any coroutine builders or other background tasks, so we're safe from the error-handling pitfalls we've learned about so far. Remember, catching errors from suspending functions works just fine. In fact, it might work a little too well! Our indiscriminate catch clause is going to interfere with our coroutine cancellation, leading to some nasty results:

museum/v4/src/main/kotlin/com/example/museum/MuseumApplication.kt
```kotlin
suspend fun main() {
  withTimeoutOrNull(15.seconds) {
    tourMuseum()
  }
}

suspend fun tourMuseum() {
  val catalog = museumService.listObjects()
  while (true) {
```

```
➤      try {
         lookAtArt(catalog.objectIDs.random())
➤      } catch (error: Throwable) {
         println("Skipping to next artwork due to $error")
       }
     }
}
```

Our program was working fine before, so these extra lines are a precaution, one that's not supposed to kick in unless something goes wrong. What are you expecting to happen when you run this code?

```
…
Skipping to next artwork due to TimeoutCancellationException
Skipping to next artwork due to TimeoutCancellationException
Skipping to next artwork due to TimeoutCancellationException
Skipping to next artwork due to TimeoutCancellationException
Skipping to next artwork due to TimeoutCancellationException
…
```

Instead of ending the tour, our program deteriorates into an endless stream of error messages. Once again, you'll need to terminate the whole application to get it to stop.

There are three questions to answer here. First, if cancellation isn't an error, why are we seeing an exception whose name is clearly related to cancellation? Second, how has our new try–catch block managed to catch an exception in what previously seemed to be a working, error-free program? And third, when we do catch the error, why won't it stay caught?

Cancellation Exceptions

The exception we just saw is doing two important things to facilitate the coroutine cancellation process. First, throwing an exception lets a suspended function skip the rest of its waiting and exit immediately without returning a result. Second, once the exception has been thrown, it acts as a control-flow shortcut that lets the coroutine make a quick and easy exit from a whole stack of functions and control structures. We'll talk more about both of those things later in the chapter once we've fixed our broken code.

Most of the time, these cancellation exceptions pass by silently and unnoticed. They're ignored by the coroutine's Job, which is why our program didn't crash when we let the exception go uncaught. So, adding a catch block didn't somehow summon a CancellationException from thin air. Instead, it intercepted and exposed an exception that was hiding there all along and, in doing so, prevented the exception from fulfilling its intended purpose.

One way to fix this code would be to check whether the exception we caught was a CancellationException and rethrow it if so. But that approach has some problems of its own, which we'll touch on later. Thankfully, there's an even simpler solution, which will work for any catch block in any coroutine. Let's apply the fix to our museum tour code, and then we'll break it down and learn more about what we've done.

The tool we'll need is a function called ensureActive(). This function is available as part of every coroutine scope and coroutine Job, and it's going to act as the emergency exit for our canceled coroutine. If it detects that the job has been canceled, it'll throw a new CancellationException of its own, giving our code a way to escape from the faulty catch block that it's become trapped in.

We can access ensureActive() via the coroutineContext property, which is available from any suspending function. To make sure cancellation doesn't take precedence over other real errors, we'll only call it when the exception we've caught is a CancellationException:

```
museum/v5/src/main/kotlin/com/example/museum/MuseumApplication.kt
suspend fun main() {
  withTimeoutOrNull(15.seconds) {
    tourMuseum()
  }
}

suspend fun tourMuseum() {
  val catalog = museumService.listObjects()
  while (true) {
    try {
      lookAtArt(catalog.objectIDs.random())
    } catch (error: Throwable) {
      if (error is CancellationException) coroutineContext.ensureActive()
      println("Skipping to next artwork due to $error")
    }
  }
}
```

Looks like the code is working again! There's no sign of any errors, and our tour stops normally when the timeout completes. Cancellation is all about finding a safe route to the nearest exit, and the call to ensureActive() is giving our canceled coroutine a way out of the catch block it was trapped in.

Not sure what we just did or how it fixed the problem? Don't worry—we'll go through it all in detail in the next part of the chapter.

Keep Clear of Cancellation Exceptions

When a scope ends, a timeout expires, or a parent task fails, the automated cancellation mechanism kicks in, and any abandoned tasks are quickly and quietly cleaned up.

But coroutine cancellation is more than an abrupt exit. The catch block we added to our museum tour code has given us a glimpse at the cleanup process that's going on behind the scenes.

In this section, you'll learn more about how cancellation works and what role these cancellation exceptions are playing. When we extend our code with a counter to track the museum's available parking spaces, we'll need to use a finally block to restore the counter to its correct value. In the process, you'll discover why cancellation is a cooperative agreement that requires each canceled coroutine to accept its own fate.

Shut It Down

Imagine we're right in the middle of our museum tour. We've requested the next item from the API, and now the coroutine is suspended while it waits for a response.

But before our data arrives, we hit the timeout, and the coroutine is canceled. What happens next?

To understand the challenges Kotlin faces here, let's think about how we might go about stopping our canceled coroutine if we didn't have the automated tools to do it for us.

Remember, our coroutine is suspended inside our Retrofit service's getObject() function. We don't want to wait for the request to finish—there's no way of telling how long that would take, and we're not going to be using the result anyway. A suspended function might be waiting for something that's going to happen long in the future, and we don't want that to prevent us from releasing its resources quickly.

What if we don't resume the suspended coroutine? If the getObject() function never returns, the coroutine will never run any more code or consume any more CPU time. Once we've canceled the underlying HTTP request and removed any other references to the task, the garbage collector will be able to clean up the still-suspended coroutine like any other discarded object.

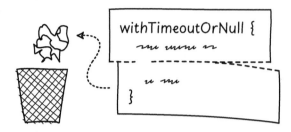

That sounds like a simple solution, but it's missing a key piece.

Slow and Steady

When you're driving on the freeway, and your engine warning light blinks on, you don't jump on the brakes and stop in the middle of the road. Instead, you continue driving normally until you reach the next exit or find another place where you can safely pull over.

Tasks in a computer program work the same way. A piece of code can't stop in its tracks—it needs to continue running until it reaches an exit. Only the task itself knows what resources it's holding onto, what data it's in the middle of modifying, and what cleanup code it needs to run to leave the program in a consistent, working state.

Let's take a look at a simple example. Imagine our art gallery visitors are all arriving by car. In our tour code, we'll add a counter that keeps track of how many parking spaces are available at the museum. When each guest arrives, we'll reduce the counter by one, showing that a parking spot has been filled. At the end of the tour, we'll increment the counter again:

```
museum/v6/src/main/kotlin/com/example/museum/MuseumApplication.kt
var parkingSpots = 250

suspend fun main() {
  withTimeoutOrNull(15.seconds) {
    try {
      parkingSpots--
      tourMuseum()
    } finally {
      parkingSpots++
    }
  }
}
```

What happens if the coroutine never resumes from the suspended Retrofit call inside the tourMuseum() function?

If the code stopped at that line and never continued, it wouldn't reach the finally block. The parkingSpots counter wouldn't get increased, and we'd continue to show that a parking spot was occupied even after the guest had taken their car and left. If the program contained other code that relied on that counter, it might go on to fail or behave incorrectly.

A canceled task might need to close files, release locks, reset counters, and do any number of other cleanup tasks to make sure it isn't leaving behind costly resource leaks or dangerous bugs. Remember, cancellation is a normal outcome, not an error. Other parts of the program need to continue functioning properly after the canceled task has gone away.

Exceptions Are the Easy Way Out

If our suspended network call can't just vanish, what other options does it have?

One option would be for the function to return normally. But in most programs, that's going to be tricky. For one thing, the Retrofit call is supposed to return a value—the response data received from the museum's API. If the request was canceled before completion, what should it return instead? You might be able to come up with a solution—maybe a dummy response or a null value—but you'd have to do the same for every single suspending function in your application and then write code to pass those values up the call stack.

What we really want is a way for the suspended function to exit early, without returning a value, while still running any finally blocks and other cleanup code.

In Kotlin's control flow toolkit, an exception is the tool that corresponds to those requirements.

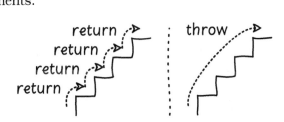

When a suspending function is canceled, it throws a cancellation exception. Not only does this let the function exit early without returning a value or waiting any longer than necessary, but it also propagates up the coroutine's call stack with no extra code required. Any cleanup operations along the way will automatically execute, and—assuming the exception goes uncaught—it'll quickly reach the top of the call stack and cause the whole coroutine to exit.

Covert Operations

So, if every suspension point throws an exception when its waiting is canceled, how come we've never seen one of these cancellation exceptions before? This certainly isn't the first coroutine we've canceled.

Well, cancellation exceptions are good at hiding—and that's by design.

As you learned in Chapter 5, Plan for Any Outcome, on page 75, a coroutine that ends with an unhandled exception will mark its Job as failed. But when it comes to cancellation, we want the quick-exit capabilities of a thrown exception without the error-handling mechanisms associated with a failed coroutine.

That's what the CancellationException class is for. When the Job sees a CancellationException or any of its subclasses, it knows that it shouldn't send it onward or trigger any error handling code. With this ability to hide in plain sight, cancellation exceptions are the undercover coroutine cops. The job hierarchy grants them—and them alone—a license to terminate coroutines and not get in trouble for it.

Carte Blanche

Cancellation exceptions only receive special handling when they reach the top of the coroutine and terminate the Job. Inside your functions and try–catch blocks, they behave like any other exception, and it's up to you to make sure you don't get in their way.

But, if you're not careful, that can leave the door open for a new problem. Nothing's ever easy, is it?

A coroutine that terminates due to a cancellation exception will never be recorded as a failure. That applies to all coroutines, not just the ones that you're trying to cancel—which means that misplaced cancellation exceptions can cause some unexpected results. Since CancellationException is a public class that you can instantiate yourself, it's easy enough to try this out:

```
suspend fun main() {
  coroutineScope {
    launch { throw CancellationException() } // don't do this!
  }
}
```

Try editing this code and replacing the CancellationException with something else—a RuntimeException, say—to see the difference in behavior. If you use any other exception here, you'll see the program crash and print a stack trace to the console. But with a cancellation exception, nothing happens at all. This program completes normally with no errors, and the coroutineScope() function—that's our parent Job—doesn't throw anything.

That might look like what happens when you cancel a coroutine, but there's an important difference. Although cancellation exceptions are closely linked to coroutine cancellation, the exception itself isn't what determines whether a coroutine has been canceled. That information is stored separately as part of the coroutine's Job. Since we never called the cancel() function, we never updated our Job's state.

That means code along the coroutine's exit route, like calls to ensureActive() or other suspending functions, won't react to this like a real cancellation. In fact, you could catch this exception and continue running code as if nothing had ever happened—something which, as you'll see later on, wouldn't be possible with a real cancellation.

To cancel a coroutine, call its cancel() function. To signal an error or other abnormal termination, use an ordinary exception—one that doesn't extend from CancellationException. Don't throw cancellation exceptions from your own code.

Double-Edged Sword

Cancellation exceptions make it much easier for a canceled coroutine to exit, but their superpowers can also be dangerous.

For an example, look at the await() function, which gets the result from an async() coroutine. When the target coroutine has failed, await() throws an exception—and when the target coroutine has been canceled, the exception that await() throws is a CancellationException.

That might not sound so bad, but be careful! A function such as await() is passing a result from one coroutine to another, and the coroutine where that hypothetical exception was thrown is not the same one that was originally supposed to be canceled.

Cancellation exceptions can crop up in other places too, including from Java functions that don't know anything about coroutines—but to a coroutine's Job, they all look the same! To avoid letting an impostor silently terminate the wrong task, don't rethrow every CancellationException you see. Instead, stick to ensureActive(), which throws a cancellation exception only when the current coroutine has been canceled, and handle everything else the way you would a normal error.

Suspend a Canceled Coroutine

You've learned how to update your catch blocks so they don't get in the way of coroutine cancellation. But we still haven't fully explained why our museum tour at the start of this chapter went so badly wrong. Why did our CancellationException get rethrown over and over again?

Cancellation is irreversible, and a canceled coroutine can never return to its active state. But there might still be some final cleanup code to run on the way out. If that code keeps running for longer than it should, the coroutine can end up in a zombie state—unable to function properly but unable to exit.

In the final section of this chapter, you'll see why it's so important for a coroutine to cooperate with a cancellation request. And before we wrap up, you'll also learn how you can safely sidestep that rule—at least temporarily—to call one last suspending function on the way out.

Downward Spiral

As you've learned, canceling a coroutine tells it to skip over any suspension points, throwing an immediate cancellation exception instead of waiting for them to resume normally. Well, that doesn't just apply to suspension points that are currently waiting. It's also true for any suspension points that the coroutine might run into in the future.

Remember, canceling a coroutine makes an irreversible change to the status of its Job. From this point on, you can think of the coroutine as being in a temporary *canceling* state. In this state, attempting to suspend the coroutine won't work and will simply throw a CancellationException instead.

That makes sense—suspending operations involve waiting around for things to happen, and a canceled coroutine's mission is to make a quick exit with as little delay as possible. We don't want to start on anything new.

Why Are We Waiting?

 Many asynchronous operations are cancellable, but not all. In Chapter 9, Upgrade Every Callback, on page 145, you'll learn why some suspension points don't have the ability to stop waiting and exit early.

That's why our museum tour at the start of the chapter ended up in an inescapable failure loop. Each time we caught an exception, we logged it and continued to the next iteration of our loop. But the coroutine is still in its canceling state, so trying to load the next museum exhibit throws another cancellation exception. A failure spiral like this one is a nasty bug that will keep on chewing through CPU cycles as it tries in vain to reach an exit.

It's vital that you don't keep trying to continue with business as usual once you detect that your coroutine's been canceled. We fixed our museum tour by adding a call to ensureActive(), which breaks out of the catch block with another cancellation exception, but anything that allows the code to exit will do the trick.

Cancellation is Cooperative

Why can't Kotlin detect that our coroutine isn't responding correctly to cancellation and terminate its execution altogether?

There are two reasons that's not an option.

First, we're reliant on marked exits in the code to provide places where the coroutine can stop safely. These come in the form of suspension points and other explicit checks, such as the ensureActive() function. Outside of these designated cancellable operations or other cooperative signaling mechanisms, there's simply no way to stop a running piece of code. In Chapter 7, Unlock Parallel Processing, on page 109, we'll see how we need to alter our code to account for this when we're running coroutines that don't contain frequent suspension points.

Second, even when we do reach a designated exit, we still need to run its finally blocks and other cleanup code. We saw this with our parking space counter, and there's no way to get around it safely. Halting a task without an orderly exit could leave the program in a completely broken state, undermining behavior guarantees made by many of the tools and functions our code relies on. We might get away with it, or we might end up with a problem worse than the one we were trying to solve.

Coroutine cancellation is a cooperative process. Calling a coroutine's cancel() function lets the task know that it should be terminating. But it's up to the code inside the coroutine to act on that request and make sure it exits—running any appropriate cleanup code on the way.

Did You Know?

Java 1.0 came with a Thread.stop() function that could force any running task to exit. By Java 1.1, the function was already deprecated due to safety concerns. Its only replacement is thread interruption—which, like coroutine cancellation, is cooperative.

Dead Coroutine Walking

As you've learned, suspending functions are off-limits for a coroutine that's already been canceled. So, what happens when the coroutine wants to suspend its execution as part of a legitimate cancellation procedure? Some cleanup operations are more complicated than others, and it's not unheard of that a piece of code needs to report to a remote server or even make some updates to the user interface before exiting.

Let's try out an example.

Earlier on, we added a counter to keep track of the museum's available parking spaces. It was missing a few crucial details, such as a check to make sure it didn't go below zero. But instead of adding all that stuff to our tour program, let's separate things out and make it the responsibility of a different service. We'll upgrade our parking lot with some automated barriers and a ticketing system. At the end of our tour, all we'll need to do is validate the guest's ticket—the parking system will take care of the rest.

Our tour's validateParking() function will need to send some information to the parking system and update the ticket database, so we'll be using a suspending function.

For now, we'll fill it in with a placeholder delay():

museum/v7/src/main/kotlin/com/example/museum/MuseumApplication.kt
```kotlin
suspend fun validateParking() {
  println("Validating your parking…")
  delay(1.seconds)
  println("Your parking ticket has been validated. Have a nice day!")
}
```

Now, we can get rid of our counter and call this function at the end of the tour. We know the tour is going to end with a routine CancellationException, so we'll use a finally block that will run when the exception is thrown:

museum/v7/src/main/kotlin/com/example/museum/MuseumApplication.kt
```kotlin
suspend fun main() {
  withTimeoutOrNull(15.seconds) {
    try {
```

```
      tourMuseum()
    } finally {
      validateParking()
    }
  }
}
```

What do you think this code is going to do?

```
...
Validating your parking...
```

Our tour completes as normal, but our validateParking() function doesn't manage to finish. We can see that it started running, but it never printed its final line of output to show that the job was done.

Our Job is still marked as inactive, and any suspension points will still throw an immediate CancellationException. Here, the culprit is a delay(), but the same thing would happen if we tried to make a suspending network call.

Stay of Execution

A canceled coroutine can't be uncanceled, but it can temporarily sidestep its cancellation status. To do that, use the withContext() function to create a protected NonCancellable code block. Code inside this block will ignore the fact that the outer coroutine has been canceled and will continue running as normal:

museum/v8/src/main/kotlin/com/example/museum/MuseumApplication.kt
```
suspend fun main() {
  withTimeoutOrNull(15.seconds) {
    try {
      tourMuseum()
    } finally {
      withContext(NonCancellable) {
        validateParking()
      }
    }
  }
}
```

This time, our code will work the way we intended, and our validateParking() function will have a chance to finish:

```
...
Validating your parking...
Your parking ticket has been validated. Have a nice day!
```

Not for External Use

 NonCancellable replaces a task's parent Job. That's fine for withContext(), which has a suspended caller to wait for its completion instead. But don't use it in coroutine builders or custom scopes—it'll create an orphaned task that leaks errors and resources.

What Have You Learned?

Coroutine cancellation is cooperative, relying on marked exits in the coroutine's code.

In this chapter, you used the ensureActive() function not just to avoid treating a CancellationException as an error but to fix a zombie coroutine and escape a broken loop. The problem was partly caused by trying to call suspending functions after cancellation—which won't work outside a NonCancellable cleanup block.

The coroutines you've written so far can cooperate with cancellation thanks to frequent suspension points, but that's not something you'll always be able to rely on. In the next chapter, you'll use coroutines to organize and parallelize CPU-intensive tasks that might not even suspend at all.

Key Concepts

Cancellability

This is the ability to respond to a cancellation request and make a quick exit. Most suspension points are cancellable and will throw a CancellationException instead of continuing to suspend a canceled coroutine.

CHAPTER 7

Unlock Parallel Processing

If a coroutine doesn't call any suspending functions, is it still a coroutine?

We started this book by describing a coroutine as something like the suspending equivalent of a thread, able to pause its execution while it waits for outside events. Since then, we've introduced all kinds of tools to make coroutines safe and easy to work with.

In this chapter, we'll use those same tools—and a couple of new ones—to speed things up not with asynchronous suspension points but with parallel execution across multiple CPU cores. When we're done, you'll be equipped to make the most of your hardware by subdividing any problem, asynchronous or otherwise, into a series of simpler tasks.

Launch Millions of Tasks

So far, we've mostly been focusing on the ways coroutines can help us make more effective use of a single shared thread. But what about code that's not confined to one designated main thread?

Coroutines and threads each provide their own form of multitasking. In this section, we'll explore the pros and cons, beginning with a simple experiment that compares the cost of each approach. As we'll find out, the best solution might turn out to be a combination of the two.

Threads or Coroutines?

When a single thread is all that's available—whether because you're writing UI code or because you're targeting a platform that doesn't offer multithreading capabilities at all—coroutines can be an invaluable tool. Blocking the thread would prevent it from carrying out its other important duties, so it's vital to swap thread-blocking operations for asynchronous or suspending calls.

But when multiple threads are at your disposal, blocking a single thread isn't necessarily such a problem. After all, your operating system is already dividing its attention among many different threads and processes. When one thread stops to wait for something, the system simply sets that thread aside and looks for another one that's ready to execute code.

Plenty of platforms, including the JVM, let you take advantage of this system-level concurrency by splitting your program's work across multiple threads. If you start a new thread for each task, you'll still get the multitasking you're looking for, even with old-fashioned functions that wait by blocking their thread.

Concurrency without the coroutines—sounds great, right? But multithreading has some downsides of its own, so don't pick your winner just yet.

Heavyweight Threads

To demonstrate the difference in cost between threads and coroutines, let's perform an experiment. We'll write a program that creates threads in an infinite loop and count how many threads it can start before the program crashes. Then, we'll do the same thing with coroutines and compare the results.

We'll use a do–while loop to launch the threads. In each thread, we're simply going to call sleep() with the maximum duration, so none of our threads will ever do anything. We'll use a loop counter to keep track of the number of threads we've started, and we'll add a finally block so we can display a message if and when the program runs into an error:

parallel/v1/src/main/kotlin/com/example/parallel/MultithreadingApplication.kt
```kotlin
fun main() {
  var threads = 0
  try {
    do {
      thread(isDaemon = true) { sleep(Long.MAX_VALUE) }
    } while (threads++ < Int.MAX_VALUE)
  } finally {
    println("Total threads: $threads")
  }
}
```

The results aren't bad, but it doesn't take long at all before the program crashes:

```
Total threads: 8169
Exception in thread "main" java.lang.OutOfMemoryError:
  unable to create native thread:
  possibly out of memory or process/resource limits reached
```

Lightweight Coroutines

Like a thread, a coroutine keeps track of the state of a running task, including its local variables and its progress through the code. Coroutines are sometimes described as *lightweight threads* because they provide a form of concurrency without the full cost of creating and switching between real threads.

If coroutines are lighter than threads, we should be able to create many more of them before the program crashes. Let's test the theory!

We'll replace the thread() and sleep() functions with launch() and delay(). Since Kotlin adds structured concurrency features that aren't provided by plain threads, we're also going to need to add a coroutineScope() to contain the new coroutines:

```
parallel/v2/src/main/kotlin/com/example/parallel/MultithreadingApplication.kt
suspend fun main() {
  var coroutines = 0
  try {
    coroutineScope {
      do {
        launch { delay(Long.MAX_VALUE) }
      } while (coroutines++ < Int.MAX_VALUE)
    }
  } finally {
    println("Total coroutines: $coroutines")
  }
}
```

One thing that's obvious right away is that this program runs for much longer. That's a good sign! It means we're managing to create more tasks before giving up:

```
Total coroutines: 35769854
Exception in thread "main" java.lang.OutOfMemoryError: Java heap space
```

With 35,769,854 total coroutines, we've managed to create over 4000 times more tasks than we could with threads. Try running the code yourself and see how your results compare! The exact number of coroutines and threads you can create will depend on the hardware and configuration of the computer you're using.

Coroutines let you create new tasks wherever and whenever you like without worrying that they're going to use up memory or slow your application down. That freedom can fundamentally change the way you think about your code's architecture, with a separate coroutine for every user, session, request, activity, event, or other stateful entity in your application. In Chapter 12,

Share Flows, Connect Channels, on page 201, we'll introduce ways for all those coroutines to communicate with one another.

Double Trouble

What makes threads so expensive? It varies by platform, but there are two major factors:

- First, each thread in a running process reserves some space in the program's memory. If you're relying on threads, you'll incur that memory cost all over again for every task you create.

- Second, there's an extra cost each time a multithreaded program wants to switch from one task to another. To switch between tasks, the operating system has to unload the state of one thread and load up another in a time-consuming process called a *context switch*.

So, threads have a double disadvantage. Not only does it take time and resources to create a new task, but it also takes time and resources to proceed from one task to the next.

All code ultimately needs to run on a thread, and that's true even when you are using an asynchronous programming style like coroutines. But as you've learned in previous chapters, coroutines save on resources by sharing the same thread among many different tasks.

If we can replace our blocking operations with suspending asynchronous alternatives, coroutines are our clear winner.

Dispatch to Multiple Cores

We've compared coroutines with threads and seen coroutines come out on top in our test. But there's one thing we've overlooked in our comparison of threads and coroutines so far. It's time we talked about parallelism.

In this section, we're going to be writing a function to generate password hashes. In the process, we'll see how multithreading isn't something we want to go without.

Rather than trying to pick between coroutines and threads, maybe we should be looking at how to combine the best bits of both. With the right dispatcher, you'll learn how to do just that.

What About Virtual Threads?

Kotlin's coroutines aren't the first attempt to fix the problems of conventional multi-threading, and they won't be the last. Lightweight threads, green threads, virtual threads, user threads, fibers—the names and details might differ, but they're all versions of the same idea across different programming languages and platforms.

Let's take a concrete example—Java 21's virtual threads. Like coroutines, they promise to make multitasking more efficient, avoiding most of the costs of thread creation and context switching. Combine virtual threads with the structured concurrency tools from more recent versions of Java, and you've replicated much of what Kotlin's coroutines can do.

Java's virtual threads even work with existing blocking functions—no need for new suspension point syntax. So, why choose coroutines instead?

No matter what platforms and frameworks your Kotlin code targets, coroutines bring all your asynchronous programming and concurrency tools together in one consistent, idiomatic programming model. Under the hood, platform-specific capabilities such as virtual threads could one day form part of a coroutine's implementation—but the same Kotlin code will continue to work on older Java versions, too, as well as bringing multitasking benefits to single-threaded platforms such as JavaScript.

Working Hard

We've been focusing our multitasking efforts on code that waits around for things to happen. But multitasking can also be useful when you have a lot of work to do and several CPU cores to run it on. Encoding videos, compiling code, simulating scientific processes, and training AI models are a few examples of compute-heavy tasks where more processor power can mean speedier results.

Let's look at a CPU-intensive task from the field of cryptography and learn how we can speed it up with coroutine-powered multitasking.

Say we're working on a login system that checks usernames and passwords against a database. To keep things secure, our software stores a computed hash in place of the actual password. If the user enters the right password, we can verify that it matches the hash we've stored. But there's no way to decode the hash and get back to the original password, so our users' secret credentials will stay hidden even if someone manages to get access to our database.

Secure Storage

Here's the function that will take a password and generate a hash:

parallel/v3/src/main/kotlin/com/example/parallel/Hash.kt
```kotlin
fun salt() = Random.nextBytes(8)

fun hash(password: String, salt: ByteArray = salt()): String {
  val sha256 = MessageDigest.getInstance("sha256")

  var hash = salt + password.encodeToByteArray()
  repeat(1_000_000) {
    hash = sha256.digest(hash)
  }

  return salt.toHexString() + hash.toHexString()
}
```

We're not going to dig into exactly what the code is doing—all that matters is that it intentionally takes some time to run. Someone with the correct password only needs to compute the hash once, so it's fine if it takes a couple of hundred milliseconds. That's barely a blink of an eye. But a hacker needs to try hundreds of trillions of possible passwords. At five attempts per second, that could take them millions of years.

We can use this as a realistic example of a long-running computation that will give our CPU a bit of a workout. But don't take the code too seriously—it's not intended to resist password-cracking attempts by a real attacker. If you're looking for actual security advice, you're going to need a different book!

Let's test the function out by computing a hash for our super secret password:

parallel/v3/src/main/kotlin/com/example/parallel/MultithreadingApplication.kt
```kotlin
fun main() {
  val (value, duration) = measureTimedValue {
    hash(password = "kotlin1")
  }

  println("Computed the hash in $duration")
  println(value)
}
```

Run the code, and you'll get something like this:

```
Computed the hash in 117.591583ms
a1560a65ab7cacdbd45c3a5c28ae0891860186d6b9848290…
```

Your hash won't be the same as this one because the salt value is generated fresh each time. It's stored alongside the hash in the database and will make sure that an attacker can't tell when two users share the same password.

Now Make 2000 of Them

Our software is proving popular, and we've signed a big new customer. They have 2000 users who are all going to need new accounts. We've been tasked with generating new credentials for each user. Each person will need a unique temporary password, which is secure enough to keep their account safe until they can change it to something more personal.

Generating the passwords is the easy part. A randomized 10-character string of letters, numbers, and symbols should do the trick:

parallel/v4/src/main/kotlin/com/example/parallel/MultithreadingApplication.kt
```
val chars = ('a'..'z') + ('A'..'Z') + ('0'..'9') + '_' + '!' + '?'

val passwords = List(2_000) {
  CharArray(10) { chars.random() }.concatToString()
}
```

This will give us a list of 2000 different random passwords. But, to assign them to our new users, we need to store them in the database. Or rather, we need to store a hash for each password. That means generating all the hashes using our hash() function:

parallel/v4/src/main/kotlin/com/example/parallel/MultithreadingApplication.kt
```
fun main() {
  val (values, duration) = measureTimedValue {
    passwords.map { hash(it) }
  }
  println("Computed ${values.size} hashes in $duration")
}
```

If you bother to wait for the code to finish, you'll see something like this:

```
Computed 2000 hashes in 1m 15.979241292s
```

Thanks to all those millions of hash iterations, the code takes more than a minute to run. The exact time will vary significantly depending on your computer.

That's a bit painful, especially if we're going to be doing this every time we need to add a batch of new user accounts. How can we make things better?

Secret Weapon

So far, we've focused on using coroutines to share a single thread among several tasks. But that approach isn't going to help speed up this code. Our program is always busy crunching numbers, and there wouldn't be any asynchronous gaps where other tasks could jump in.

Add another thread, though, and the story changes. Why? Most modern systems have more than one CPU core. A program that divides its work into multiple threads can benefit from parallel execution, with one thread running on each available CPU core.

Okay, but we don't want to make a new thread for each of our password-hashing tasks, do we? Not only will each of those 2000 threads cost us some extra time and memory, but we won't get any of the error handling and resource management features that coroutines would have given us. How can we get access to CPU-level multitasking without giving up our lightweight tasks and structured concurrency benefits?

Thread Pools

Our earlier comparison between threads and coroutines wasn't a fair one. We started one thread per task and then switched to coroutines for a huge improvement.

But if you've used threads for parallelization in a real program, you probably didn't create a new thread for each piece of work. Depending on the size and number of tasks, the cost of thread creation and context switching might outweigh the benefits of parallel execution altogether.

A better strategy is to use a small group of threads, or *thread pool*, large enough to provide the required level of parallelism. One common setup is to have the threads in the pool execute tasks from a shared work queue. When you want to run a task, you don't start it as a new thread—you add it to the queue, and it'll be executed by one of the existing worker threads. In plain Java, you might be used to doing this via an Executor or ExecutorService.

We can do the same thing for the coroutines in a Kotlin program. In our first chapter, you learned that coroutines get allocated to threads by a dispatcher. Well, a coroutine dispatcher can be backed by a pool of threads in the same way as a Java Executor.

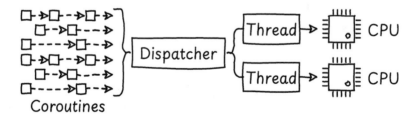

Running coroutines on a multithreaded dispatcher is like submitting tasks to a multithreaded Executor—except now, those tasks have all the benefits of suspending functions and structured concurrency as well. Let's try it out!

Shared Mutable State

With multiple coroutines running on multiple threads, it's not safe to have mutable data structures and variables that might be accessed by more than one task at once.

But the techniques you're used to using to solve that problem in non-coroutine code, such as locks and synchronized sections, are built for use with threads and won't work correctly with coroutines.

Kotlin does offer a suspending Mutex utility, but you might find you never need it. The tools and techniques we've been using so far—such as concurrent decomposition with async() and await()—are instead designed to avoid the need for shared mutable state altogether. In Chapter 12, Share Flows, Connect Channels, on page 201, you'll learn even more tools that let coroutines meet up and exchange data safely at designated suspension points.

Parallel Coroutines

We'll create our coroutines using the same familiar recipe that you learned in Chapter 4, Split Up to Speed Up, on page 59. For each piece of work, we'll start a new async() task. Once they're all running, we can sit back and let the awaitAll() function take care of collecting the results.

To make sure we have access to multiple CPU cores, we'll configure our coroutines to use Dispatchers.Default. This is the second coroutine dispatcher we've introduced, and unlike Dispatchers.Main, this one doesn't confine all its coroutines to just one thread. Instead, it has a small pool of threads like the executors or thread pools you might have used in Java:

```
parallel/v5/src/main/kotlin/com/example/parallel/MultithreadingApplication.kt
suspend fun main() = withContext(Dispatchers.Default) {
  val (values, duration) = measureTimedValue {
    val results = passwords.map {
      async { hash(it) }
    }
    results.awaitAll()
  }

  println("Computed ${values.size} hashes in $duration")
}
```

The amount of work is the same, but now our program runs more than six times faster:

```
Computed 2000 hashes in 12.379590167s
```

Notice that we've also added the suspend modifier to our main() function—we have to do that if we want to call withContext(). Like the coroutineScope() function, withContext() creates a scope and waits for all the coroutines inside it. Waiting for other tasks means suspending the current one. Asynchronous events don't have to originate outside the program—they can come from other computations and calculations in your own code, too!

Your Mileage May Vary

 When you run this code yourself, you might not see the same six-fold improvement. The speed boost here comes from distributing coroutines among more than one CPU core, so it's completely dependent on how many cores you have and how busy they are.

Concurrency and Parallelism

The speed increase we're getting here isn't the same asynchronous multitasking that we've seen before. After all, our password-hashing coroutines don't contain any suspension points or asynchronous operations.

Instead, the code's running in parallel on separate CPU cores. This isn't an illusion created by switching back and forth between different tasks—we really are running multiple tasks simultaneously.

Once again, it's concurrency that makes this possible. Without concurrency, a program is just a list of instructions that must be executed in the same order that they're written. Each task has to finish before the next one can begin. Concurrency removes those ordering constraints, so it's a crucial building block for any program that wants to take advantage of parallel execution.

However, our code doesn't contain any instructions about how many threads to use or how to distribute the work among them. Keeping those concerns separate from our business logic is going to make our whole program easier to read, maintain, and test—more on that last part in Chapter 13, Unit Test Without Delay, on page 229.

Terminology Time Out

Let's stop to quickly review some terminology to make sure we're keeping all these things straight:

- *Concurrency* means breaking up a problem into independent tasks that don't depend on one another. Because they're independent, these concurrent chunks don't have to be executed in a fixed order. In Kotlin, you can add concurrency by launching coroutines.

- *Parallelization* means executing several tasks at the same time. Each task will run on a different CPU core.

A program can't work on two tasks at once unless you divide it into tasks in the first place, so concurrency is a prerequisite for any kind of multitasking, including parallelization.

That means we've now seen two different benefits that we can get by using coroutines to describe the separate tasks in our program:

1. When our tasks contain asynchronous suspension points, we'll save time and resources by multitasking between them.

2. If we're running on a platform that provides multithreading capabilities and we have multiple CPU cores, we'll save even more time by running multiple coroutines simultaneously.

In practice, many programs will take advantage of both of these at the same time. Just add some coroutines, pick the default dispatcher, and let Kotlin take care of the rest.

Sensible Defaults

The dispatcher we've been using, Dispatchers.Default, is designed to be a good choice for general coroutines whether they contain CPU computations, asynchronous tasks, or a mixture of the two.

Environmental Adaptation

 On the JVM, Dispatchers.Default has one thread for each CPU core. In JavaScript web applications, it uses the browser's single-threaded event loop, the same as Dispatchers.Main. Either way, you write the same code, and it adapts to the platform.

It's called the *default dispatcher*, but that doesn't mean it's going to be auto-matically cropping up all over the place. Remember, coroutine context is inherited, and most of the time, you'll be working with a coroutine or coroutine scope that already has a dispatcher. Launch a coroutine in Android's lifecycle-Scope, for example, and you'll always get Dispatchers.Main. If you want to switch back to Dispatchers.Default for its parallelization capabilities, you'll need to select it explicitly.

The default is there for Kotlin to fall back on when you launch a coroutine with no dispatcher at all in its starting context.

When would you ever have a scope with no dispatcher? One example is the built-in bare-bones GlobalScope. You also end up with no starting dispatcher if you start a new application with a suspending main() function.

Since that's exactly what we just did—calling async() from a suspending main() function—we technically didn't need to specify our password hashing pro-gram's dispatcher explicitly. With no starting dispatcher selected, Kotlin will automatically fill in the blank with Dispatchers.Default. However, relying on the default isn't a great strategy, since code can get moved around as the program evolves. We'll talk more about that in the next chapter when we introduce the concept of main-safety.

Suspending with No Dispatcher

 Child coroutines always have a dispatcher, but in the top-level main() function itself, be aware that suspension points outside a withContext() block could resume on an unexpected thread.

Teach a Selfish Function to Share

Thanks to the multithreaded default dispatcher, we've got the best of both worlds. We can divide our program into as many coroutines as we like, and the dispatcher will distribute them across a small, cost-efficient pool of threads.

Once we introduce parallelism, concurrency is useful for more than asyn-chronous multitasking. That means coroutines can make sense even when they don't include any suspension points! Structured concurrency and the rules of jobs are as useful for parallel tasks as they are for asynchronous ones.

But without the suspension points, we've lost some other things, too. In this section, we'll look at what happens when a coroutine runs for a long time without encountering any suspending functions. You'll see how that can cause problems for other tasks in your program, and you'll learn how to make sure your coroutines can still be good neighbors, even when they're working flat-out on tasks that don't include any waiting.

How Slow Can You Go?

Our password hashing function creates security by taking a long time to run. But as we've seen, a more powerful computer with extra CPU cores can make the job easier. Let's make our hashing algorithm configurable so that hackers can't overcome all our defenses by buying a more powerful computer:

parallel/v6/src/main/kotlin/com/example/parallel/Hash.kt

```kotlin
const val iterations = 200_000_000

fun slowHash(password: String, salt: ByteArray = salt()): String {
  val sha256 = MessageDigest.getInstance("sha256")

  var hash = salt + password.encodeToByteArray()
  repeat(iterations) {
    hash = sha256.digest(hash)
  }

  return salt.toHexString() + hash.toHexString()
}
```

Two hundred million iterations should slow it down plenty! Okay, maybe that's a bit extreme—but with an adjustable number of iterations, we can tune it later to find the right balance between performance and security.

Let's test our new slowHash() function on one password and see how long it takes now:

parallel/v6/src/main/kotlin/com/example/parallel/MultithreadingApplication.kt

```kotlin
fun main() {
  val (value, duration) = measureTimedValue {
    slowHash(password = "kotlin1")
  }

  println("Computed the hash in $duration")
  println(value)
}
```

```
Computed the hash in 8.370272792s
0ba2d16763766162a702a8adfab7d39e07aa5b31ae54b019…
```

Great—that should keep those hackers busy.

Play by the Rules

Now that this function takes longer to run, there's a new problem we need to think about. Let's see what happens to this program if we try to add a time limit using the withTimeoutOrNull() function:

parallel/v7/src/main/kotlin/com/example/parallel/MultithreadingApplication.kt
```kotlin
suspend fun main() {
  val (value, duration) = measureTimedValue {
    withTimeoutOrNull(5.seconds) {
      slowHash("kotlin1")
    }
  }

  println("Computed the hash in $duration")
  println(value)
}
```

What do you think is going to happen when you run this code? Can you predict the output?

```
Computed the hash in 8.494025s
0e8ba295bcb4a52d823ef0814cc7583573de604a60081252…
```

Huh? The five-second timeout didn't seem to do anything at all. The output is exactly the same as it would have been if the withTimeoutOrNull() function wasn't there at all.

What went wrong?

In a way, that's a trick question. The withTimeoutOrNull() function is designed for use with suspending operations, such as the long-running network requests and timed delays that made up our museum tour program in the last chapter. It'll wake up a suspended coroutine if it's been waiting for too long.

But our slowHash() function isn't a suspending function at all, and it doesn't include any waiting. It doesn't have a clue that it's running in a coroutine, and with no suspension points or other cancellation checks, it'll never find out that the coroutine has been canceled. Remember, cancellation is cooperative—the only way to stop a task is to ask it nicely and hope it's paying attention.

That's not great! This function uses a lot of resources, and since we're going to be using coroutines to run it in parallel, we want it to play by the rules. If its parent Job fails or gets canceled, the task should exit promptly instead of continuing to spend CPU time on a calculation that will never be used.

There are a few ways we could think about adding cancellation checks to our slowHash() function. Maybe you already have an idea of how you might modify the function and its loop condition to solve the problem. Before we take care of it, though, let's have a look at another problem we might run into when we use this code in a coroutine.

Don't Be Selfish

Let's add some parallelization back into our program. That's the reason we want coroutines in the mix, after all.

Our function will take much longer to run now, so we'll reduce the number of passwords we're processing. Even so, we're just going to get a blank console until it's done. Maybe we could add some sort of output to keep track of progress and show how long the program's been working.

We'll start with one password-hashing task for each CPU core. On top of that, we'll add one additional coroutine to measure the elapsed time and display our output. This extra task will only wake up once every second, so it'll barely add any extra demand on our system's resources. Even so, we're not going to get the behavior we want when we try running this code. Can you guess what the problem is?

```
parallel/v8/src/main/kotlin/com/example/parallel/MultithreadingApplication.kt
suspend fun main() = withContext(Dispatchers.Default) {
  val startTime = TimeSource.Monotonic.markNow()
  val numberOfCores = Runtime.getRuntime().availableProcessors()

  val passwordJob = async {
    passwords.take(numberOfCores) // one task for each CPU core
      .map { async { slowHash(it) } }.awaitAll()
  }

  launch {
    while (passwordJob.isActive) {
      delay(1.seconds)
      println("Time taken so far: ${startTime.elapsedNow()}")
    }
  }

  val values = passwordJob.await()
  println("Computed ${values.size} hashes in ${startTime.elapsedNow()}")
}
```

Notice how we're putting our structured concurrency skills to use by using the passwordJob as a parent for each of our other async() tasks! Our new timer coroutine will run for as long as that Job and its children are still doing work.

All our coroutines are supposed to be running at once, so we should start seeing the output from our timer coroutine right away. But instead, it doesn't seem to do anything at all until the program's almost over:

```
Time taken so far: 27.5s
Time taken so far: 28.5s
Computed 10 hashes in 29.4s
Time taken so far: 29.5s
```

Why did the final coroutine take more than twenty seconds to start?

It's because all our dispatcher's threads were already busy doing other work. Our slowHash() function is selfish—once it's got hold of a thread, it's going to keep it. As you learned way back at the start of our journey, an ordinary non-suspending function like this one can't give up its thread until it reaches the end and exits.

So, by the time our final coroutine comes along, all the threads have already been taken! The default dispatcher has the right number of threads to match our system's processor cores—any more would be wasteful. But with all those threads already busy running uncooperative coroutines, there's no way for other tasks to get a look in.

If we were using a dedicated thread for each task, this wouldn't be a problem. Instead of relying on cooperative suspension points, threads allow for *preemptive multitasking*, where the system can swap between tasks whenever it likes. But it can only work with the threads we give it, and all our dispatcher's threads are already loaded up with password-hashing tasks. The timer coroutine was the last to be started, and it won't be allocated to a thread at all until the dispatcher has completed at least one of its other tasks.

Sharing Is Caring

You've just seen two problems with running our slowHash() function in a coroutine. First, it can't exit early when the coroutine is canceled because it doesn't know anything about coroutines or cancellation. Second, it can't cooperate by sharing its thread with other tasks. As an ordinary function with no suspension capabilities, it's bound to its thread until it's completed its entire execution.

We can fix both of these problems by giving the slowHash() some suspension points. That might sound strange since it doesn't have any asynchronous operations or outside events to wait for. But suspending is as much about cooperating with other coroutines as it is about waiting for outside events. If there are several coroutines waiting to execute, we can suspend the current function and let another task run for a while.

That's the job of the yield() function.

Think of it like the *yield* or *give way* sign at a traffic intersection. It marks a point where you need to pause and check for other vehicles—but you only have to stop if there's something coming. If there aren't any other coroutines waiting, the yield() function doesn't suspend at all, and the current task keeps right on running.

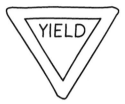

Let's try it out in our code. We'll call yield() once every 200,000 iterations:

parallel/v9/src/main/kotlin/com/example/parallel/Hash.kt
```kotlin
suspend fun slowHash(password: String, salt: ByteArray = salt()): String {
  val sha256 = MessageDigest.getInstance("sha256")

  var hash = salt + password.encodeToByteArray()
  repeat(iterations) { i ->
    if (i % 200_000 == 0) yield()
    hash = sha256.digest(hash)
  }

  return salt.toHexString() + hash.toHexString()
}
```

Run the program again with this upgraded slowHash() function, and everything works the way we want. Our extra timer coroutine can print its output once every second. The same change will also fix the previous version of the app, letting our timeout code cancel the work promptly.

Striking a Balance

 Consider using yield() to keep everything running smoothly if you're doing CPU work for more than a few dozen milliseconds. But don't go overboard, or you might end up with more task-switching than actual work.

Any suspension point, whether it's a delay() or a network request, creates a gap where the task can give up its thread and let other coroutines take a turn. So the yield() function is only necessary when a coroutine runs for a long time without encountering any other suspending functions. Like any other suspension point, it also checks for cancellation, throwing a CancellationException when the task is no longer needed.

Notice how we had to add the suspend modifier directly to our slowHash() function this time—not just to the main() function that's going to wait for its parallel execution. That's because yield() is a suspending function—even if it only ever waits for other coroutines and not outside events. Since coroutines use suspension points for cooperative multitasking, being able to suspend is a useful trait for any long-running function that wants to be a good neighbor while running on a coroutine dispatcher.

What Have You Learned?

We split this chapter's work into thousands of individual coroutines, all for only a fraction of the cost of threads. After that, all we had to do for an automatic parallelization speed boost was select the multithreaded Dispatchers.Default in our coroutine context.

With no suspension points, our code didn't cooperate correctly with other tasks and cancellation requests—but we fixed that with a few calls to yield().

Even so, this CPU-intensive code is probably too heavy for an app's main UI thread. In the next chapter, you'll learn how to keep the two safely separated. Not only that, but we'll introduce a third dispatcher that will finally bridge the gap between coroutines and old-fashioned blocking code.

Key Concepts

Lightweight threads

These are thread-like tasks that don't incur the full cost of creating and switching between real operating system threads. Kotlin's coroutines are a great example.

Parallelization

This is when multiple tasks run simultaneously on different CPU cores. Use Dispatchers.Default to run coroutines in parallel on supported platforms.

Cooperative multitasking

This is periodically giving up control from the current task so that another task can take over. Coroutines yield control at each suspension point or with explicit calls to yield().

Part II

Better Together

Call old-fashioned blocking functions from new suspending code. Transform existing callbacks into seamless suspension points. Pipe Reactive Streams right into your Kotlin functions, and link tasks and data with shared flows and channels.

The second part of this book is all about connecting coroutines with other code. With a complete lineup of tools and techniques for integrating with every other asynchronous programming style you can think of, you will bring all your established libraries and skills with you into the new world of coroutines.

CHAPTER 8

Call Blocking Functions Safely

Coroutines rely on suspending functions to wait without blocking threads.

But that doesn't mean you need to throw away all your existing code or replace every network call and outside input with a new suspending function. In this chapter, we'll bring old blocking code with us into the new world of coroutines, and you'll learn the tools and best practices that make it a breeze to mix the two.

After completing this chapter, you'll be able to wrap any blocking call in a suspending function that's safe to access from anywhere. You'll know the simple conventions that keep your coroutines out of trouble, no matter what they do or how they're called.

Keep Your Functions Honest

We've spent a good part of our journey learning about the headline benefit of suspending functions. A suspending function doesn't block its thread, so it's safe to call from anywhere—right?

The suspend modifier gives us access to the right ingredients for efficient execution, but a misplaced blocking call will still lock up its thread, whether it's in a suspending function or not. In this section, we'll write a function that's misrepresenting itself, and you'll learn some ground rules to make sure it doesn't happen in the real world.

Blank Canvas

On our journey so far, you've used suspending functions to download images from the Internet. But network calls aren't the only reason you might need to wait for data. Let's go back to the image viewer code we last saw in Chapter 4, Split Up to Speed Up, on page 59 and try some other suspending operations in place of our photo download.

Here are the dependencies you'll need:

gallery/v1/build.gradle.kts
```
dependencies {
  implementation("org.jetbrains.kotlinx:kotlinx-coroutines-core:1.10.1")
  runtimeOnly("org.jetbrains.kotlinx:kotlinx-coroutines-swing:1.10.1")
}
```

We'll reuse the same abstract ImageViewer class that we used for our astronomy photos, though we won't be making any network requests in this chapter:

gallery/v1/src/main/kotlin/com/example/gallery/ImageViewer.kt
```
abstract class ImageViewer : WindowAdapter() {
  val coroutineScope = MainScope()

  override fun windowOpened(e: WindowEvent) {
    val window = e.window as JFrame
    coroutineScope.launch {
      update(window)
    }
  }

  protected abstract suspend fun update(window: JFrame)

  override fun windowClosed(e: WindowEvent) {
    coroutineScope.cancel()
  }
}
```

Don't forget the createWindow() function, which you'll need when you want to run the app:

gallery/v1/src/main/kotlin/com/example/gallery/Helpers.kt
```
fun createWindow(title: String, listener: WindowListener) {
  SwingUtilities.invokeLater {
    val window = JFrame(title)
    window.defaultCloseOperation = JFrame.DISPOSE_ON_CLOSE
    window.size = Dimension(400, 300)
    window.add(JLabel("Loading your image…", JLabel.CENTER))
    window.addWindowListener(listener)
    window.isVisible = true
  }
}
```

I Can't Believe You Just Blocked Me

To implement our abstract ImageViewer class, we need to fill in the update() function. Since update() has the suspend modifier, it'd be easy to assume that the program will always run safely on our Swing app's UI thread, no matter what implementation we provide.

But watch out! As well as being able to call other suspending functions, a function with the suspend modifier can still call ordinary non-suspending code. Technically, there's nothing to stop a suspending function from calling a function that blocks its thread.

We can see the problem if we add a Thread.sleep() to our update() function:

gallery/v1/src/main/kotlin/com/example/gallery/ImageViewerApplication.kt

```kotlin
fun main() = createWindow("Image Viewer", object : ImageViewer() {
  override suspend fun update(window: JFrame) {
    Thread.sleep(10_000)
  }
})
```

Just like the blocking network call in our first chapter, this code freezes the whole app. The loading text shows up this time since it's added before the coroutine starts—but once the faulty coroutine is running, you won't be able to interact with the window. The UI thread is blocked by the call to Thread.sleep(), so it can't redraw the interface or process new inputs.

Warning Signs

Depending on your IDE version and its configuration, you might see a warning about this misplaced Thread.sleep(). Keep an eye out for these warnings, but don't rely on them—more on that later.

Remember, the suspend modifier is there to unlock new capabilities, not change existing ones. Unlike Java's fancy virtual threads, coroutines don't change the way your old code runs or magically convert blocking calls to asynchronous ones. A suspending function only lets go of its thread when it reaches a suspension point. The rest of the time, it behaves like any other piece of code.

Call a blocking function from a coroutine, and it'll block the thread like it would anywhere else. But coroutines don't own their threads; they share them—and you'll see in this chapter that blocking a shared thread can cause more problems than UI freezes.

Great Power, Great Responsibility

You already know how to fix this program. All you need to do is replace the thread-blocking sleep() function with Kotlin's suspending delay().

In a moment, we'll take a look at another example where things aren't so straightforward. But before we do that, let's take a closer look at the problem we've created. Our function's being dishonest—its suspend modifier says one thing, but its implementation does something else.

Callers such as our Swing application choose suspending functions over regular functions when they want to wait for something without the risk of blocking a thread. So, by concealing a blocking call to Thread.sleep, our update() function is misleading its consumers and blocking a caller that was not expecting to be blocked. It's like writing *decaf* on a regular cup of coffee—there's nothing stopping you from doing it, but your customers aren't going to be too happy with you.

Treat the suspend modifier as an agreement with your function's callers. They came for asynchronous operations that don't block threads, and that's what they should get.

Open a File

With access to the right libraries, it's easy enough to replace a blocking function with a suspending alternative—like when we swapped blocking execute() for suspending awaitResponse() in our first Retrofit app.

But things aren't always so easy. Let's see what happens when we want to load a picture from a file.

First, we'll prompt the user to ask which file we should open:

gallery/v2/src/main/kotlin/com/example/gallery/Helpers.kt
```kotlin
fun promptForFile(context: JFrame? = null): File? {
  val dialog = FileDialog(context)
  dialog.isVisible = true
  return dialog.files.singleOrNull()
}
```

Nothing to See Here

 This FileDialog does some waiting of its own, and Swing has its own way to make sure it doesn't freeze the rest of our UI. It won't affect our coroutines, so we'll skip over it and focus on reading the file's contents.

We'll also add a displayImage() function, which we can call inside update() to remove our loading text and replace it with a picture:

gallery/v2/src/main/kotlin/com/example/gallery/Helpers.kt
```kotlin
fun displayImage(window: JFrame, image: Image) {
  window.contentPane.removeAll()
  window.add(JLabel(ImageIcon(image)))
  window.pack()
}
```

We've written a version of the same function before, but this one's slightly different. It accepts an Image object, which will give us some new options for providing our image data.

Ready-Made Solution

Once again, our task is to implement the suspending update() function. After we call our promptForFile() function, we'll read the contents of the file into an Image and call displayImage().

Java has a purpose-built function for that in its ImageIO class. Let's try putting it to use:

gallery/v2/src/main/kotlin/com/example/gallery/ImageViewerApplication.kt
```kotlin
fun main() = createWindow("Image Viewer", object : ImageViewer() {
  override suspend fun update(window: JFrame) {
    val file = promptForFile(window) ?: return
    val image = ImageIO.read(file) // oops!
    displayImage(window, image)
  }
})
```

Opening a file shouldn't take long, so you might not see a problem when you run this code. But that read() function is loading data from outside our application, and it's doing that by blocking its thread. Use this code to open a large file from a slow storage device or a network location, and we might be right back where we were before, with a frozen user interface.

So, what do we do?

In Chapter 9, Upgrade Every Callback, on page 145, we'll try our hand at building a non-blocking replacement for ImageIO.read(). But that'll require some new tools and techniques—and it might not be feasible to start replacing or rewriting core functionality like this in a real project.

Apart from the blocked thread, the ready-made ImageIO.read() function has exactly the signature and functionality we need. If we can keep it clear of the UI thread, we won't need to throw out the existing implementation or write any new file-handling code of our own.

Switching threads is the job of the coroutine dispatcher, and there's a dedicated dispatcher we can use to fix our image viewer. But before we jump to the right solution, let's quickly go over some other ideas.

Into the Background

Outside the world of coroutines, you might fix this file-loading problem with a SwingWorker—a built-in class for moving tasks off the UI thread.

Android Equivalent

 Java's SwingWorker is similar to the deprecated AsyncTask in Android. Both update the UI on completion of a background task.

Maybe we can use that here?

It's easy enough to make the change. To create a SwingWorker, we provide two functions—one that runs in a separate background thread and another that updates the UI when the data is ready:

```
gallery/v3/src/main/kotlin/com/example/gallery/ImageViewerApplication.kt
fun main() = createWindow("Image Viewer", object : ImageViewer() {
  override suspend fun update(window: JFrame) {
    val file = promptForFile(window) ?: return

    val worker = object : SwingWorker<Image, Nothing>() {
      override fun doInBackground() = ImageIO.read(file)
      override fun done() = displayImage(window, get())
    }

    worker.execute()
  }
})
```

Now that ImageIO.read() is safely tucked away in the doInBackground() function, it won't put our UI responsiveness at risk. If we weren't using coroutines, that would be the end of the story.

But update() is still a suspending function, so starting a background task is a bit of a problem.

Why? Once again, it's down to the expectations that we create when we use the suspend modifier.

Be True to Your Keyword

A suspending function is supposed to wait for its asynchronous tasks to finish. That's what suspending means, after all. But our SwingWorker doesn't wait. Its execute() function returns immediately, letting the rest of the code continue elsewhere.

What happens when the SwingWorker fails and throws an exception? What if someone tries calling our image viewer's show() function in a loop, expecting each iteration to complete its work before moving on to the next? And what happens when the coroutine that called show() is canceled?

All of these are things that are normally taken care of by suspending functions, and callers of our suspending show() function will be expecting the same level of service. But our SwingWorker doesn't know anything about that, and its errors, code, and resources are going to leak free from our coroutine's control.

The suspend modifier tells callers that a function is going to wait for all its work to complete before returning. We might not have asked for this code to be inside a suspending function, but now that it is, it's going to have to follow the rules.

By convention, suspending functions don't leak tasks or introduce concurrency. Any new coroutines, threads, or callbacks need to be wrapped up before the function returns. If you want to start truly asynchronous work that outlives the current function, don't mislead callers by adding the suspend modifier.

Keep Your Coroutines Contained

Starting a coroutine with launch() or async() means kicking off a new task without waiting for it to finish. That's why you can't call one of these coroutine builders directly from a suspending function—you need a function such as coroutineScope() that can wait for the tasks to complete.

If you get creative, you'll be able to come up with ways to get around this. For example, you might try using the currentCoroutineContext() function to make a CoroutineScope that inherits the current function's context without forcing the function to wait.

But conjuring a coroutine scope like that is only going to obscure your intentions and confuse your callers. If you want your function to start new coroutines without waiting for them, leave out the suspend modifier. Instead, provide an explicit coroutine scope in some other way, out in the open where everyone can see it.

Let's recap. You've seen two *suspending function conventions*—rules that aren't enforced by the compiler but that you need to follow if you want your coroutine code to be safe for public consumption:

1. Suspending functions don't block their caller's thread. In the next part of this chapter, you'll learn how coroutines can still use blocking functions without breaking this rule.

2. Suspending functions finish what they start. If a function doesn't wait for all its threads, coroutines, or callbacks, it shouldn't have the suspend modifier.

There are two kinds of functions—ones that wait and ones that don't—and we're relying on the suspend modifier to tell us which of those two we're dealing with. Keep the two separate, and you'll make life easier both for yourself and for your colleagues.

Block That Thread, Not This One

Our suspending update() function shouldn't block its thread, and it shouldn't start new tasks without waiting for them to finish. Without changing the ImageViewer base class, what other options do we have?

In this section, we introduce a new dispatcher to help us solve the problem.

Who Needs Background Tasks?

You've seen how you could use a SwingWorker to move the blocking readBytes() function off the UI thread. But that means starting a background task and taking away the suspending-function benefits that your callers could be relying on.

Maybe we need a way to suspend update() until our SwingWorker has done its thing?

That might work, but it's a more complicated solution than we need. Offloading blocking calls to background tasks is an idea that comes from other asynchronous programming models where waiting is all jumbled up with concurrency. But there's no reason we need to multitask here. We don't need to do two things at the same time—we need to do them on two different threads.

Since we're working with suspending functions, that's not a problem. Remember, a coroutine is free to move between threads, like the jigsaw puzzle tray moving from one table to another in our first chapter. All we need to do is pick a new dispatcher, and we can switch threads right in the middle of an existing function. No background tasks are needed!

In fact, this is the same mechanism that we're using to get our code running on the UI thread in the first place, with Dispatchers.Main. But which dispatcher should we use if we want a thread that we can safely block?

A Safer Way to Block

For coroutines that need to call old-fashioned blocking code on multithreaded platforms such as Java, Kotlin provides Dispatchers.IO. Let's use it right away to fix our image file viewer:

gallery/v4/src/main/kotlin/com/example/gallery/ImageViewerApplication.kt

```kotlin
fun main() = createWindow("Image Viewer", object : ImageViewer() {
  override suspend fun update(window: JFrame) {
    val file = promptForFile(window) ?: return
    val image = withContext(Dispatchers.IO) {
      ImageIO.read(file)
    }
    displayImage(window, image)
  }
})
```

What we've written here is a single function that runs on two different threads. Most of the time, it's on the main UI thread, thanks to the withContext() block wrapping the whole thing. But when it's time to call readBytes(), it uses a second withContext() block to briefly switch to Dispatchers.IO. When we reach displayImage(), we have left that inner code block, so we are back where we need to be on Dispatchers.Main.

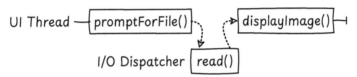

If you want to prove it's working, try adding an extra Thread.sleep() to the innermost withContext() section. Since it's no longer running on the UI thread, the app will still respond to inputs while it's waiting.

General Purpose

 It might be called the I/O dispatcher—short for *input/output*—but Dispatchers.IO isn't just for files and networking. It's designed for any code that blocks its thread.

Wait for Me

So what thread is Dispatchers.IO using, and why is that one safe to block?

The I/O dispatcher works by keeping hold of a few spare threads—ones that don't have anything else important to do. When you need a thread that doesn't mind being blocked, it loans one out to you.

You can think of it like hiring an assistant to stand in line for you at a busy event venue or product launch. You can carry on with your day, and your new minion will drop you a message when your turn finally comes around.

The more blocking operations you use in your coroutines, the more sacrificial threads the I/O dispatcher will need to create. That means it's a compromise solution. It comes with some cost since you're still creating and blocking threads—but at least you won't be freezing your app by blocking the all-important UI thread.

In Chapter 9, Upgrade Every Callback, on page 145, we'll try out some truly non-blocking file operations that don't need to use a thread at all. When we get to Chapter 10, Go with the Flow, on page 161, you'll see how the costs of this thread-switching solution can quickly add up if you use it in loops and repeating data streams.

Bring Your Own Dispatcher

Now that we're using the right dispatcher, our update() code is following the two suspending function conventions that we've learned. It won't block its caller's thread, and it'll wait for all its work to finish.

But our solution feels fragile. What if a future change to our codebase moves this code somewhere else and forgets to bring the dispatcher with it? How about when we need to reuse the same solution somewhere else?

To make this more robust and reusable, we can write a single suspending readImage() function that encapsulates both the file operation and its dispatcher.

gallery/v5/src/main/kotlin/com/example/gallery/ImageViewerApplication.kt
```
suspend fun readImage(file: File): Image =
  withContext(Dispatchers.IO) {
    ImageIO.read(file)
  }
```

Make It Cancellable

 Need cancellation capabilities? Swap withContext() for runInterruptible(). The runInterruptible() function allows coroutine callers to cancel blocking functions using Java's thread-interruption mechanism.

It's a small change, but a useful one. Now that this function's bringing its own dispatcher, nothing outside the function ever needs to know that it contains blocking code. Our update() function can focus on its UI updates and call readImage() the same way it would call any other suspending function:

gallery/v5/src/main/kotlin/com/example/gallery/ImageViewerApplication.kt
```
fun main() = createWindow("Image Viewer", object : ImageViewer() {
  override suspend fun update(window: JFrame) {
    val file = promptForFile(window) ?: return
    val image = readImage(file)
    displayImage(window, image)
  }
})
```

We've taken the blocking ImageIO.read() function and wrapped it up into a suspending readImage() function that's safe to call from anywhere. You can use the same technique to make life easier for your callers whenever you need a house-trained suspending version of an unruly blocking function. Not only that, but you can safely assume that when a function has the suspend modifier, it's safe to call from any dispatcher.

Make It Main-Safe

Functions that are safe to call from the main UI thread—which all suspending functions should be—are referred to as *main-safe*. An important part of writing main-safe code is that you should never assume you're already running on a particular thread. Remember, by adding the suspend modifier, you're advertising that your function is safe to call from any dispatcher.

Our new readImage() function is a great example of a properly behaved main-safe function. Its caller doesn't need to worry about what's inside the function. No matter what dispatcher we're running on when we call readImage(), the function will switch to the right dispatcher to perform the file operation and then switch back again when it's done.

Avoiding blocking calls is an important part of main-safety, and any suspending function that follows the conventions we've learned has this one covered already. In the next section, we'll look at the other thing main-safe functions need to consider.

Identify Blocking Calls

If we're going to make sure we don't block our coroutines, we'll need to know which functions block threads and which don't.

Tools such as IntelliJ IDEA and Android Studio can sometimes spot potential thread-blocking threats. Depending on which IDE and compiler versions you're using, you might see warnings when you use Thread.sleep() and ImageIO.read() in a suspending function. But even when you know which functions to watch out for, making a positive identification of a blocked thread isn't always straightforward. Take a look at this code:

gallery/v5/src/main/kotlin/com/example/gallery/ByteArrayImageViewer.kt
```
abstract class ByteArrayImageViewer(val data: ByteArray) : ImageViewer() {
  override suspend fun update(window: JFrame) {
    val image = ImageIO.read(data.inputStream())
    displayImage(window, image)
  }
}
```

Does the update() function block its thread?

An InputStream can represent many things—including open files and network connections—so code-checking tools will most likely warn you that passing an InputStream to ImageIO.read() could be a blocking operation. But when you look beyond that single line of code, it's pretty obvious that the data only ever comes from a ByteArray that's already in memory. This particular call won't ever block its thread because there's nothing it needs to wait for.

Unlike a suspending function, blocking code doesn't come with a helpful keyword to signal its intentions. Identifying which calls need offloading to a different dispatcher often comes down to context and common sense. Keep an eye out for signs of network calls, filesystem operations, and interactions with other tasks, processes, or threads. If the code waits for something that's not in its control and returns a result without any suspension points, callbacks, or asynchronous wrappers, that's a blocking call.

Unreliable Indication

 Blocked-thread warnings often use clues from a Java function's throws clause. That can cause false positives—but in Kotlin, where @Throws is optional, it can also lead to false negatives. Don't assume a function never blocks just because there's no IDE warning.

Make Hard Work Look Easy

You've turned a blocking function into a suspending one and used it to load a photo into a coroutine.

But waiting for outside input isn't the only way to tie up a thread. To end this chapter, let's see what happens when we make our main UI thread work too hard. Even if the thread's not technically blocked, heavy workloads can still cause problems. To fix it, we'll use the same technique we've just learned but with a different dispatcher.

Blocked or Not?

What's next for our image viewer? How about some computer-generated artwork? Instead of fetching a photo from outside our program, we're going to write our own code to create one from scratch.

We'll use Java's BufferedImage class and fill in each pixel with a different color based on its position:

gallery/v6/src/main/kotlin/com/example/gallery/ImageViewerApplication.kt
```
fun generateImage(): Image {
  val image = BufferedImage(10240, 7680, BufferedImage.TYPE_INT_RGB)
  for (x in 0 until image.width) for (y in 0 until image.height) {
```

```
    val hue = (x + y).toFloat() / ((image.width - 1) + (image.height - 1))
    image.setRGB(x, y, Color.HSBtoRGB(hue, 1f, 1f))
  }
  return image.getScaledInstance(1024, 768, Image.SCALE_SMOOTH)
}
```

Can you guess what the picture's going to look like? Don't worry if you can't—the details of what's inside this function aren't important. What matters is that it returns an Image, which we can drop right into our ImageViewer code. Let's take a look:

gallery/v6/src/main/kotlin/com/example/gallery/ImageViewerApplication.kt
```
fun main() = createWindow("Image Viewer", object : ImageViewer() {
  override suspend fun update(window: JFrame) {
    val image = generateImage()
    displayImage(window, image)
  }
})
```

Beautiful—you're an artist!

This program is deliberately inefficient, and while it's taking its time to fill in all those individual pixels, the user interface is unresponsive. It's like the familiar behavior we've seen when we accidentally called blocking functions on the UI thread.

In technical terms, this thread isn't blocked. It's still doing work, and it never needs to stop and wait for anything outside its own control. But to a UI programmer, that's not much comfort. The thread still isn't responding, whether it's doing its own work or waiting for someone else's.

How can we fix it?

Get Off My Thread

Just like our blocking file operations, we can move this work to a different dispatcher. But since we're doing more than waiting around, Dispatchers.IO isn't the right choice. This is a heavy compute task, and as you learned in Chapter 7, Unlock Parallel Processing, on page 109, those belong on Dispatchers.Default:

gallery/v7/src/main/kotlin/com/example/gallery/ImageViewerApplication.kt
```
suspend fun generateImage(): Image = withContext(Dispatchers.Default) {
```

The rest of the function stays the same—this first line is all we need to change. Now we have a main-safe generateImage() function, and we can run this code without freezing up our user interface. You can use the same technique for any heavy workloads that you want to move off the UI thread.

It might seem strange to add the suspend modifier to a function that doesn't do any suspending—and it might not be the right choice in all cases. But remember, we've done something like this before when we added suspend to our slowHash() function in the last chapter.

Combine and Cooperate

 Using the skills you picked up in Teach a Selfish Function to Share, on page 120, how would you modify the suspending generateImage() function to help it cooperate with other coroutines?

Main-safety isn't just about blocked threads—it's about anything that could interfere with UI responsiveness.

Working Hard, or Hardly Working?

You've learned that the I/O dispatcher is for idle waiting, while the default dispatcher is for doing work. But in both cases, the goal is the same—get the code off the main thread and keep the UI responsive. So why two different dispatchers?

Allocating your tasks to the correct dispatcher is how you let Kotlin know what you'll be using your thread for. That, in turn, lets Kotlin know how many threads it should create, based on two goals—keep the total number of threads small, but always have enough threads to make full use of the CPU.

By running a coroutine on Dispatchers.Default, you're asking Kotlin to provide both a thread and a CPU core to run it on. For these tasks, Kotlin reserves a number of threads equal to the number of processor cores. Creating more threads would be a waste of resources because there wouldn't be any free processor cores for them to run on.

Since the default dispatcher only reserves one thread for each processor core, the rules of main-safety are important for more than your user interface code. If you accidentally block one of the default dispatcher's threads, it'll have fewer running threads than processor cores. Your coroutines won't be able to make full use of your CPU, and your app will run slower. Like a UI thread, the default dispatcher's reserved threads are a fixed and finite resource.

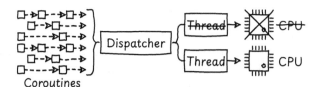

When you switch to Dispatchers.IO, you're letting Kotlin know that your coroutine will be using a thread without occupying a processor core. That means you want more threads than processor cores, at least temporarily. These extra threads are pure overhead, spending most of their time doing nothing, so the I/O dispatcher creates them only when needed and cleans them up again after use.

> ## Deadlock Danger
>
> Say you want to use Dispatchers.Default to run some coroutines in parallel, but you're not in a suspending function. You can't suspend to wait for the coroutines—but in an ordinary function, there's no rule saying you can't wait for them by blocking the thread instead. There's even a built-in runBlocking() function that will block its thread to run coroutines and wait for their completion. Sounds great! But be careful.
>
> The hypothetical function where you've just added a call to runBlocking() can be used from anywhere, coroutine or not. What happens when you call it from a coroutine that's already running on the default dispatcher? As you've learned, stealing a thread from the default dispatcher risks leaving the CPU underutilized—but that's not the real danger here. After runBlocking() takes over the thread, it's going to submit your parallel tasks ... to the default dispatcher. Oops! You'd better hope the dispatcher has more than one free thread. Otherwise, your new coroutines are waiting to run on the same thread that's now blocked, waiting for them to finish. Did somebody say *deadlock*?
>
> Don't leave traps like this in your code! Use runBlocking() with extreme caution, and only in those rare functions that are absolutely guaranteed to run on a non-coroutine thread.

Dispatcher Recap

The I/O dispatcher is the third dispatcher we've seen and the last one we're going to cover in this book. That makes this a great time to review them all:

- Dispatchers.Main lets you run coroutines on a single main thread. It's available when you're using one of the supported UI frameworks, including Android and Swing. Suspending functions should always be safe to call from here.

- Dispatchers.Default can be used to offload heavy computations from the main thread or for general tasks in non-UI applications. On platforms such as Java, it's backed by a pool of threads, with one thread for each CPU core. In a JavaScript browser application, Dispatchers.Default and Dispatchers.Main are the same since there's just one thread to work with.

- Dispatchers.IO is for functions that block their thread. No other coroutine should have its thread blocked, so all blocking calls belong here. You won't find this dispatcher when targeting JavaScript, since browser apps don't generally deal with multiple threads or functions that block them.

These three dispatchers should be all you need for most applications. If you do have more specific requirements, it's also possible to build your own. For example, a Java Executor can be converted to a coroutine dispatcher using the asCoroutineDispatcher() extension function.

There is one other built-in dispatcher, but it's not one you'll need to use often, if at all. It's called Dispatchers.Unconfined, and it lets coroutines behave more like callbacks, running directly in whatever background thread triggered each suspension point to resume. The result is a coroutine that can appear to swap between threads unpredictably.

What Have You Learned?

Suspending functions finish all their work before returning and don't block their caller's thread. It's up to you to make sure that stays true! Use the I/O dispatcher to wrap blocking operations in main-safe suspending functions that can be called from anywhere and offload heavy computations to Dispatchers.Default.

You've learned how to integrate coroutines with old-fashioned blocking code. But what about all the callbacks, futures, and promises in your other asynchronous libraries? In the next chapter, you'll find out how to turn any asynchronous operation into a coroutine-compatible suspending function.

Key Concepts

Main-safety

> This makes a function safe to call from the main UI thread. Send thread-blocking operations to Dispatchers.IO and offload heavy computations to Dispatchers.Default.

CHAPTER 9

Upgrade Every Callback

One of Kotlin's greatest strengths is its ability to integrate with other languages and frameworks. That's true for coroutines, too.

In this chapter, we'll bridge the divide between suspending functions and other asynchronous programming styles. We'll use built-in tools to convert a Java CompletableFuture to a coroutine and back, and then we'll go a step further when we build a custom suspension point from scratch.

By the end of this chapter, you'll be able to upgrade any asynchronous operation to a Kotlin suspending function, no matter what style it started out in. Not only that, but you'll have a deeper insight into the relationship between coroutines and callbacks.

Mix Coroutines and Futures

We've talked a lot in this book about suspending functions, blocking functions, and callbacks.

But there's another flavor we haven't explored as much, though we've come across it once or twice—asynchronous functions that work by returning some sort of object to represent their future outcome.

We're going to get this chapter started by exploring some built-in integrations that can connect coroutines to the asynchronous futures and promises found in all kinds of other libraries and languages.

Future Possibilities

Let's start by writing a simple function that can make a request via Java's built-in HttpClient:

```
gallery/v8/src/main/kotlin/com/example/gallery/DownloadAsync.kt
val client = HttpClient.newHttpClient()

fun downloadAsync(url: String): CompletableFuture<HttpResponse<ByteArray>> {
  val request = HttpRequest.newBuilder(URI(url)).build()
  return client.sendAsync(request, BodyHandlers.ofByteArray())
}
```

As the name suggests, sendAsync() is an asynchronous function. Since it comes from Java, it works the old-fashioned way without any suspending. So, where's its callback?

Instead of accepting a follow-up code block as an argument, sendAsync() creates a separate CompletableFuture object to manage its callbacks. You can think of this as a callback go-between. The completed HTTP request will deliver its result to the CompletableFuture, and the CompletableFuture will forward the result to any callbacks we've added. Not only that, but each callback step can create a new CompletableFuture of its own.

Let's try it out. After we call downloadAsync(), we'll use thenApply() to add a couple of extra steps, turning our initial ByteArray result into an Image:

```
gallery/v8/src/main/kotlin/com/example/gallery/DownloadAsync.kt
fun downloadImageAsync(url: String): CompletableFuture<Image> =
➤   downloadAsync(url)
      .thenApply { it.body().inputStream() }
      .thenApply { ImageIO.read(it) }
```

We're still splitting the code up into isolated chunks that can run outside the starting thread, but now they're arranged more like the lines of a sequential program. It's a good compromise—not as powerful or flexible as a coroutine, but certainly better than the nesting pyramids of callback hell. As a result, it's an attractive and popular solution for ergonomic asynchronous calls in plain Java.

Now, let's say we've inherited this downloadImageAsync() function as part of an existing codebase. We can keep the function's current implementation and Java-compatible return type and still use suspending functions to wait for it in our Kotlin coroutines.

That Looks Familiar

You can think of a CompletableFuture as a placeholder for the future result of an asynchronous task.

We've seen something like that before. It's a lot like the Deferred result that's returned by an async() coroutine. Since the two classes implement the same underlying idea, Kotlin makes it easy for us to convert from one to the other.

Let's write a coroutine-powered image viewer that can display an image provided by Java code. Once we call asDeferred() to turn the CompletableFuture into a Kotlin Deferred result, we'll be able to await() the download task as we'd wait for an async() coroutine. To display the logo, we'll use the same ImageViewer base class and helper functions that we've been using in previous chapters:

gallery/v8/src/main/kotlin/com/example/gallery/ImageViewerApplication.kt

```
fun main() = createWindow("Image Viewer", object : ImageViewer() {
  override suspend fun update(window: JFrame) {
    val url = "https://kotlinlang.org/docs/images/kotlin-logo.png"
➤   val image: Deferred<Image> = downloadImageAsync(url).asDeferred()
➤   displayImage(window, image.await())
  }
})
```

Two in One

In fact, we can combine those two steps into one since Kotlin provides the await() function directly as an extension for CompletableFuture:

gallery/v9/src/main/kotlin/com/example/gallery/ImageViewerApplication.kt

```
fun main() = createWindow("Image Viewer", object : ImageViewer() {
  override suspend fun update(window: JFrame) {
    val url = "https://kotlinlang.org/docs/images/kotlin-logo.png"
➤   val image: CompletableFuture<Image> = downloadImageAsync(url)
    displayImage(window, image.await())
  }
})
```

Since CompletableFuture is a general-purpose interface for all kinds of Java code, we've unlocked suspending access to hundreds of existing asynchronous libraries and tools. Any time a function returns a CompletableFuture, Kotlin can use asDeferred() or await() to integrate it seamlessly into a coroutine.

The await() function does more than wait for the CompletableFuture to provide a result. It'll also throw an exception if the request fails and abort the request if the waiting coroutine is canceled. Turning futures into suspension points upgrades them with the extra power and safety of coroutines and structured concurrency.

Would You Like Cancellation with That?

 Deferred.await() and CompletableFuture.await() are not entirely equivalent—they have different behavior when the waiting coroutine is canceled. Check the documentation to find out which one suits your needs.

Two-Way Trip

Now you know how to wait for futures in your coroutines. But what about when you need to go the other way?

Let's take a coroutine and turn it into a CompletableFuture. The coroutine will be able to call your Kotlin suspending functions, but its asynchronous result will be fully compatible with your non-coroutine code.

This time, we'll get some image data from a file, much like we did in our last chapter. We'll start by setting up a suspending getImageFromFile() function that wraps up two functions we've already written—promptForFile(), from the code on page 132, followed by readImage(), from the code on page 138:

gallery/v10/src/main/kotlin/com/example/gallery/GetImageFromFile.kt
```
suspend fun getImageFromFile(): Image = withContext(Dispatchers.Main) {
  val file = promptForFile() ?: error("No file selected")
  readImage(file)
}
```

Thanks to that suspend modifier, this function is currently reserved for Kotlin callers only. If we want to share the same functionality with code that doesn't use coroutines, we'll need to provide an alternative entry point. How can we take the suspending function that we've already written and translate it into a CompletableFuture that Java will understand?

We'll start by launching an async() coroutine, which will give us a Deferred result. Starting a coroutine requires a CoroutineScope, so we'll have this step take one as its receiver parameter—more on that in a moment. Once we have our Deferred value, we can call asCompletableFuture() to perform the same conversion as before, but going the other way this time:

gallery/v10/src/main/kotlin/com/example/gallery/GetImageFromFile.kt
```
fun CoroutineScope.getImageFromFileAsync(): CompletableFuture<Image> {
  val imageTask = async { getImageFromFile() }
  return imageTask.asCompletableFuture()
}
```

Once again, there's also a shortcut that will skip the conversion and combine the two steps into one. Instead of starting with an async() coroutine, we can call future() to create a CompletableFuture directly:

gallery/v11/src/main/kotlin/com/example/gallery/GetImageFromFile.kt
```
fun CoroutineScope.getImageFromFileAsync(): CompletableFuture<Image> =
    future { getImageFromFile() }
```

Other Brands Are Available

Java's CompletableFuture is just one implementation of a concept that's used in many languages and frameworks. Here are a few asynchronous result types that Kotlin integrates with, either in its core library or via an extra download. But don't worry if you don't see your favorite! By the end of this chapter, you'll be able to build your own integrations like these:

Language/Library	Result Type	Package
Java	CompletableFuture	kotlinx-coroutines-core
JavaScript	Promise	kotlinx-coroutines-core
Guava	ListenableFuture	kotlinx-coroutines-guava
Play Services	Task	kotlinx-coroutines-play-services

All these types have asDeferred() and await() functions. Names will vary when going the other way—for instance, on JavaScript, it's promise() to create a Promise coroutine directly or asPromise() to convert from a Deferred.

For now, we're sticking to single-shot result types that represent the unique outcome of an already-running task. Later on, in Chapter 11, Operate the Reactive Way, on page 183, we'll talk about operations that produce multiple values as well as run-on-demand task objects such as Reactor's Mono.

Alternate Future

 One that you won't find on the list is Java's Future class, which some older code still uses. Unlike a CompletableFuture, a plain Future can only wait by blocking its thread. It's no good as a building block for non-blocking asynchronous code.

Who's in Charge Here?

Our new getImageFromFileAsync() function needs a coroutine scope and can't be called without one. That's a change from the suspending getImageFromFile() function. If a CompletableFuture is just Java's version of a suspending function, why do we need a scope for one and not for the other?

In Kotlin, a suspending function is executed by its caller. Until the function is invoked, it's not doing anything. But in plain Java, our asynchronous tasks have to be executed in the background—the caller can't do it because that would mean blocking the caller's thread. It's the same problem that we had when we wanted to use a suspending function from our Android activity in Chapter 3, Start It, Scope It, Stop It, on page 39.

To create a CompletableFuture, we also need to create a background task that will produce the result. That's exactly what we're doing when we call async(), promise(), or future(). Once we've created the task, it's responsible for its own execution, regardless of which other code might be using its result. The scope is there to take charge of the new task's lifecycle and to guard against resource leaks.

Okay, that's fair enough. But earlier in the chapter, we wrote a non-suspending downloadImageAsync() function that returned a CompletableFuture, too. Why didn't that one have any sign of a parent scope? Let's compare the two different approaches:

- The downloadImageAsync() function is doing things the Java way. Its background task isn't a coroutine, and it doesn't benefit from Kotlin's structured concurrency.

- In getImageFromFileAsync(), our background task is a coroutine that's linked to its parent scope. Errors will propagate upwards, and when the scope exits, any incomplete tasks will be canceled.

Remember the Rules

 Like async() coroutines, errors from a future() task can pop up in two places—the parent scope and the code consuming the task's result. For a refresher on how that works and how to change it, check back in with Chapter 5, Plan for Any Outcome, on page 75.

You've already seen plenty of ways to find and select a coroutine scope, depending on how long a task should be allowed to continue running. As with any coroutine, look for a scope that best matches the boundaries within which the task and its result are used, whether that's a viewModelScope, a lifecycleScope, a coroutineScope() block in an existing function, or some other component in your application.

On the other hand, if you're calling getImageFromFileAsync() from code that's already set up to deal with errors and resources in Java-style unstructured tasks, you might decide that Kotlin's extra safety features are redundant. In that case, you can opt out of structured concurrency by using GlobalScope to call the function.

Future Freedom

 Calling GlobalScope.future() will create an independent task with no parent, similar to what you'd get from a Java function such as CompletableFuture.supplyAsync(). It'll be up to the consumer to make sure the task's errors and resources are correctly handled.

Build Your Own Suspension Point

If a function returns a supported asynchronous result such as a CompletableFuture or Promise, you now know how to use it in your coroutines.

But what about custom asynchronous results from other libraries or asynchronous functions that only offer a plain callback with no futures or promises in sight?

In this section, we'll go beyond the built-in integrations and find out how we can make our own. You'll create a custom suspension point that's based on a callback, and you'll learn the template that you can use to do the same for any asynchronous operation.

Advanced File Operations

In the first part of this chapter, we loaded an image from a file. The readImage() function we used comes from the code on page 138, and it's backed by the thread-blocking ImageIO.read() function. When we wrote that function, we used Kotlin's I/O dispatcher to make it safe for use from any coroutine.

But it's not a perfect solution, since it still uses a blocked thread behind the scenes. This time, let's go the extra mile and look for a truly asynchronous solution that will get rid of that blocked thread once and for all.

To make this a little simpler, we'll split the problem into two parts. First, we'll focus on loading the file. Once we've done that, we'll be able to convert its contents into an Image using a trick we've already seen.

To load a file asynchronously, we'll use Java's NIO.2 API. We'll create an AsynchronousFileChannel and use it to load the file's contents into a ByteBuffer. You don't need to follow all the details here, and in fact, real apps might be better off sticking to Java's more mature blocking InputStream API. But notice how the file channel's read() function provides its results via an asynchronous callback instead of waiting to return the data directly.

That makes it a great way for us to explore the integration between callbacks and coroutines:

```
gallery/v12/src/main/kotlin/com/example/gallery/GetImageFromFile.kt
fun readFile(file: File) {
  AsynchronousFileChannel.open(file.toPath()).use { channel ->
    val buffer = ByteBuffer.allocate(channel.size().toInt())

    channel.read(buffer, 0, null, object : CompletionHandler<Int, Any?> {
```

```
    override fun completed(result: Int, attachment: Any?) {
      // TODO: do something with the data
    }

    override fun failed(exc: Throwable, attachment: Any?) {
      // TODO: handle errors
    }
  })
  }
}
```

Does that CompletionHandler object look familiar?

It's almost exactly like the Retrofit Callback object we used all the way back in the code on page 34. Once again, we've got two callback functions—one for successful completion and one for failure.

Wait Right There

We might not have a handy CompletableFuture object or a built-in await() function this time, but we can still turn this asynchronous operation into a suspending function. We'll just need to do it by hand.

To do that, we'll start with the suspendCoroutine() function. It does exactly what its name suggests and suspends the current coroutine. Before it does that, it runs a block of code that we provide. That's where we can start our asynchronous call and register a callback that will tell the coroutine when it's time to get back to work.

Since we're going to be suspending our function, we'll need to start by adding the suspend modifier:

gallery/v13/src/main/kotlin/com/example/gallery/GetImageFromFile.kt
```
suspend fun readFile(file: File): ByteArray =
  AsynchronousFileChannel.open(file.toPath()).use { channel ->
    val buffer = ByteBuffer.allocate(channel.size().toInt())

➤   suspendCoroutine { continuation ->
      channel.read(buffer, 0, null, object : CompletionHandler<Int, Any?> {
        override fun completed(result: Int, attachment: Any?) =
➤          continuation.resume(buffer.array())

        override fun failed(exc: Throwable, attachment: Any?) =
➤          continuation.resumeWithException(exc)
      })
    }
  }
```

Continuing the Coroutine

 Notice how the functions for resuming a suspended coroutine are packaged together in a *continuation* object. Remember this object—it'll be important in the next part of the chapter.

The asynchronous read() function returns right away, and once it's done that, we're at the end of the suspendCoroutine() block. From that point on, the coroutine is suspended, and the suspendCoroutine() function won't return.

At least, not until we tell it to. We've assumed manual control of the suspension point's outcome, and we can now interact with it from any other background thread or callback. When we're ready for it to return a value, we call resume(). If we want it to throw an error instead, there's a separate resumeWithException() function.

Simplified Suspending

The suspendCoroutine() function can be hard to get your head around at first. After all, it rewrites the rules on how functions are supposed to work.

Let's take a look at it without the file loading in the mix and add some println() calls to make it clearer what's going on:

```kotlin
timers/v18/src/main/kotlin/com/example/timers/TimerApplication.kt
val timer = java.util.Timer()

suspend fun main() {
  println("1. Coroutine is running")

  val result = suspendCoroutine { continuation ->
    println("2. Suspending the coroutine for 5 seconds")

    timer.schedule(5000) { // enqueue callback for later execution
      println("4. Time's up: resuming the coroutine")
      continuation.resume("Hello!")
      timer.cancel()
    }

    println("3. Now, we wait…")
  }

  println("5. Coroutine resumed with result: $result")
}
```

When you run the program, notice how the timer delays not just the code inside the callback but also the code that appears after the suspension point. We've paused our original coroutine and then used that background timer callback to resume it again later:

1. Coroutine is running
2. Suspending the coroutine for 5 seconds
3. Now, we wait…
4. Time's up: resuming the coroutine
5. Coroutine resumed with result: Hello!

The suspendCoroutine() function suspends the coroutine after running the entirety of its own code block but before returning to its caller. That's why we see the third line of output right away—it's the last thing that happens before we arrive at the suspension point proper.

If you want to visualize it, you can think of the suspendCoroutine() block's final closing brace as being the place where the program stops to wait. Execution won't continue past that line until our timer callback calls resume(). When that happens, the value that's passed to resume() becomes the value returned by the whole suspendCoroutine() operation.

In a real program, you'd replace this simple timed suspension point with the built-in delay() function. In fact, if you take a look at the delay() function's source code, you'll see something not too dissimilar to what we've written here.

Okay—now we've got a better idea of what's going on, let's get back to loading that image.

Pretty As a Picture

Using suspendCoroutine(), we turned our asynchronous callback into a suspending function. Now, we need to take our data and convert it into a displayable Image. We can do that by passing our ByteArray to the ImageIO class, which won't need to block its thread this time, since we've already loaded the data:

gallery/v13/src/main/kotlin/com/example/gallery/GetImageFromFile.kt
```kotlin
suspend fun readImage(file: File): Image {
  val data: ByteArray = readFile(file)
  return ImageIO.read(data.inputStream())
}
```

This function has the same signature as the one we made in the last chapter, so the full program should look familiar—we've written this one before. But without the blocked thread inside readImage(), its implementation should be a little more efficient:

gallery/v13/src/main/kotlin/com/example/gallery/ImageViewerApplication.kt
```kotlin
fun main() = createWindow("Image Viewer", object : ImageViewer() {
  override suspend fun update(window: JFrame) {
    val file = promptForFile(window) ?: return
    val image = readImage(file)
```

```
    displayImage(window, image)
  }
})
```

Cancel a Callback

Our suspending readFile() function is nearly complete, but there's one thing missing. As you learned in Chapter 6, Cooperate with Cancellation, on page 91, suspension points need to cooperate with cancellation, stopping what they're doing so the coroutine can make a quick exit. Right now, our function always waits until it's finished reading the entire file. We haven't provided a way to interrupt the operation early if the coroutine is canceled. With large files or slow storage, that could mean holding onto valuable resources for much longer than necessary.

To fix it, we can replace suspendCoroutine() with suspendCancellableCoroutine():

gallery/v14/src/main/kotlin/com/example/gallery/GetImageFromFile.kt
```kotlin
suspend fun readFile(file: File): ByteArray =
  AsynchronousFileChannel.open(file.toPath()).use { channel ->
    val buffer = ByteBuffer.allocate(channel.size().toInt())

    suspendCancellableCoroutine { continuation ->
      continuation.invokeOnCancellation { channel.close() }

      channel.read(buffer, 0, null, object : CompletionHandler<Int, Any?> {
        override fun completed(result: Int, attachment: Any?) =
          continuation.resume(buffer.array())

        override fun failed(exc: Throwable, attachment: Any?) =
          continuation.resumeWithException(exc)
      })
    }
  }
```

When suspendCancellableCoroutine() is canceled, Kotlin will trigger its invokeOnCancellation() block. That's our chance to interrupt the operation early. To do that, we've added a new call to channel.close(). This one isn't about cleaning up resources after the read() operation is done—our use() function already had that covered. Instead, we're relying on the fact that calling close() early will cause the ongoing read() operation to fail, skipping the remainder of its work. Other callbacks will offer different ways to cancel their background task and release their resources, so this recipe will vary depending on the library you're using.

If you don't have a way to interrupt your asynchronous task, stick to the non-cancellable suspendCoroutine() function so Kotlin knows there's no early-exit cleanup system in place. Canceling a suspended coroutine without canceling its underlying callback sounds a lot like another task leak—so when a callback can't be reliably canceled, the only safe course is for the coroutine to stick around until it completes normally instead.

> ## Indefinite Suspension
>
> After a call to suspendCoroutine() or suspendCancellableCoroutine(), the coroutine's no longer in control of its own execution. It'll only continue running when some other task, event, or timer calls resume().
>
> So, what if that never happens?
>
> If resume() isn't called, the suspension point waits forever. That might not sound like a great idea, but it can be useful—it even exists in the core library:
>
> ```
> suspend fun awaitCancellation(): Nothing = suspendCancellableCoroutine {}
> ```
>
> As the name suggests, the only way to leave this function is to cancel it. Otherwise, the suspension point never resumes—hence the Nothing return type. We'll find a use for this strange-sounding function in Chapter 12, Share Flows, Connect Channels, on page 201.

Lift the Continuation Curtain

You've learned how to convert any asynchronous operation to a coroutine-compatible suspension point. But how exactly can Kotlin jump so easily between different asynchronous styles? It's all to do with the *continuation* object that we used to resume our suspended coroutine.

In the last part of this chapter, we'll take a look at how continuations are related to callbacks. We won't introduce any new concepts, but we'll add some context to the things we've already learned. In doing so, we'll take some of the mystery out of the compile-time transformation that turns callbacks into coroutines.

Continuations All the Way Down

Way back in Chapter 2, Escape From Callback Hell, on page 17, you learned that a suspending function isn't much more than a callback in disguise.

Now you know how to wrap your own callbacks in that same disguise by using the suspendCoroutine() and suspendCancellableCoroutine() functions. But these aren't just convenient helpers for integrating coroutines with the occasional callback. In fact, this continuation-capturing operation is the fundamental building block that defines how Kotlin's coroutines work. Every single suspension point cuts a slice through its coroutine, saving the second piece in a continuation for later execution.

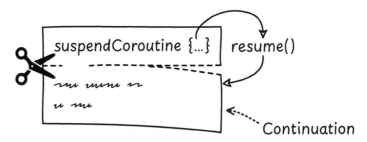

Peek at the source code of the CompletableFuture.await() function that we used earlier in the chapter, the awaitResponse() function that we saw in some of our early Retrofit code, or even something as simple as the built-in delay() function, and you'll find the same suspendCancellableCoroutine() operation that we've been using in this chapter.

If a function needs the suspend modifier, it's because it eventually calls through to a suspending operation such as suspendCoroutine() or suspendCancellableCoroutine(). These are the suspension-point nuts and bolts that we mentioned right back in our first chapter.

Smoke, Mirrors, and Indentation

Swapping callbacks for continuations is the trick that makes a coroutine read like a sequential program. If we were using callbacks, each one would be a new function with its own braces and indentation. A continuation is like a callback without the brackets—it just attaches to the end of the function we're already in. We can chain together as many of them as we like, and we'll still have a single sequence of instructions.

It sounds like obscure compiler magic, but the difference between a continuation and a callback is smaller than you might think. We can prove it by doing a magic trick of our own. All we'll need is a text editor and a few callbacks.

Back in Chapter 2, Escape From Callback Hell, on page 17, we used Java's Timer class to demonstrate some simple callbacks. We'll use it again here with a sequence of nested callbacks that form a countdown:

timers/v19/src/main/kotlin/com/example/timers/TimerApplication.kt
```kotlin
val timer = java.util.Timer()

fun main() {
  println("3…")
  timer.schedule(1000) {
    println("2…")
```

```
    timer.schedule(1000) {
      println("1…")
      timer.schedule(1000) {
        println("Lift-off!")
        timer.cancel()
      }
    }
  }
}
```

With the suspending delay() function, we could easily remove all that nesting or even replace the whole thing with a loop. But let's try something different. Instead of changing any code, let's reformat it a little. Delete some whitespace here, add some more over there, and … abracadabra!

timers/v20/src/main/kotlin/com/example/timers/TimerApplication.kt
```
val timer = java.util.Timer()

fun main() {                                      /* Secret hidden brackets */
  println("3…")
  timer.schedule(1000)                                 {
  println("2…")
  timer.schedule(1000)                                 {
  println("1…")
  timer.schedule(1000)                                 {
  println("Liftoff!")
  timer.cancel()                                       } } }
}
```

Take a moment to convince yourself it's the same code. All we've done is move some brackets and indentation around. It might be a misleading and unexpected way to format the function, and you'll get some funny looks if you do it in a real codebase, but it'll technically work just fine.

Now—hold your hand in front of the page and cover up all those pesky brackets in the right-hand margin.

You just invented continuations!

Kotlin's real continuations are more involved than this, and as you know, they handle things—such as loops and exceptions—that callbacks can't. All the same, this formatting trick is a great way to visualize the principle that's at play every time you use suspending functions to disguise your asynchronous code as a sequential program.

Superficial Differences

It's because callbacks and continuations are so closely related that coroutines can integrate so easily with any other asynchronous style. When you use suspendCoroutine() or suspendCancellableCoroutine(), the continuation you're creating can be passed in place of a callback to any other asynchronous operation.

Now that you understand continuations, you know more than you might think about how coroutines work. As you learned in Chapter 3, Start It, Scope It, Stop It, on page 39, starting a background task is the same thing as submitting a callback for execution by some other thread, event loop, or thread pool. Well, submit a continuation instead of a callback, and you've created a coroutine dispatcher.

When the launch() function wants to start a new coroutine, it creates the first link in the continuation chain, passing it to the dispatcher for immediate execution. After that, any time the coroutine resumes after a suspension point, it submits the next continuation to the dispatcher.

A coroutine is simply a sequence of connected continuations, each submitted for execution when the previous suspension point is done waiting. That's why coroutines are called *lightweight*—there's nothing to them beyond that chain of chopped-up chunks of code.

What Have You Learned?

Like Kotlin itself, coroutines are designed to integrate with other languages, libraries, and tools. You've used a ready-made solution to connect with a Java CompletableFuture, and you've learned how the suspendCancellableCoroutine() function can upgrade a callback into a fully featured suspension point. Along the way, you've uncovered some valuable insights into the mostly hidden continuations that make coroutines tick.

Continuations are a powerful tool, and their uses aren't limited to asynchronous programming. In the next chapter, you'll learn how Kotlin's lazy sequences and flows can use the same continuation-powered suspension points to generate multiple results from a single piece of code.

Key Concepts

Continuation

This is the saved control state of a suspended coroutine. It represents the remainder of the coroutine's work and can be invoked like a callback to have the coroutine resume execution.

CHAPTER 10

Go with the Flow

Functions follow a familiar structure, whether they're the suspending variety or not. Take some inputs, run some code, and return a single result.

But does that always have to be true?

In this chapter, you'll see how suspension points can change the rules. We'll start by using Kotlin's sequence() builder to enter and exit the same function call more than once, returning a new value each time. Then, we'll upgrade our simple Sequence to a suspending Flow, adding asynchronous capabilities and extra safety.

By the end of the chapter, you'll be able to write a single piece of code that generates an ongoing stream of values. You'll know how to encapsulate a data producer's code and resources so its consumers don't have to worry about what's behind the scenes.

Run, Return, Resume, Repeat

Let's put coroutines to one side for now. Instead, we're simply going to add together some numbers to form a sequence. No inputs, outputs, or background tasks are necessary here—thank you very much.

Why does a program like that belong in a book about asynchronous programming and coroutines? After we answer that key question, we'll use the same approach to step through the lines in a text file. We'll separate the code that's using the values from the file reader that's producing them, making a complex loop easier to read, maintain, and test.

Fibonacci Numbers

The *Fibonacci sequence* can trace its origins back more than 2000 years to the study of ancient Sanskrit poetry. Today, it has applications and appearances in mathematics, computer science, biology, physics, finance, art, music, and more.

Let's use it as the basis for our next program. To generate each value, we need to add together the two numbers that came before it. We'll use Kotlin's handily named sequence() function to track the two most recent values and produce each subsequent element in turn:

```
fibonacci/v1/src/main/kotlin/com/example/fibonacci/FibonacciApplication.kt
val fibonacci = sequence {
  var prev = 1; var next = 0

  while (true) {
    yield(next)
    prev = next.also { next += prev }
  }
}
```

Each time we calculate a value, we pass it to the sequence builder's special yield() function.

Control Flow Cousins

 No, this isn't the same yield() function that you used back in Chapter 7, Unlock Parallel Processing, on page 109. You might spot some common traits between the two, but they don't get invited to the same parties.

Infinitely Lazy

That looks a lot like an infinite loop. So, when does this sequence stop?

If this was an ordinary function, it would never end. The loop condition is always true, and there are no break, return, or throw statements to offer an alternative way out. We already said we're not using coroutines, so cancellation is off the table, too. Good guess, though.

Our sequence could happily keep adding numbers and producing values forever—at least until the numbers get too big for our program to store.

But it doesn't because sequences like this one are evaluated *lazily*. Instead of preparing all its values ahead of time, a Sequence will only execute each step when the consumer asks for it. Right now, we're not asking for any values, so our program does nothing at all.

Let's fix that by adding a main() function that will run our code. To iterate through the sequence's values, we need a regular for loop. When we get to 5000, we'll use a break instruction to end the loop:

```
fibonacci/v1/src/main/kotlin/com/example/fibonacci/FibonacciApplication.kt
fun main() {
  for (f in fibonacci) {
    if (f < 5000) print("$f ") else break
  }
}
```

Perfect!

```
0 1 1 2 3 5 8 13 21 34 55 89 144 233 377 610 987 1597 2584 4181
```

Creating a sequence() is like declaring a function—it won't run until we call it. And when we do that, we can decide how much of the sequence we want to execute before we stop.

To Me, To You

Infinite loops aside, it's easy enough to understand what our program is doing. But take a closer look, and there's something interesting going on. We'll see it more clearly if we add some extra println() output to our code:

```
fibonacci/v2/src/main/kotlin/com/example/fibonacci/FibonacciApplication.kt
val fibonacci = sequence {
  var prev = 1; var next = 0

  while (true) {
➤    println("  sequence(): producing the next value ($next)")
    yield(next)
    prev = next.also { next += prev }
  }
}

fun main() {
➤  println("main(): starting the loop")

  for (f in fibonacci) {
➤    if (f < 5000) println("main(): consuming the next value ($f)")
    else break
  }
}
```

Run the code, and you'll be able to see the program switching its attention back and forth between the main() function and the sequence() function:

```
main(): starting the loop
  sequence(): producing the next value (0)
main(): consuming the next value (0)
  sequence(): producing the next value (1)
main(): consuming the next value (1)
  ...
  sequence(): producing the next value (2584)
main(): consuming the next value (2584)
```

```
  sequence(): producing the next value (4181)
main(): consuming the next value (4181)
  sequence(): producing the next value (6765)
```

An ordinary function could not do this. Once we return a value from a function—suspending or not—the function call is complete, and we can't go back in. Calling the same function again will start it again from the beginning—a blank slate with a fresh set of variables.

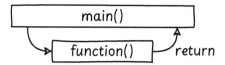

But our sequence() block isn't following the ordinary rules. Instead of computing each value from scratch, it needs to keep hold of the state of its variables—because each Fibonacci number is calculated by looking back at the previous two. It's able to save its current progress, give control back to the main() function, and then resume later from where it left off.

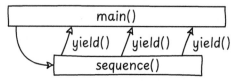

Sound familiar? Yes, it's powered by suspension points—but more on that later.

Generator Functions

Our sequence-building code block is an example of a *generator function*, though that's not a term you'll find much in Kotlin's own documentation. Ordinary functions return once, but a generator function can use its special *yield* operation to return control to its caller many times during the course of its execution.

You might be familiar with the same concept if you've used the yield keyword in languages such as Python, C#, and JavaScript. Remember back in Chapter 4, Split Up to Speed Up, on page 59 when we compared Kotlin's async() function to the async keyword found in other languages? Yes, yield() is the other place where Kotlin uses some suspension-point tricks to swap a keyword for a function.

Getting Fired Up

The sequence() builder function isn't just for generating numbers. It can help with any repeating task or loop. Let's try it out on a program that loops through the lines in a text file.

First, we'll need the file and some text to put in it. Open up your favorite text editor and jot down the items on our day's to-do list:

todo/v1/src/main/resources/todo.txt
```
Go to space
Build a mobile app
Plan a party
Make some coffee
Visit the museum
Pick a new password
```

We'll load this text file as a system resource—so if the code's in src/main/kotlin/, the to-do list needs to be at src/main/resources/todo.txt:

todo/v1/src/main/kotlin/com/example/todo/TodoApplication.kt
```
fun getTaskList(): InputStream =
  ClassLoader.getSystemResourceAsStream("todo.txt") ?: error("Not found")
```

Next, we'll read each line from the list we've loaded. Our program doesn't contain any suspension points or shared threads, so some old-fashioned blocking I/O will be fine for now. To help us stay motivated, let's also include some code to add an extra message to each task.

For now, we'll start with a sequence-free version:

todo/v1/src/main/kotlin/com/example/todo/TodoApplication.kt
```
val hype = listOf("You got this!", "Crush it!", "Let's go!", "Easy!")

fun main() {
  val reader = getTaskList().bufferedReader()
  try {
    while (true) {
      val task = reader.readLine()
      if (task != null) println("$task. " + hype.random()) else break
    }
  } finally {
    reader.close()
  }
}
```

Nice work! Run the program to see the hyped-up list of tasks:

```
Go to space. Easy!
Build a mobile app. Crush it!
Plan a party. Let's go!
Make some coffee. Let's go!
Visit the museum. Easy!
Pick a new password. You got this!
```

It looks like we've already done all these in our previous chapters, so we can check them all off right away. Talk about an anticlimax.

One Line at a Time

Right now, most of our code is hanging out in the main() function. But there are at least three different things going on—reading the lines from the file, adding the hype messages, and displaying the output.

How can we separate the different responsibilities and make our program easier to maintain and test?

We could try making a separate function that loads all our tasks and returns them as a List, but that would change our code's behavior. We'd be loading the whole file all at once instead of processing one line at a time. It's not a problem here, but for a bigger file, it could chew through a lot of time and memory.

Instead, let's use a lazily evaluated sequence() as we did for our Fibonacci numbers:

todo/v2/src/main/kotlin/com/example/todo/TodoApplication.kt
```
val tasks = sequence {
  val reader = getTaskList().bufferedReader()
  try {
    while (true) {
      val task = reader.readLine()
      if (task != null) yield(task) else break
    }
  } finally {
    reader.close()
  }
}
```

Loop Blueprint

 We've swapped println() for yield(), but notice how our loop code is otherwise almost identical to the way it looked before. You can think of a generator as a blueprint or template where each yield() operation is a blank to be filled in by the caller.

With all that code extracted into a separate block, the main() function can shrink to only a few lines:

todo/v2/src/main/kotlin/com/example/todo/TodoApplication.kt
```
fun main() {
  for (task in tasks) {
    println("$task. " + hype.random())
  }
}
```

Since our tasks sequence runs each step on demand, we haven't changed the code's behavior at all. We are still reading a single line from the file, adding the message, displaying the output, and then going back to the still-open file to grab another line.

Separate the Strands

By loading our task-list entries as a lazy sequence(), we've separated a single block of code into two different areas of responsibility without changing the order in which it executes.

The task-list sequence is the *producer*, and all it has to worry about is providing a stream of values for the program to use. It doesn't need to know anything about where the data is going next—it spits out a value and then waits until it's time to produce another.

Meanwhile, our main() function acts as the *consumer*, grabbing each value from the sequence in turn. It doesn't need to know where the task-list entries are coming from—so, when it comes time to test this program or swap out that text file for a database, we've made our lives a whole lot easier!

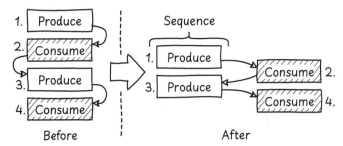

That's the power of generator functions—they can encapsulate a repeating process, along with all of its state, even when the program has other things to think about between each iteration.

But our tasks sequence isn't perfect yet. In the next section, let's talk about two ways we can make it even better.

Wrap It Up Safely

You've seen how to swap an ordinary function's one-time return for the multiple values produced by a generator.

For a simple sequence of numbers, the kind of code we've been writing so far is a great solution. But when we start working with outside resources like files, we're stretching the limits of what the sequence() builder can do. If we want to get the best out of our code, we're going to need some of the full-fledged coroutine tools from our previous chapters.

In this section, we'll take a closer look at what's going on inside the yield() function and see why sequences have a unique relationship with suspending functions. Then we'll upgrade our to-do list with proper coroutine capabilities, fixing two important problems with its reliability and responsiveness.

End of the Line

Operating systems place a limit on the total number of open files and network connections. So, when we're done using one, we need to make sure we close it again—at least if we're going to continue using the same program for other things. In our task-list program, we're doing that with a finally block that calls our reader's close() function.

We can see it working if we add an extra println() call inside the finally section:

todo/v3/src/main/kotlin/com/example/todo/TodoApplication.kt
```kotlin
val tasks = sequence {
  val reader = getTaskList().bufferedReader()
  try {
    while (true) {
      val task = reader.readLine()
      if (task != null) yield(task) else break
    }
  } finally {
    println("Closing the file…")
    reader.close()
  }
}
```

Run the code using the same main() function as before, and when the program finishes, you'll see that extra line of output, letting you know the file's been closed:

```
Go to space. Easy!
…
Pick a new password. You got this!
Closing the file…
```

Early Exit

Everything looks good so far—but there's a hidden problem with this code. To see the issue, we need to end our loop early:

todo/v3/src/main/kotlin/com/example/todo/TodoApplication.kt
```kotlin
fun main() {
  for (task in tasks) {
```

```
    println("$task. " + hype.random())
➤   if (task.contains("party")) {
➤     error("Can't do any more tasks, it's party time!")
    }
  }
}
```

What output are you expecting to see from this code?

```
Go to space. Easy!
Build a mobile app. Crush it!
Plan a party. Let's go!
java.lang.IllegalStateException: Can't do any more tasks, it's party time!
```

After the first three tasks, our program throws an error and terminates the loop. It's party time!

But what happened to closing the file? No matter what happens, a finally block is always supposed to run when the program leaves the corresponding try section—even when we're exiting because of an error. And yet, there's no sign of our final println() message.

Back in Chapter 6, Cooperate with Cancellation, on page 91, you learned how important it is for every running task to get the chance to clean up its resources and make an orderly exit. It's not safe to discard a piece of code in the middle of its execution—but that's exactly what's happening when we end this sequence() early. If we use this code repeatedly as part of a bigger program, it could result in a resource leak, eventually leaving the system unable to open new connections and files.

Unfinished Iteration

Like many loops, our sequence consumer's for loop is backed by a hidden Iterator object. The iterator holds the sequence's current state, and each time the consumer loop steps forward, the iterator runs just enough code to generate the next value.

Sequences and Iterators

The sequence() function's partner in crime is the iterator() builder. Both have the same syntax, with a generator block that can yield() values. Each Iterator can only be used once, so the sequence() builder is a handy shortcut to make a reusable version.

An Iterator has two functions—hasNext() and next()—which drive its entire operation. That explains why our sequence's finally block isn't always being executed. There's no extra mechanism to close or clean up an in-progress iterator, so when we stop our consumer loop early, there's no way to let the producer code know what's happened. The partially completed operation that's saved inside the iterator gets forgotten.

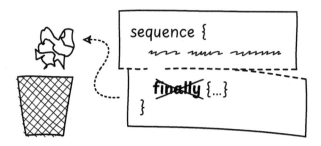

Blocked Again

The sequence() builder is great for encapsulating simple repeating tasks, but it can't safely manage a resource such as our text file InputStream. In a moment, we'll fix it by upgrading from a Sequence to a Flow. But first, since we're on the subject of file operations, let's look at another place where our sequence() falls short.

It's time to talk about that blocked thread. Our call to reader.readLine() needs to fetch data from outside our program, and it'll hold onto its thread while it's waiting. That's not breaking any rules, since we're not running in a coroutine—more on that in a moment—but all the same, it would be nice to fix it. As it stands, it would be all too easy for an unsuspecting caller to invoke our sequence from the UI thread and end up with an unresponsive app.

Sounds like it's time for some suspending functions. This is where you'll need the core coroutines package if you haven't already added it:

todo/v4/build.gradle.kts
```kotlin
dependencies {
    implementation("org.jetbrains.kotlinx:kotlinx-coroutines-core:1.10.1")
}
```

In a coroutine, we'd use the withContext() function to unblock our thread by offloading the work to a different dispatcher. There are a couple of clues that our sequence might be able to use suspending functions—more on those in a second—so let's give it a try:

todo/v4/src/main/kotlin/com/example/todo/TodoApplication.kt
```kotlin
val tasks = sequence {
    val reader = getTaskList().bufferedReader()
    try {
        while (true) {
```

```
    val task = withContext(Dispatchers.IO) { // error!
      reader.readLine()
    }
    if (task != null) yield(task) else break
  }
} finally {
  println("Closing the file…")
  reader.close()
}
}
```

No luck. Instead, when we try to use coroutine functionality here, we get an interesting complaint from the compiler:

```
> Task :compileKotlin FAILED
Restricted suspending functions can invoke member or extension suspending
functions only on their restricted coroutine scope.
```

Huh? What's a *restricted suspending function*? This error message is giving us a peek behind the scenes at how our sequence program's back-and-forth control flow works.

Suspicious Suspension

Our sequence can be used from anywhere, coroutine or not, so it can't do anything that might try to suspend its caller's execution.

But if you're following along with the code in your IDE, you might have noticed that the yield() function comes with a suspension-point icon.

$$-\looparrowright \mid \text{yield(task)}$$

Didn't we just say suspending functions were off-limits?

A *restricted suspending function* is one that can use its own in-house suspension points but can't call other suspending functions from the outside world. The sequence() builder's code block is a restricted suspending function, and the only time it's allowed to suspend its execution is to call its own yield() function.

When yield() suspends the sequence producer's execution, it's not pausing an entire task. Instead, it's passing control back to another piece of code in the same thread or coroutine, like a game of control-flow tennis. Since the consumer takes over control directly from the producer each time it stops, and vice versa, there's never any need for an actual coroutine to be suspended—so the resulting sequence can be used from non-suspending code. When you look at the documentation or source code, you'll see that the suspend modifier applies only to the sequence's restricted inner code block and not to the sequence() function itself.

Restricted suspending functions aren't common. The sequence()–yield() pair might be the only example you ever come across, and it's unlikely you'll ever need to make your own.

Call That a Coroutine?

The word *coroutine* was coined as far back as 1958 by programmer Melvin Conway. Originally, it was a type of function—think *subroutine*, only with different control-flow rules. In languages using that definition, a generator function like our sequence() block might be called a *semicoroutine*.

Since Conway wrote his first coroutines in low-level assembly language, different programming languages have come to use the term in a variety of different ways.

When we talk about coroutines in this book and in Kotlin at large, we're talking about the standalone thread-like tasks that execute suspending functions. A sequence generator fails to qualify on both counts—it can't suspend its caller, and it needs an existing coroutine or thread to drive its execution. Still, Kotlin's sequence generators are closely related to the wider concept of coroutines, and you'll find some coroutine references in their source code.

Flowing Smoothly

We've seen two problems with our sequence. It can't clean up its resources if it ends early, and it can't offload blocking work to a different thread. To fix both those things, it's time we upgrade our program to use coroutines.

Let's replace our sequence() builder with a coroutine-enabled flow(). It's going to look almost exactly the same as before, though it does replace the yield() function with a new one called emit():

todo/v5/src/main/kotlin/com/example/todo/TodoApplication.kt
```
val tasks = flow {
  val reader = getTaskList().bufferedReader()
  try {
    while (true) {
      val task = withContext(Dispatchers.IO) {
        reader.readLine()
      }
      if (task != null) emit(task) else break
    }
  } finally {
```

```
    println("Closing the file…")
    reader.close()
  }
}
```

The code inside our flow() block is now a proper suspending function. That gives us a responsibility to avoid blocking our thread, but it also gives us a solution in the form of the dispatcher-switching withContext() block.

Does it Block?

 Now that we're in a coroutine, your IDE might suggest using Dispatchers.IO to call reader.close() as well. That can be important for network connections, but it's less likely to matter when closing a file.

Good enough for now—but there's still room to improve this code later. Like a regular suspending function, our Flow is going to start its execution on a dispatcher provided by its caller. On every iteration of the loop, we'll be switching to the I/O dispatcher to read the data and then switching back to the caller's dispatcher to collect the emitted value. Try this code with a larger file, and you might see all that thread switching start to slow things down significantly.

Switching dispatchers inside a flow() comes with some pitfalls, and we'll come back to this later. After you learn about flow operators, you can try using flowOn() and buffer() to rewrite this loop and reduce the number of times it needs to switch threads.

Collect the Results

Like the sequence() builder, flow() creates a generator function that can deliver multiple values. On the producer side, the two are strikingly similar—but when it's time to consume the values, things get a bit more interesting. Now that we've upgraded from a Sequence to a Flow, an Iterator isn't going to cut it anymore.

For one thing, our flow() block contains a real suspending call, where it waits for the withContext() function to run code on a different thread, so the code that consumes our upgraded task list is going to need the ability to suspend its own execution. That's not something an ordinary iterator's hasNext() and next() functions can do.

Without an iterator, we won't be able to use a for loop to consume the values. Instead, a Flow comes with its own collect() function. Let's use it to process the entries from our task list:

todo/v5/src/main/kotlin/com/example/todo/TodoApplication.kt

```
suspend fun main() {
  tasks.collect { task ->
    println("$task. " + hype.random())
  }
}
```

Like the loop we used before, the collect() function passes control between itself and the flow(). Each time the flow() block calls emit(), the collect() function runs the resulting value through its own code block.

Since the flow() can contain asynchronous suspending functions, and the collect() function is responsible for running the code inside the flow(), collect() itself is a suspending function. That means our main function needs the suspend modifier too.

Still Not a Coroutine

 It might be able to call suspending functions now, but our flow() still isn't a coroutine in its own right. It's being executed by the single coroutine that runs our suspending main() function, and our program is only doing one thing at once.

Orderly Exit

With our iterator-based loop swapped for a dedicated collect() function, our resource-management problem is fixed as well. Let's take a look:

todo/v6/src/main/kotlin/com/example/todo/TodoApplication.kt

```
suspend fun main() {
  tasks.collect { task ->
    println("$task. " + hype.random())

    if (task.contains("party")) {
      error("Can't do any more tasks, it's party time!")
    }
  }
}
```

This time, the file is properly closed when we hit that error:

```
Go to space. Easy!
Build a mobile app. Crush it!
Plan a party. Let's go!
Closing the file…
java.lang.IllegalStateException: Can't do any more tasks, it's party time!
```

So, what changed?

Iterators are manually operated, relying on their caller to invoke the hasNext() and next() functions. You can call those functions from anywhere at any time—you don't have to enter a specific function or code block before you start. That means no designated exit route either and no place for the iterator to perform automatic cleanup when you're done. Manual cleanup isn't possible either, since the Iterator interface doesn't have a close() function. In short, the only way to end the iteration early is to stop asking for new values and hope there weren't any important resources to clean up at the end.

A Flow's collect() function encapsulates and automates the entire iteration process and adds a proper exit route. To start receiving values, you have to enter the collect() function. When collection stops, whether it's due to an error, a coroutine cancellation, or a successful completion, the collect() function ends.

Like any other function, collect() can run cleanup code on the way out. It uses that capability to make sure that the code producing its values also exits properly instead of stopping in its tracks:

		One value	Many values	Can suspend?	Stops safely
fun	return	✓			✓
suspend fun	return	✓		✓	✓
sequence(), iterator()	yield()		✓		
flow()	emit()		✓	✓	✓

- Use a sequence() for self-contained tasks that don't need to deal with external resources.

- Use a flow() for tasks that have a managed lifecycle or that need to suspend and wait for outside data and events.

Download Page After Page

To wrap up this chapter, let's take what we've learned and put it to use in the image viewer application we've been building.

We'll display a whole series of images using a Flow to power the loop behind our slideshow. When our data arrives, it'll be split across several pages, and we'll need to flatten them out into a single stream of values. In the process, you'll see how the flow() builder can completely encapsulate the details of a data-producing operation, hiding complexity from its consumers.

Cats or Dogs?

There's a lot of great stuff on the Internet. We started our journey by looking at some amazing astronomy photos courtesy of NASA. But online, there's one thing that counts above all else and that's cat pictures. Or was it dog pictures? Not to worry—this part is a choose-your-own-adventure!

Ready to make your choice?

If you're a fan of fluffy felines, you'll be starting here:

pets/v1/src/main/kotlin/com/example/pets/PetService.kt
```kotlin
const val url = "https://api.thecatapi.com/v1/"
```

Or, if you're all about those cuddly canine companions, just swap that line for this one:

pets/v1/src/main/kotlin/com/example/pets/PetService.kt
```kotlin
const val url = "https://api.thedogapi.com/v1/"
```

The downloadable code for this chapter includes both URLs and an import statement you can alter to make your choice. Both APIs provide their data in the same form, so from now on, all the code will be the same.

Return of the Retrofit

You're an expert with Retrofit by now, so we can race through this part. The dependencies are the same as usual:

pets/v1/build.gradle.kts
```kotlin
dependencies {
  implementation("org.jetbrains.kotlinx:kotlinx-coroutines-core:1.10.1")
  implementation("com.squareup.retrofit2:retrofit:2.9.0")
  implementation("com.squareup.retrofit2:converter-moshi:2.9.0")
  runtimeOnly("org.jetbrains.kotlinx:kotlinx-coroutines-swing:1.10.1")
}
```

For the service itself, we've got three different methods. First, we'll fetch a list of breeds. Next, we'll grab some information about the picture associated with each. Finally, we'll download the image data itself, so we can display it in our gallery:

pets/v1/src/main/kotlin/com/example/pets/PetService.kt
```kotlin
interface PetService {
  @GET("breeds")
  suspend fun listBreeds(
    @Query("limit") limit: Int,
    @Query("page") page: Int
  ): List<Breed>

  @GET("images/{id}")
  suspend fun getImageInfo(@Path("id") id: String): ImageInfo

  @GET
  suspend fun downloadImage(@Url imageUrl: String): ResponseBody
```

```
    data class Breed(val name: String, val reference_image_id: String)
    data class ImageInfo(val id: String, val url: String)
}
```

Great! Now, we need to have Retrofit put everything together. Here's where you'll need that URL you selected earlier:

pets/v1/src/main/kotlin/com/example/pets/PetService.kt
```
private val executor = Executors.newCachedThreadPool { task ->
    Thread(task).apply { isDaemon = true }
}

private fun createHttpClient() = OkHttpClient.Builder()
    .protocols(listOf(Protocol.HTTP_1_1)).dispatcher(Dispatcher(executor))

➤ val petService = Retrofit.Builder().baseUrl(url)
    .client(createHttpClient().build())
    .addConverterFactory(MoshiConverterFactory.create())
    .build().create<PetService>()
```

The Animals Went in Page by Page

Our list of animal breeds will arrive in several pages, so we'll be calling list-Breeds() more than once. That's why the function accepts two parameters. We'll pass a limit to control the number of items per page and a page number to select which portion of the list we want.

But when we come to display our images, we don't want them grouped into pages. We want to loop through them as a single stream, pausing to display each one.

That means this is a perfect place to use a flow(). By remembering its state, our generator code block will be able to keep track of the current page number and emit() the items from each page one by one. Let's see it in action:

pets/v1/src/main/kotlin/com/example/pets/PetPicsApplication.kt
```
val breeds = flow {
    var i = 0
❶   while (true) {
        val page = petService.listBreeds(limit = 5, page = i++)
❷       if (page.isNotEmpty()) for (item in page) emit(item) else break
    }
}
```

Notice the two loops inside our flow() builder:

❶ The outer while loop is iterating page by page.

❷ Then, for each page, the inner for loop goes through the individual items.

Since the code is executed on demand, each new page is fetched only when the consumer is ready to start using its items.

No More Nesting

Let's collect() our animals and start downloading some images:

pets/v1/src/main/kotlin/com/example/pets/PetPicsApplication.kt

```
suspend fun main() {
  breeds.collect { breed ->
    val info = petService.getImageInfo(breed.reference_image_id)
    val imageResponse = petService.downloadImage(info.url)
    val image = ImageIO.read(imageResponse.byteStream())

    // TODO: do something with the image

    delay(5.seconds)
  }
}
```

Our flow() block might contain a couple of nested loops, but in our collect() function, there's no sign of them. By wrapping our data in an asynchronous generator function, we've hidden all the details of the underlying API and its pagination choices. From now on, we can loop through the breeds as a single stream of values without worrying about what's going on behind the scenes.

Wait for a Window

Okay, it's time to add some user interface components and turn this stream of images into a real application.

In our earlier chapters, we wrote a createWindow() function and used it to start a new window with its own background coroutines. For our slideshow viewer, let's upgrade our approach. Instead of sending the window to run in the background, we'll write it as a suspending function:

pets/v2/src/main/kotlin/com/example/pets/Helpers.kt

```
suspend fun createWindow(
  title: String,
  onWindowOpened: suspend CoroutineScope.(JFrame) -> Unit
): Unit = withContext(Dispatchers.Main) {
  val window = JFrame(title)
  window.defaultCloseOperation = JFrame.DISPOSE_ON_CLOSE
  window.size = Dimension(400, 300)
  launch {
    window.addWindowListener(object : WindowAdapter() {
      override fun windowClosed(e: WindowEvent) = this@launch.cancel()
    })
    window.isVisible = true
    try {
```

```
          coroutineScope { onWindowOpened(window) }
    } finally {
      window.dispose()
    }
  }
}
```

The new function accepts an onWindowOpened() lambda function as its final parameter, letting us provide a custom code block where we'll fetch and display our photos. Notice the suspend modifier in the lambda function's type, which will let us use suspending functions in the code we provide. When we invoke the onWindowOpened() code block, we'll also give it its own coroutineScope(), which it can use to launch additional child coroutines. It'll definitely need to include some long-running code or child tasks because as soon as that coroutineScope() block finishes, we're calling dispose() to close the window.

Scope or Suspend?

The suspend modifier tells callers that a function is going to wait for its asynchronous tasks, while a CoroutineScope parameter signals that the function is going to launch background tasks without waiting for them. Putting both in the same function signature is usually a bad idea since it's confusing for the caller. Does the function wait for its tasks or not?

In lambda parameters like this one, though, the combination works since we know the outer createWindow() function is going to wait for everything anyway. Callers would be able to add a coroutineScope() inside the suspending lambda block if they wanted to. Adding it outside the lambda is a handy shortcut that means they don't have to. You've seen the same thing in the launch() and async() coroutine builders, which let you launch new coroutines directly from their suspending inner code block.

Start the Slideshow

Representing a long-lived task like a window as a function might seem strange if you're used to functions that block threads. But with suspending functions, it's fine. Think of the window and all its code as a single task, which starts when the window opens and ends when the window closes. A big advantage of this approach is that any errors inside the window's code will be thrown back to the function's caller. That's an improvement over the self-contained background windows we made before, where the scope was disconnected from its creator and had no choice but to handle its errors in-house.

Suspend When You Can, Scope When You Can't

Custom scopes are vital when background tasks are your only option, like in an Android activity. But when you have access to suspending functions, try to design tasks and resources that are simply linked to their caller instead.

All we need to do now is fill in the blanks to collect our flow and display the pictures:

pets/v2/src/main/kotlin/com/example/pets/PetPicsApplication.kt

```
suspend fun main() = createWindow("Slideshow") { window ->
  breeds.collect {
    val imageInfo = petService.getImageInfo(it.reference_image_id)
    val imageResponse = petService.downloadImage(imageInfo.url)
    val image = ImageIO.read(imageResponse.byteStream())

    window.contentPane.removeAll()
    window.add(JLabel(ImageIcon(image)))
    window.pack()

    delay(5.seconds)
  }
}
```

Run the code to see a slideshow of your favorite furry friends!

There's plenty more we can do to improve this code, so keep hold of it. In the next chapter, we'll use some flow operators to make the program more readable and more responsive.

What Have You Learned?

In this chapter, you've paused and resumed a single code block to create a lazily evaluated stream of values, cleanly separating a data producer from its consumers.

The sequence() builder we started out with might be powered by suspension points, but it can be called from anywhere and can't make use of external suspending functions. When you needed safe handling for external file resources, you had to upgrade to a coroutine-capable flow().

But there's much more to a Flow than the flow() builder function—we've barely scratched the surface. Next, we'll chain asynchronous steps together with operator functions such as map() and filter(), and you'll learn how a Flow connects with similar tools from other libraries and frameworks.

Key Concepts

Generator

This is a code block that can remember its state over a series of invocations, producing a new value each time. The iterator(), sequence(), and flow() builder functions all create generators—though there are plenty of other ways besides generators to create an Iterator, Sequence, or Flow.

Sequence

This is a lazily evaluated pipeline that produces values on demand as they're consumed. It can be generated using the sequence() builder or backed by some other Collection or Iterator.

Flow

This is similar to a Sequence, but with full access to call suspending functions. It's always consumed by a single call to its collect() function so that outside resources are safely encapsulated.

CHAPTER 11

Operate the Reactive Way

Why does Kotlin choose the name *flow* for its asynchronous repeating tasks?

In this chapter, we'll refactor our code into a connected pipeline, where values flow from stage to stage and operator to operator. We'll see how flows fit into the wider world of reactive programming, creating paths for data and events to follow through an entire application.

Once you complete this chapter, you'll be ready to construct powerful asynchronous pipelines from a simple set of modular building blocks. You'll have the tools to connect Kotlin's flows with other languages and frameworks, and you'll understand how to build your own operators and integrations that go beyond the built-in foundations.

Transform from Flow to Flow

In our last chapter, we split up a repeating process into an encapsulated producer and consumer. But why stop there? Using flows, we can keep dividing our code further, just like we'd divide up any other code into smaller and smaller functions.

Our slideshow's image-flow consumer code still contains more than one step. In this section, let's introduce some operator functions that will make it easy to break things down. You'll learn how to chain together individual functions and stages, forming a pipeline for your data and events to flow through.

Too Many Responsibilities

We'll be continuing straight on from Chapter 10, Go with the Flow, on page 161, so make sure you've completed the PetService and its createWindow() function before you jump into this section.

When we left off, we'd just finished building a slideshow. We started with a Flow containing our animal breeds and used its collect() function to display an image for each one in turn.

Let's review what the program currently looks like. This is how we left it in the code on page 180:

```
pets/v2/src/main/kotlin/com/example/pets/PetPicsApplication.kt
suspend fun main() = createWindow("Slideshow") { window ->
    breeds.collect {
        val imageInfo = petService.getImageInfo(it.reference_image_id)
        val imageResponse = petService.downloadImage(imageInfo.url)
        val image = ImageIO.read(imageResponse.byteStream())

        window.contentPane.removeAll()
        window.add(JLabel(ImageIcon(image)))
        window.pack()

        delay(5.seconds)
    }
}
```

We used the flow() builder to factor out some of our code, but this main() function is still doing too many things:

❶ Our first network call, along with all its pagination, is encapsulated in the breeds flow that we've already created.

❷ But we've still got two more network calls to make in the main() function, fetching an Image for each animal breed.

❸ Finally, we need to update our user interface and display the picture for five seconds.

Displaying a slideshow is one chunk of responsibility and downloading images from our PetService is another. Can we package up the rest of the network calls, too, and give our main() function a fully prepared Flow<Image>? That way, we'll be able to reuse the same slideshow code with any source of data, and the whole program will be easier to maintain and test.

We can use some more Flow functionality to separate things out.

Pull It Apart

In our last chapter, we used the collect() function to execute our Flow. Functions that work with flows are called *operators*, and it's time for you to learn a few more of them.

The collect() function is a *terminal operator* because it's the final step we need to execute a flow once we're done building it.

Terminal Operators

 A *terminal operator* is a suspending function that immediately executes the code inside a flow. If the flow's contents are like a function, applying a terminal operator is like calling the function.

But before we call collect() and execute the flow's code, we can also use *intermediate operators* to modify the flow's behavior.

Let's try out an intermediate operator. We'll use map(), which applies a function to transform each element of a flow. We can use it to go from Flow<Breed> to Flow<Image>, encapsulating the image download portion of our code. For now, we'll focus on building the image flow, and we'll leave out the user interface code:

pets/v3/src/main/kotlin/com/example/pets/PetPicsApplication.kt
```kotlin
val images: Flow<Image> = breeds.map {
  val info = petService.getImageInfo(it.reference_image_id)
  val imageResponse = petService.downloadImage(info.url)
  ImageIO.read(imageResponse.byteStream())
}
```

Intermediate Operators Are Lazy

Does that map() function look familiar? You've probably used something similar when converting from one List to another. But with flows, there's one important difference.

Like the Flow it's using for its input, the map() operator is lazy. Calling map() doesn't execute any code, and it won't collect the breeds flow right away. Everything's wrapped inside our new images flow, and it's only when we execute that one that it'll need to start collecting values from the breeds flow we gave it as input.

Since our program isn't doing anything, we don't have a main() function right now, and there's no need for us to do any suspending.

Intermediate Operators

 An *intermediate operator* returns a new Flow which, when executed, will collect() and transform the original. Those transformations might include suspending calls, but the operator isn't a suspending function because it doesn't run the code itself.

Tidy It Up

Before we move on, let's make one more change to tidy things up a little. We'll extract the body of our map() call into a new downloadImage() function:

pets/v4/src/main/kotlin/com/example/pets/PetPicsApplication.kt
```kotlin
suspend fun downloadImage(breed: PetService.Breed): Image {
  val info = petService.getImageInfo(breed.reference_image_id)
  val imageResponse = petService.downloadImage(info.url)
  return ImageIO.read(imageResponse.byteStream())
}
```

With the code wrapped up into a function, our map() operation shrinks to a single line:

pets/v4/src/main/kotlin/com/example/pets/PetPicsApplication.kt
```kotlin
val images: Flow<Image> = breeds
  .map { downloadImage(it) }
```

Great! Our images flow is looking nice and tidy. That'll help when we start adding more operators.

Chain Operators Together

Every intermediate operator function has the same distinctive shape, with a Flow as its input and another Flow as its output.

$$Flow<A> \longrightarrow map\ \{...\} \longrightarrow Flow<B>$$

Since the output is the same shape as the input, we can chain functions like this together in a row. Let's add a couple more intermediate operators to our program:

pets/v5/src/main/kotlin/com/example/pets/PetPicsApplication.kt
```kotlin
val images = breeds.filter { it.reference_image_id.isNotBlank() }
  .onEach { println("Downloading the next image...") }
  .map { downloadImage(it) }
  .take(10)
```

Each operator returns an updated Flow, letting us chain more operators right onto the end:

❶ filter() removes non-matching elements from the flow. We'll use it to make sure we only let through valid image IDs. Can't be too careful!

❷ onEach() runs some extra code between each element emitted by the flow. Adding a println() statement will make it easy to see what the program is doing.

❸ map() is the one we've already seen. It transforms each element by applying some code to it. This is where we're downloading our Image.

❹ take() will stop the flow's execution after it's emitted a given number of elements. Remember this one—it's a bit different from the others, and we'll talk more about it later on.

We Got Ourselves a Convoy

By chaining operator functions onto an existing Flow, we've begun to create a lazily evaluated *pipeline* of connected modular operations. It's a series of steps for our data to flow through. Each time we ask for more output, the next value will move through the pipeline, passing each step in turn until it reaches the end. The output of each step forms the input for the next one.

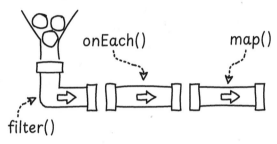

This is a *declarative* programming style that focuses on describing the path our data and events will follow. In a complex program that deals with many different inputs and outputs, building programs this way can make it much easier to see at a glance how everything fits together.

Imperative or Declarative

 Picture a car factory. An old-fashioned loop is like having one workstation to build the whole vehicle, start to finish. A Flow pipeline splits the work into an assembly line instead—one station for building the chassis, one for the engine, and so on.

There are dozens of operators to discover and use, and we won't try to cover them all in this book. It's up to you to look at the Flow documentation and find the specific operator functions that will suit your needs. Don't worry if you come up empty—by the end of the chapter, you'll be able to write your own operator functions, too!

To help us work with pipelines, let's introduce a couple of new words to describe how they fit together. If one step happens before another step in the pipeline, we'll describe the first one as *upstream* and the second one as *downstream.* For instance, our filter() operation is a couple of steps upstream of the map() stage and its image download.

Write a Terminal Operator

Our flow pipeline is looking great, but it still doesn't do anything. The output from those println() calls is nowhere to be seen because they're part of a flow that's not being executed. We've only used intermediate operators, and we're still missing the all-important collect() call.

Let's write our terminal operator function. Remember, a terminal operator is a suspending function that calls collect() and executes the flow's code. We already know what ours needs to do, and we can copy most of its implementation from the createWindow() code we put to one side at the start of the chapter:

pets/v6/src/main/kotlin/com/example/pets/PetPicsApplication.kt
```kotlin
suspend fun Flow<Image>.displaySlideshow() {
  createWindow("Slideshow") { window ->
    collect { image ->
      window.contentPane.removeAll()
      window.add(JLabel(ImageIcon(image)))
      window.pack()
      delay(5.seconds)
    }
  }
}
```

That's great—we've got a reusable displaySlideshow() operation that will work for any source of images in any application.

Finish the Pipeline

Let's go ahead and add our terminal operation to the end of our existing flow pipeline. We'll also need to add a suspending main() function since we're finally executing those network calls from inside the flow:

pets/v6/src/main/kotlin/com/example/pets/PetPicsApplication.kt
```kotlin
suspend fun main() {
  breeds.filter { it.reference_image_id.isNotBlank() }
    .onEach { println("Downloading the next image…") }
    .map { downloadImage(it) }
    .take(10)
    .displaySlideshow()
}
```

Keep an eye out for the println() statements in the program's output, and notice how the slideshow stops after 10 images. Our intermediate operators are modifying the flow's behavior.

Each typical flow pipeline has one or more intermediate operators, followed by a single terminal operator. You'll spot the terminal operator by its suspension point icon, indicating that it's going to execute your flow's suspending code.

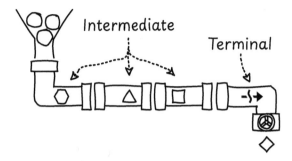

We wrote our own displaySlideshow() function that calls collect(), but there are a couple of other built-in terminal operators as well, such as count() and toList().

Watch Out for Terminators

 A List might look similar to a Flow, but don't mistake toList() for an intermediate operator. Calling toList() tells the flow to generate all its values right away—an expensive mistake if you accidentally use it with a long or infinite stream of data.

End a Flow Early

In this chapter, we've been working with flows that have a finite number of elements and a clear point of exit. For instance, we know that our pet-pictures flow is going to come to an end when we reach the end of the final page of animal breeds.

But not all loops terminate, and not all code blocks complete successfully. In this section, you'll write your own intermediate operator and use it to make an infinite flow. Once it's working, we'll see how exceptions and size-limiting operators can both be used to stop it from running forever. You'll learn how to handle exceptions safely as they propagate through the stages of a pipeline.

Infinite Flows

Just like the sequences we saw in the last chapter, a flow is executed on-demand, and it can use an infinite loop to keep on producing new values indefinitely.

Let's add another step to our pet-images flow and turn our fixed-length slideshow into an infinitely repeating series of images. We'll define a simple function called repeat() that takes our original Flow as its input:

```
pets/v7/src/main/kotlin/com/example/pets/PetPicsApplication.kt
fun <T> Flow<T>.repeat(): Flow<T> = flow {
  while (true) {
    collect { item ->
      emit(item)
    }
  }
}
```

① ②

Inside the function, the first thing we do is use the flow() builder function to create a new Flow.

To grasp how it works, it's important to understand that collect() and emit() are coming from two different places:

❶ The collect() function we're calling belongs to the Flow<T> that we received as input—that's our repeat() function's own extension receiver.

❷ Meanwhile, the emit() function belongs to the output flow and comes from the flow() builder that's wrapping our code.

We're collecting one flow and emitting values to another. When we get to the end of the source flow's collect() operation, our while loop will send us back around to collect it all over again.

Don't forget, since this is all happening inside a flow()-builder code block, none of it will run until the resulting Flow is collected.

When Are We Waiting?

By convention, a suspending function shouldn't return a Flow—and functions that return a Flow shouldn't have the suspend modifier. That's the rule that distinguishes intermediate operators from terminal operators, but it applies to other kinds of code, too.

So, what's the problem? Well, mixing flows with suspending functions makes it hard to tell when the suspending is going to happen. Imagine a function called fetchDelayed() which has the suspend modifier and also returns a Flow:

```
suspend fun fetchDelayed(): Flow<String> // don't do this!
```

Does this function wait for a while and then return a Flow? Or does it return a Flow that will do some waiting when you collect() it? It could be either—or even both—and you'll have to look at the function's implementation to find out.

If you return a Flow, make sure any suspending calls go inside the flow, not outside. You can always wrap an existing flow in a new flow() builder if you need to add some more suspending code. That way, the function itself doesn't need the suspend modifier, and it'll be much easier for callers to understand, invoke, and test.

Artisanal Operators

Take a closer look at that repeat() function we just wrote, and you should spot some familiar characteristics. The function takes one Flow as input and returns a new Flow that will collect() the first one. That means it's an intermediate operator.

Just like any other intermediate operator, we can slot it right into our flow pipeline:

```
pets/v7/src/main/kotlin/com/example/pets/PetPicsApplication.kt
suspend fun main() {
  breeds.map { downloadImage(it) }
    .repeat()
    .displaySlideshow()
}
```

Now, the slideshow goes on forever until you close the window.

In fact, this recipe is what's behind every other intermediate operator function we've used, too. Take a look at the Flow interface, and you'll only see one function—collect(). The other operators are extension functions, and they all follow the same simple template:

1. Create a new flow().
2. Inside the new flow(), collect() the original one.
3. emit() values to the new flow.

You already know how to write your own terminal operators—make a suspending function that calls collect(). With the addition of the flow() builder, you've got all the tools you need to create your own intermediate operators, too.

Operators in Operators

 If you think about it—but not too hard—an intermediate operator is a terminal operator that's being called inside a new flow().

Using flow(), collect(), and emit() as your building blocks, how would you implement your own version of the map() operator? Look back at the repeat() function we just wrote if you need some clues.

Set a Size Limit

Our repeating images flow can produce as many images as we like. But that doesn't mean we have to use them all. It won't fetch them until we ask for them—so if we stop collecting, it'll stop repeating.

When we wrote our Fibonacci sequence generator at the beginning of Chapter 10, Go with the Flow, on page 161, we used a for loop with a break instruction.

Flows rely on the safer collect() function, which will always try to execute the entire flow and all the code it contains. That's an important rule, and we'll talk a little more about it later on. Because of this design difference, we don't have access to the break instruction that we'd have in a for or while loop. So how do we stop?

In fact, you saw the answer when you used the take() function earlier in the chapter. If collect() is always going to execute the entire flow, what we need is a way to make the flow shorter. A size-limiting operator such as take() does exactly that. Give it a long or even unlimited flow as input, and it'll return a truncated one that stops after emitting a fixed number of items.

Let's say we always want to end the slideshow after exactly 100 slides. We don't know how many pictures there are in the original flow or how many times it might need to loop around before it reaches 100. By combining our repeat() function with take(), we can keep looping until we reach the limit and then stop:

```
pets/v8/src/main/kotlin/com/example/pets/PetPicsApplication.kt
suspend fun main() {
    breeds.map { downloadImage(it) }
        .repeat()
        .take(100)
        .displaySlideshow()
}
```

Great! We've limited our infinite flow to 100 items, and we've used the take() function to stand in for the missing break operation.

Handle a Failed Flow

The collect() function is always going to try and make it to the end of the flow, and you've seen how size-limiting operators such as take() can make that happen sooner. But reaching the end isn't the only way to exit. Like an ordinary function, a multivalued Flow can stop its execution early by throwing an exception. What happens to the rest of our Flow pipeline when one of its stages fails?

Let's replace our image download with an error, simulating a problem with our PetService network call:

```
pets/v9/src/main/kotlin/com/example/pets/PetPicsApplication.kt
suspend fun main() {
  val images: Flow<Image> = breeds
    .map { throw Exception("Oh no, something went wrong!") }

  try {
    images.displaySlideshow()
  } catch (error: Exception) {
    println("Caught an error: $error")
  }
}
```

As you should be expecting by now, the error isn't going to be thrown when we call map(). It's the terminal operator that will throw the error since that's where the flow's code is being executed. In our case, that's the collect() call inside our displaySlideshow() function:

```
Caught an error: java.lang.Exception: Oh no, something went wrong!
```

Since the flow collection fails, the displaySlideshow() function doesn't complete successfully. Instead, we end up in the catch block—as if we'd caught an error from any other function. And since we linked our window's lifecycle to the function that created it, the window closes automatically when the function fails.

Operator, Could You Help Me Catch This Error?

 If your code does something with a Flow, there's a good chance you can wrap up that code in a reusable lazy operator and slot it into a pipeline. That works for error handling, too, and Kotlin includes a pre-built catch() operator.

That's Not My Fault

When you add a catch() operator or wrap collect() in a try–catch block, you're handling the error from an upstream flow that's already failed. But just as with a regular suspending function, you might also want to recover from errors inside the flow() builder itself, and let the flow continue running. When you do that, there's one important pitfall to watch out for.

Let's see the problem in action.

Our original breeds flow emits several pages of data, making a fresh HTTP request for each one. To guard our code against network outages or problems with the remote server, let's try adding some error handling inside the flow() builder itself. If one of the downloads fails, we'll skip it and move on to the next one. That way, consumers won't need to worry about the problem:

pets/v10/src/main/kotlin/com/example/pets/PetPicsApplication.kt

```kotlin
val breeds = flow {
  var i = 0
  while (true) {
    try {
      val page = petService.listBreeds(limit = 5, page = i++)
      if (page.isNotEmpty()) {
        for (item in page) emit(item) // careful!
      } else {
        break
      }
    } catch (error: Exception) {
      println("Skipped one page due to $error")
    }
  }
}
```

We don't need to display the whole slideshow, so we'll use the take() operator to limit it to one image for now:

pets/v10/src/main/kotlin/com/example/pets/PetPicsApplication.kt

```kotlin
suspend fun main() {
  breeds.map { downloadImage(it) }
    .take(1)
    .displaySlideshow()
}
```

What are you expecting to see when you run this code? Unlike our last example, we're not throwing any errors of our own this time. We're guarding against potential problems, but if the server's up and running, everything should work fine.

It starts out okay, displaying the slideshow window and loading the first image with no problems. But after that, things start to deteriorate:

```
Skipped one page due to kotlinx.coroutines.flow.internal.AbortFlowException:
  Flow was aborted, no more elements needed
Skipped one page due to java.lang.IllegalStateException:
  Flow exception transparency is violated: Previous 'emit' call has thrown
  exception [...], but then emission attempt of value [...] has been detected.
...
```

What did we do wrong?

Unexpected Error

Much like a canceled coroutine, a failed or truncated flow uses an exception as a shortcut to make a quick exit. That makes sure the producer has a chance to run its finally blocks and other cleanup code before the flow terminates—which is one of the reasons we switched from a Sequence to a Flow in the first place, back in Chapter 10, Go with the Flow, on page 161.

Like a canceled coroutine, a terminated flow remembers that it's supposed to be terminating. It won't let you emit any more items, even if you suppress the original exception. That's why we saw an error in the program we just wrote.

This isn't the same as coroutine cancellation, though. A flow doesn't have its own coroutine or Job, so the ensureActive() function won't help. Instead, make sure your emit() calls never happen inside a try–catch–finally block or any other code block that catches errors. Let the error make its way back to the consumer, and you'll be able to handle it in the downstream code where it belongs.

Size-limiting operators end the flow with a special AbortFlowException, but emit() can throw other exceptions, too, and none of them should be caught. When emit() fails, it means the downstream flow has failed or been terminated. No matter what the exception is, it needs to continue propagating upward, interrupting each stage in the flow pipeline until it eventually makes its way back to the flow collector where it originated. This principle is called *exception transparency*.

Internal Only

 The only way to end a flow early without having it throw an error is to use a built-in operator. You can't write your own size-limiting operators from scratch because the AbortFlowException class isn't accessible from your own code.

Publish a Reactive Stream

Outside the world of suspending functions, plenty of other languages and frameworks have their own take on multivalued asynchronous operations. Many of these solutions are part of the *Reactive Streams*[1] initiative, which defines a shared blueprint for reliable, efficient, and cross-compatible data streams across the Java ecosystem and beyond.

You've already learned how to integrate single-valued futures and promises with your coroutines. In the final section of this chapter, we'll do the same for streams that produce multiple values. Kotlin might not implement the Reactive Stream interfaces, but its Flow API is built on the same core principles, making flows and Reactive Streams work naturally together.

---

1. https://www.reactive-streams.org/

We'll use RxJava for our examples in this section, but you can use the same tools and techniques to integrate your Kotlin coroutines with other tools, including Reactor's Flux and Java's own Flow.Publisher.

From Future to Flowable

We'll start this section by adding a new dependency. This will give us access to the RxJava library and the tools to integrate it with our Kotlin coroutines and flows:

pets/v11/build.gradle.kts
```
dependencies {
  implementation("org.jetbrains.kotlinx:kotlinx-coroutines-core:1.10.1")
  implementation("org.jetbrains.kotlinx:kotlinx-coroutines-rx3:1.10.1")
  implementation("com.squareup.retrofit2:retrofit:2.9.0")
  implementation("com.squareup.retrofit2:converter-moshi:2.9.0")
  runtimeOnly("org.jetbrains.kotlinx:kotlinx-coroutines-swing:1.10.1")
}
```

In Chapter 9, Upgrade Every Callback, on page 145, we wrote an asynchronous downloadImage() function that returned a CompletableFuture. Let's grab the same code again—we can repurpose it to make a simple RxJava Flowable:

pets/v11/src/main/kotlin/com/example/pets/DownloadAsync.kt
```
val client = HttpClient.newHttpClient()

fun downloadAsync(url: String): CompletableFuture<HttpResponse<ByteArray>> {
  val request = HttpRequest.newBuilder(URI(url)).build()
  return client.sendAsync(request, BodyHandlers.ofByteArray())
}

fun downloadImageAsync(url: String): CompletableFuture<Image> =
  downloadAsync(url)
    .thenApply { it.body().inputStream() }
    .thenApply { ImageIO.read(it) }
```

We'll wrap this asynchronous function with some RxJava code—the kind of thing you might find if you were working with Reactive Streams in a non-coroutine application:

pets/v11/src/main/kotlin/com/example/pets/PetPicsApplication.kt
```
val logoPublisher: Publisher<Image> = Flowable.defer {
  val url = "https://kotlinlang.org/docs/images/kotlin-logo.png"
  Flowable.fromCompletionStage(downloadImageAsync(url))
}
```

The Publisher type is defined in Java, and it's a shared interface for all Reactive Stream implementations. Flowable is a specific subtype of Publisher belonging to RxJava.

Don't worry about following exactly how this RxJava code works. We just need any old Flowable to use as an example so we can explore how you'd write a Kotlin consumer for a Publisher or Flowable that you might already have in your existing Java code.

Use RxJava with Coroutines

How can we pass this non-coroutine stream of images to the suspending displaySlideshow() function that we've already written?

Easy! The dependency we already added comes with an asFlow() function that will convert from a Java Publisher to a Kotlin Flow:

pets/v11/src/main/kotlin/com/example/pets/PetPicsApplication.kt
```
suspend fun main() {
  logoPublisher.asFlow().displaySlideshow()
}
```

You can use the same Publisher.asFlow() function for any stream that implements the shared Publisher interface. That includes RxJava, Project Reactor, and Java 9's standard library Flow implementation. Just check the Kotlin coroutines library's online documentation to find out which dependencies you need for your integration.

Similar, but Not the Same

 Some RxJava operators will be identical to Kotlin's, while others might have differences in name or behavior. The same goes for other Reactive Stream implementations. Use the documentation to translate from one framework to another.

Write in Kotlin, Run in Java

We've used asFlow() to bring an existing Reactive Stream into a coroutine-powered slideshow application, making it safer and easier to use. What about when we need to go the other way? Let's take a piece of code that's written with Kotlin flows and suspending functions and call it from an application that's built with RxJava.

Our animal pics are a good candidate for conversion since we only have them in Kotlin-compatible Flow form so far. For easy access from other code, we'll start by wrapping the Flow<Image> in a getImages() function:

pets/v12/src/main/kotlin/com/example/pets/PetPicsApplication.kt
```
fun getImages(): Flow<Image> =
  breeds.map { downloadImage(it) }
```

This isn't a suspending function, so we'll be able to call it from Java or from other non-suspending functions in Kotlin. But without coroutines, this function still won't be of much use to us. We won't be able to call the all-important terminal operators, so we'll have no way to execute the code inside.

Or will we? As we've seen before, Kotlin's suspending functions are just one way to represent an asynchronous operation. Suspension points might make Kotlin's flows easy to write and consume, but the asynchronous operations they contain are no different from any other. To call a Flow from RxJava, we need to convert it using asFlowable(). We'll use RxJava's blockingForEach() function to demonstrate:

pets/v12/src/main/kotlin/com/example/pets/PetPicsApplication.kt

```
val images: Flowable<Image> = getImages().asFlowable()

fun main() = images.blockingForEach { image ->
  // TODO: do something with the images
}
```

When we did something similar to convert a single-valued suspending function to a CompletableFuture in Chapter 9, Upgrade Every Callback, on page 145, we needed a coroutine scope. Why don't we need one here? Well, unlike a CompletableFuture, our Flowable on its own doesn't represent a running task. It's a lazy stream that runs on demand like the Kotlin Flow it's based on.

Swap asFlowable() for asObservable(), asFlux(), asPublisher(), and so on, depending on what framework you're using and what specific type you need. You'll also find some other functions that can replace the flow() builder directly and build a different type of stream, similar to how we replaced an async() coroutine with the future() builder when we integrated coroutines with Java futures.

Use Android LiveData with Coroutines

 Using LiveData instead of Reactive Streams for your observable state on mobile? Just add Android's LiveData KTX dependency to get access to Flow.asLiveData(), LiveData.asFlow(), and a liveData() builder function that can emit() values.

Suspend or Subscribe?

Why use Kotlin flows instead of Reactive Streams?

Like futures and promises, Reactive Streams are built on callbacks, and they come with all the same problems as their single-valued counterparts. You've already seen how suspending functions can make asynchronous code easier to read, write, and maintain. Flows let you take those benefits and apply them to multivalued streams, too.

In fact, you've seen some of these benefits in the last chapter when you upgraded from a Sequence to a Flow. Unlike a sequence's Iterator, a Reactive Stream Subscription does at least provide some functions to clean up its resources—but you still have to remember to invoke those functions at the right time.

Flows solve the problem by making sure the whole stream is collected in a single suspending function call. As you saw earlier in the chapter, a terminal operator such as collect() will always try to execute the entire flow—it can only be interrupted by an exception. And like an ordinary function, its state and variables no longer exist after it completes or fails. That means no task leaks to worry about.

Of course, with the right coroutine scope in place, you can run your flows in background coroutines like any other suspending code—but more on that in the next chapter.

Leave Backpressure Behind

Suspension points take care of backpressure, too!

If you've used Reactive Streams, you might have had to worry about what happens when the producer task is sending values faster than the consumer can handle them. Thanks to suspending functions, a Kotlin flow can often avoid that problem altogether. When producer and consumer are running in the same coroutine, it's impossible for one to overtake the other. The producer only runs while the consumer suspends to call emit(), and the consumer only continues running when emit() returns a value.

That suits us for now, but we'll come back to it in the next chapter when we add a buffer that will let us adjust our flow's backpressure and start down-loading each slideshow image ahead of time.

Suspending for Singles

Many Reactive programming tools work with single values as well as streams. RxJava has the Single type, while Reactor has Mono. You won't find a single-valued counterpart for the Flow class in Kotlin, though. Why not?

Remember, we started our Kotlin data stream journey by learning that a Flow is a way to write a suspending function that can return multiple values. In other words, a suspending function is already the single-valued equivalent of a Flow. Suspending functions don't come with the Flow-style operators you'd get from a Mono or Single, but since they can slot into ordinary control-flow structures, that's less of a problem than you might think.

When you do need to integrate a single-valued suspending function with a Reactive framework, there are functions to convert suspending operations to and from Single, Mono, and so on.

What Have You Learned?

You've refactored a flow into modular stages and learned about the anatomy of a flow pipeline. You know how to write your own operator functions, and you can spot the difference between intermediate and terminal operators.

After we fixed some errors in our flow pipeline, we looked at how to integrate flows with code that doesn't use coroutines. A flow is one way to represent an asynchronous stream of data or events, and you've learned how to make the simple conversion between suspending Kotlin flows and subscriber-based Reactive Streams. With those tools at your disposal, you'll be able to integrate coroutines with even more of your existing code.

The flows we've looked at so far do all their work in a single coroutine, so we don't have to worry about background tasks or backpressure. In the next chapter, we'll upgrade our flows with some new tools that let multiple coroutines collaborate on a single stream of data.

Key Concepts

Intermediate operator

This is a function that takes a Flow as input and returns a modified Flow. Combine intermediate operators to build a modular pipeline.

Terminal operator

This is a suspending function, such as collect(), that executes the code inside a Flow.

Reactive Stream

This is an asynchronous data pipeline with callback-style subscribers for programs that don't have access to Kotlin's suspending functions and flows.

CHAPTER 12

Share Flows, Connect Channels

Coroutines are at their most powerful when they're working together. You already know how to launch a group of subtasks where each contributes one part of a larger task. Now, let's put that together with your new Flow skills. What happens when each subtask is producing not just one result but an ongoing stream of data?

In this chapter, you'll learn how coroutines can work together to produce or consume a combined stream of values. First, we'll connect two tasks using a channel. Next, we'll introduce shared flows that can broadcast their data more widely. Along the way, you'll pick up a handy recipe for integrating recurring callbacks and event listeners with your coroutines.

After you complete the chapter, you'll know the right tool to collect and distribute tasks and events in any situation.

Communicate Between Coroutines

Over the course of the last two chapters, you've learned all about the flow() builder, which can emit multiple values from a single block of code. In this simple form, the flow is produced and consumed by a single coroutine. Each time the collector needs another value, it steps back into the flow to run more of its code.

That's a great way to package up a repeating producer process that generates its own data. But what about values that originate somewhere else? In a real application, streams of data and events can come from all over the place—sensors, message queues, user inputs, and more.

In this section, let's introduce some tools to let our flows communicate with the outside world. We'll create a stream of incoming UI events and use it to control our image viewer app.

Under Pressure

We're nearing the end of our journey now, and you'll be consolidating what you've learned by combining a flow builder with the concurrency tools from Chapter 4, Split Up to Speed Up, on page 59. If you're following along with the code, you'll need a working version of the flow-based image viewer from our previous chapter.

We've made great progress refactoring our slideshow application. But when you run the code and watch the screen for a while, you might notice a slight performance hiccup.

The displaySlideshow() function uses delay() to add a five-second interval between each photo. But in reality, we're going to see each slide for slightly longer than that because we're also waiting for the network requests that fetch the images.

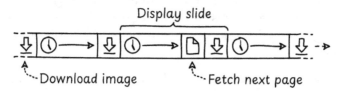

It's an inconsistent viewing experience, and it's something we should be able to improve. There's plenty of time available to perform those downloads, after all. We need to use that time more effectively.

Multivalued Multitasking

Like any other suspending function, flows run their code sequentially, doing one thing at a time. Each instruction has to be completed before the next one can start, and the producer can't act until the consumer hands over control. So, when our slideshow code calls delay(), it has to finish that operation before it can do anything else. That means we're not making the most effective use of the time available.

If you can remember all the way back to Chapter 4, Split Up to Speed Up, on page 59, then this problem should sound familiar. In that chapter, we divided a task into coroutine subtasks. That allowed our program to run faster by using the gaps in one task to make progress on another. Can we do the same thing here?

What we want is to be able to run the next downloadImage() step during the delay() function's downtime. It's time for some more concurrency!

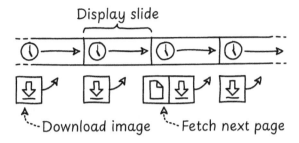

Like much of what we've been doing with flows, there's an operator for this—and it has some tricks we can't easily pull off for ourselves. We'll get to that, but let's take the scenic route and see how far we can get without relying on the built-in version. Along the way, you'll pick up a vital new set of tools and techniques that you can use in your own code.

Launch a Background Task

Remember, to add concurrency and let our program do two things at once, we need to launch additional coroutines.

Let's start writing a new function that will add concurrency to our image pipeline. We'll call it produceInBackground() since our goal is to launch a background coroutine that can start downloading images while the slideshow is busy displaying them.

Just like the last time we sped things up with multitasking, our starting point is going to be the coroutineScope() function. That'll create a scope that can start new child coroutines and then wait for them to finish. Since the flow() builder's code block is a suspending function, we're free to call coroutineScope() inside it.

This code is not going to work, by the way—we're missing some crucial pieces. But let's write it out anyway and see what we can learn as we go:

```kotlin
pets/v13/src/main/kotlin/com/example/pets/PetPicsApplication.kt
fun <T> Flow<T>.produceInBackground(): Flow<T> = flow {
  coroutineScope {
    launch {
      collect { value ->
        emit(value) // oops!
      }
    }
  }
}
```

It's a plausible attempt. We're launching a new coroutine and using it to collect our upstream flow. Let's give it a spin. What do you think will happen?

```
pets/v13/src/main/kotlin/com/example/pets/PetPicsApplication.kt
suspend fun main() {
  getImages()
    .produceInBackground()
    .displaySlideshow()
}
```

The user interface loads up as normal, but it won't display any images. Instead, the program complains that we're trying to emit values from the wrong coroutine:

```
java.lang.IllegalStateException: Flow invariant is violated:
  Emission from another coroutine is detected.
```

What did we do wrong?

That's Not My Coroutine!

Calling emit() is like using return—it only works inside the function that you're trying to emit a value from. Writing emit() inside a launch() block might not cause the same compilation failure that you'd get with a misplaced return, but the underlying problem is still the same.

Remember, our flow is a generator function that can return to its caller more than once. When we emit() a value, we're not sending it off to some separate consumer process or coroutine. Instead, the emit() function itself is handing back control directly to the flow's caller as part of the current coroutine's continuing execution.

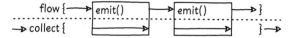

Our displaySlideshow() caller is already running in one coroutine, but when we attempt to emit() a value to it from our launch() block, we're trying to continue its execution in a second one.

Imagine waking up in a different bed from the one you went to sleep in—or even in two different beds at the same time—and you'll understand why the slideshow's collect() function isn't too happy about this. It wants to keep running in the coroutine it started out in, and it'll throw an error if it finds itself waking up in the wrong place.

Context Preservation

You'll see the same error if you try using emit() inside a dispatcher-switching withContext() block. A flow's emit() function must always be invoked from the same coroutine context as the flow collector.

Even if our code could run without throwing an exception, it wouldn't solve our problem. Our goal is to do two things at once, and for that, we need the producer and consumer to run in their own separate coroutines. How do we move our image producer into a background task without accidentally dragging the flow's collector along for the ride?

Create a Channel

Okay, let's rethink. We want our image producer to run in a new coroutine, but we need its output in the original coroutine where the flow is being collected.

If we were launching a coroutine to generate a single value, we'd solve that problem with the async() builder. It returns a Deferred result, letting the new coroutine pass a value back to its creator.

But, an async() coroutine's await() function waits for the entire task to finish before providing a single result. That's not what we need here. Our image producer is going to generate an ongoing stream of data, so we don't want to wait for its completion. Instead, we need a tool that will let us send a series of values back to the caller while both tasks continue running.

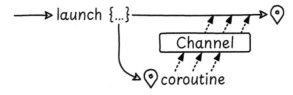

What we're looking for is a Channel.

Let's make a simple program where we can see it in action. We will need two coroutines—a sender and a receiver. To send our values, we will create a new background coroutine with launch(). Meanwhile, our starting coroutine—the one that runs our suspending main() function—can play the role of the receiver:

```kotlin
// channels/v1/src/main/kotlin/com/example/channels/ChannelsApplication.kt
suspend fun main() = coroutineScope {
    val channel = Channel<Char>()

    launch { // sender
        for (outgoingChar in "Hi!") {
            println("Sending '$outgoingChar'…")
            channel.send(outgoingChar)
            delay(100)
        }
    }
}
```

```
repeat(3) { // receiver
  val incomingChar = channel.receive()
  println("Received '$incomingChar'")
}
}
```

Communicate, Don't Mutate

When you need to share data between tasks, use a Channel instead of a shared variable or mutable data structure. Channels are safe for concurrent use by many different coroutines and unlock many new ways to organize your code.

Learn to Communicate

The send() and receive() operations are both suspending functions, and the simple channel we've created here will act as a handoff point between our two coroutines. When the sender calls send(), it waits at the meeting point for the receiver to arrive—and when the receiver calls receive(), it does the same to wait for the sender. Once both coroutines have arrived, a value is passed from sender to receiver, and the program continues.

Did you run the code yet? The output looks like this:

```
Sending 'H'…
Received 'H'
Sending 'i'…
Received 'i'
Sending '!'…
Received '!'
```

It's easy to see how the values are being passed between the two coroutines as each task continues with its own work.

So, what have we gained that we couldn't do with a flow? Multitasking! Don't forget, a flow on its own is just a single task. With two communicating coroutines, we can now do two things at once.

If flows are like the multivalued equivalent of suspending functions, it can sometimes be helpful to think of a Channel as the multivalued equivalent of a Deferred. In fact, there's even a produce() coroutine builder that will create and return its own Channel, similar to how async() returns a Deferred. We could have used it in our program just now, but we'll leave it as-is for the time being—our goal is to understand the moving parts, not hide them.

	Code It	Launch It	Retrieve It
One value	suspend fun	scope.async()	Deferred
Many values	flow()	scope.produce(), or flow.produceIn(scope)	Channel

This comparison will help you choose the right tool, but it's not an exact parallel, and it won't hold up to scrutiny in every situation.

Close a Channel

Our simple channel arranged a face-to-face meeting between our coroutines, but that doesn't always have to be the case. A channel can also include its own buffer capacity, allowing it to accept items immediately from the sender and hold onto them until the receiver arrives. Think of it like a concierge who will hold your deliveries and packages for you if they arrive while you are not home.

We'll talk a bit more about this when we introduce the flow buffer() operator later on.

If the channel holds data, what happens to those waiting messages when the receiver stops receiving? For some programs, the answer is easy—nothing. When both the sender and receiver have gone away, the channel—and any data it might have been holding onto—can be garbage collected like any other object or collection. Channels themselves don't hold resources, so they don't necessarily need to be manually cleaned up after use.

But even if the channel itself doesn't need cleaning up, the coroutine it's connected to might! If our sender coroutine fails or finishes, we don't want our receiver to continue waiting for messages that will never come. The receiver might even have its own cleanup code that it needs to run. That's why the sender has access to an additional close() function, which will let any receiving code know that it should stop waiting. Once a channel is closed, it can't be used again.

Just Looking Out for You

 On its own, a channel doesn't need closing. The close() and cancel() functions are there to help you manage the other tasks and resources that are using the channel.

In our example, we knew how many items to expect, and we called receive() the correct number of times before stopping. Let's change that and have our sender use close() to signal the end of the stream:

channels/v2/src/main/kotlin/com/example/channels/ChannelsApplication.kt

```kotlin
suspend fun main() = coroutineScope {
  val channel = Channel<Char>()

  launch { // sender
    for (outgoingChar in "Hi!") {
      println("Sending '$outgoingChar'…")
      channel.send(outgoingChar)
      delay(100)
    }
    channel.close()
  }

  for (incomingChar in channel) { // receiver
    println("Received '$incomingChar'")
  }
  println("Done!")
}
```

Now that our stream of characters has an end, we can replace our three explicit receive() calls with a simple for loop. Channels have a special suspending iterator, so this loop will pause each time it needs to wait for an item. When the sender closes the channel, the loop will come to an end.

Close That Message

 You can send any object you like via a Channel. So, what if the messages themselves are closeable resources? The optional onUndeliveredElement handler lets you run cleanup code on in-flight messages when the receiver goes away. Check the docs for details.

Closed, Canceled, or Crashed?

Like an async() coroutine's Deferred result, a Channel can also be used to signal a failure or to send a cancellation request.

Let's go over all three ways that a channel can be closed, starting with the one we've already seen:

- As the *sender*, call close() with no arguments to signal the end of the data. Calling send() after this is an error, but items that have already been sent will still make it to the receiver. Once everything's delivered, iterator-backed loops complete normally, while manual calls to receive() throw an error.

- As the *sender*, pass an exception to close() to signal that something went wrong while producing the data. This has two key differences from a normal channel closure. First, iterator-backed receiver loops will end with an error instead of terminating normally. Second, explicit calls to send() and receive() will throw the exception you provided instead of a generic ClosedSendChannelException.

- As the *receiver*, call cancel() to signal that you don't want to receive any more items. All in-flight items are discarded—there's nowhere for them to go. Both sender and receiver will get a CancellationException if they keep trying to use the channel.

Be Careful with Canceled Channels

 As you learned in Chapter 6, Cooperate with Cancellation, on page 91, sending cancellation signals between coroutines can cause some unexpected problems. Take care if you think you might encounter a canceled channel in a non-canceled coroutine.

If that sounds like a lot of errors, don't panic! There are alternative functions, such as trySend() and tryReceive(), for situations where closed channels are an expected part of your program's normal operation.

Put Channels to Work

Okay, that's more than enough time spent learning about channels. With those background details covered, you know how data and control signals can travel from one coroutine to another. Now it's time we put that knowledge to use in our slideshow program.

When we left off, we were looking for a way to produce images in a background coroutine and then send them to the original coroutine that's collecting our flow. Now you know how to use a Channel to do just that.

In a moment, you'll learn a built-in flow operator that provides this functionality and more. But let's try building it ourselves first so we understand what's going on behind the scenes:

```kotlin
pets/v14/src/main/kotlin/com/example/pets/PetPicsApplication.kt
fun <T> Flow<T>.produceInBackground(): Flow<T> = flow {
  coroutineScope {
    val channel = Channel<T>()

    launch {
      onEach { value -> channel.send(value) }
        .onCompletion { cause -> channel.close(cause) }
        .collect()
    }

    for (value in channel) emit(value)
  }
}
```

Now that we've got two separate coroutines—our original parent task and the new child task we made with launch()—we've created concurrency. Our program will be able to work on two different things at the same time, just like when we first introduced multitasking for single-valued functions.

Smooth and Steady

Time to run the code. Our main() function stays the same as before:

```
pets/v14/src/main/kotlin/com/example/pets/PetPicsApplication.kt
suspend fun main() {
  getImages()
    .produceInBackground()
    .displaySlideshow()
}
```

Now that emit() is being called within the main flow-collecting coroutine, it delivers its values without any errors.

Meanwhile, our background coroutine gets a head start on fetching each photo. It can advance right up to the send() function without worrying about whether the consumer is ready. That means when the slideshow finishes up with its delay(), the photo is right there waiting at the handoff location. Our slideshow is looking much more consistent, and once the first image has loaded, the time between slides is a steady five seconds.

The background coroutine can't get too far ahead, though. Channels create backpressure automatically because send() and receive() are suspending operations that can each pause to wait for one another. Once the producer calls send(), it's suspended until the Channel is ready to accept the value.

When the receiver loop continues to its next iteration, it implicitly picks up the waiting item and completes the exchange as if we'd explicitly called receive(). That not only gives us our next image but also wraps up the corresponding call to send(), letting the producer get back to work downloading the next file in the background.

Take the Easy Route

Our new produceInBackground() function has plenty of the same benefits that we got when we added concurrency to an ordinary suspending function. We're taking a Flow<T> as input and returning a Flow<T> as output—so consumers don't need to know anything about the extra coroutines inside. The caller doesn't need to provide a coroutine scope because all the new coroutines will be contained inside the flow's own execution.

We've created a simple recipe that'll let a flow's producer run concurrently with its consumer. But you won't need to use this recipe much in your own code, if at all. That's because the same functionality is already provided by Kotlin's built-in buffer() operator.

We briefly mentioned the relationship between channels and buffering earlier in the chapter when we talked about how channels can be configured with extra space to hold in-transit items. So far, we have been using a channel with a default capacity of zero, which means the sender has to stop and wait for the receiver to accept each item it produces. This stop-and-wait message handoff is called a *rendezvous*.

The built-in buffer() operator uses the same two-coroutine recipe, but it swaps the zero-capacity rendezvous channel for one that holds a few items.

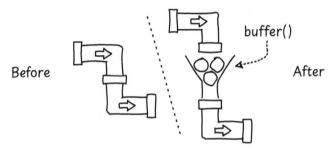

While the buffer channel has free space, the sender can continue producing items without waiting for the receiver. And while the buffer contains items, the receiver doesn't have to stop and wait for the sender. This will reduce the number of times the two coroutines each have to stop work and suspend their execution, helping the program make more efficient progress.

Changing Context

One advanced Flow operator we aren't covering in this book is flowOn(). Its job is to set different coroutine contexts for the different stages in your pipeline. When the whole flow runs in a single coroutine, it can take some time to grasp how and when those context switches will happen.

But there's one simple way to use flowOn() that's still worth mentioning here.

Remember, buffer() starts its own coroutine. Place a call to flowOn() right after the buffer() operator, and it'll set the context just for that producer coroutine without affecting the consumer. If you need to produce values on the I/O dispatcher, try using buffer().flowOn(Dispatchers.IO) instead of adding a withContext() block to the upstream flow. You'll cut down on unnecessary thread switching, and you'll be free to call emit() without worrying about what thread or coroutine it's running in.

No Space? No Problem

Adding a buffer isn't what we want for our slideshow. That would let the background coroutine go racing ahead, downloading dozens of images to fill the channel before we'd even reached the second slide. We need a more measured approach—downloading each photo just before we need it but not fetching extra ones that we might never need.

To get that behavior from the built-in buffer() operator, we need to specify that we want a zero-capacity buffer:

```
pets/v15/src/main/kotlin/com/example/pets/PetPicsApplication.kt
suspend fun main() {
  getImages().buffer(capacity = 0).displaySlideshow()
}
```

What's the use of a buffer that doesn't buffer anything at all? Well, even when we set its capacity to zero, the buffer() operator is still going to start a new background coroutine as we did in our produceInBackground() function. That's enough to give the producer a one-step head start, which is just what we're looking for. This code will behave exactly the same as the version we wrote before.

Operator Fusion

The buffer() function will use its arguments to configure its Channel. But that doesn't mean every call to buffer() will add a whole new buffer to your flow pipeline.

Several other flow builders and operators use channels under the hood—as you'll learn in our next section—and when you use one of these channel-aware operators with an existing flow, it might just resize and replace a channel that was already in place. This is called *operator fusion*, and it can make your flow pipelines more predictable and efficient.

As a result, if you look at the source code for buffer(), you'll find there's more going on than there was in the simple produceInBackground() function we wrote. Operator fusion isn't something you can easily replicate in your own code, so the built-in flow operators will often perform better than the ones you write yourself.

In the next section of this chapter, we'll need a new flow builder that comes with its own built-in channel. You'll see how operator fusion lets it pair with the buffer() operator to control its backpressure.

React to a Repeating Callback

Now that you know how to transfer data between coroutines, you have unlocked a whole new world of possibilities for how to design and structure your programs.

In this section, we'll add a new component to our user interface and send messages between two different screens. You'll learn how to turn a callback-driven event listener into a suspending flow. In the process, you'll discover some new ways to use the buffer() operator to choose your backpressure strategy and handle surplus messages.

Create a Button

Right now, our slideshow app is running on a timer. Let's change it so that it's manually controlled. We'll add an extra control bar to our user interface and use a button to advance from one slide to the next.

We'll put our button in a new window to keep it separate from the code we've already written. Let's use the same createWindow() function we've been using to display our slideshow:

pets/v16/src/main/kotlin/com/example/pets/PetPicsApplication.kt
```
suspend fun main() = createWindow("Control Panel") { window ->
  window.size = Dimension(250, 100)
  val button = window.add(JButton("Click me!")) as JButton
}
```

Huh? When you run this code, the program exits immediately, and there's no sign of our control panel. Why isn't our window showing up?

If you think back to when we wrote our createWindow() function, you'll remember that it's designed to keep the window open only for as long as its code block is running. That's a good choice for our slideshow, where the flow collector keeps running as long as there are images to display. But it's not so great here, where we don't have any suspended code or background coroutines.

We'll fix this when we upgrade our button to do some suspending of its own. But for now, we can simply use the awaitCancellation() function to keep the window open, You might remember this function from Chapter 9, Upgrade Every Callback, on page 145. It suspends the current coroutine but doesn't set up any triggers or callbacks to tell it to resume—so the only way its waiting can end is when the coroutine is canceled:

pets/v17/src/main/kotlin/com/example/pets/PetPicsApplication.kt
```
suspend fun main() = createWindow("Control Panel") { window ->
  window.size = Dimension(250, 100)
```

```kotlin
  val button = window.add(JButton("Click me!")) as JButton
  awaitCancellation()
}
```

Looking good! Well, good enough.

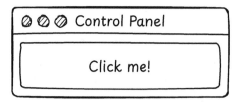

Next, we want to make our button do something. We'll use Swing's addAction-Listener() function to set up our button action:

pets/v18/src/main/kotlin/com/example/pets/PetPicsApplication.kt
```kotlin
suspend fun main() = createWindow("Control Panel") { window ->
  window.size = Dimension(250, 100)
  val button = window.add(JButton("Click me!")) as JButton
  button.addActionListener {
    println("The button was clicked")
  }
  awaitCancellation()
}
```

Run the program, and watch for the console output each time you click the button.

Wait More Than Once

That action listener is a callback that responds to an outside input event. That means it comes with all the same callback problems you've seen before—unwanted thread switching, clunky control-flow restrictions, and the potential for leaked tasks, resources, and errors.

If we can transform it into a suspension point, we'll eliminate all those issues. How can we use the button callback to resume our suspended slideshow?

You learned how to manually resume a suspended coroutine from a callback in Chapter 9, Upgrade Every Callback, on page 145. But this callback has one important difference—it can be triggered more than once. That means the suspendCoroutine() function, which is designed to pause and resume a task just once while it waits for a single asynchronous operation, isn't going to be the right tool for this job.

Rather than a suspending function, which returns a single value, we need a suspending operation that can produce multiple values over time. That's a flow!

But if we try to wire up our button callback to a flow() builder, we're going to run into an all-too-familiar problem:

pets/v19/src/main/kotlin/com/example/pets/PetPicsApplication.kt
```kotlin
suspend fun main() = createWindow("Control Panel") { window ->
  window.size = Dimension(250, 100)
  val button = window.add(JButton("Click me!")) as JButton
  val clicks = flow {
    button.addActionListener { event ->
      emit(event) // error!
    }
  }
  clicks.collect {
    println("The button was clicked")
  }
}
```

The compiler won't allow us to call the suspending emit() function directly from our action-listener callback's non-suspending code. Even if we could find a way past that obstacle, the callback is still going to run as a separate background task. As you've already learned, emit() can't run just anywhere. It needs to be called from the exact same coroutine that originally began collecting the flow, so there's no way we can use it here.

Channels to the Rescue

Once again, adding a Channel is the answer. It'll let us send values from our button-click background callback to our flow-collector coroutine.

We could create our channel by hand like we did last time, but let's take a shortcut. The coroutines library comes with a purpose-built callbackFlow() function that has a channel built right in:

pets/v20/src/main/kotlin/com/example/pets/PetPicsApplication.kt
```kotlin
suspend fun main() = createWindow("Control Panel") { window ->
  window.size = Dimension(250, 100)
  val button = window.add(JButton("Click me!")) as JButton
  val clicks = callbackFlow {
    button.addActionListener { event ->
      channel.trySendBlocking(event)
    }
  }
  clicks.collect {
    println("The button was clicked")
  }
}
```

We'll remove our awaitCancellation() call—the flow collector is doing the waiting for us now. At least, it should be. If you run the program, you'll see right away that we've missed an important part of our flow-builder code, which we'll need to revisit in a moment.

Will It Block?

Since our button callback is a user interface event, it's going to run on Swing's main UI thread. Blocking that thread is a bad idea, so you might have some well-founded concerns about the trySendBlocking() function we just used. Why do we need to block a thread here, and is it safe to do so?

When we used the suspendCoroutine() function to upgrade a simple callback, we called the continuation's resume() function to return control to our coroutine. That function doesn't need to suspend or block anything because we know that our suspended coroutine is always going to be right there waiting for us to hand control back to it.

But when we're dealing with a callback event that happens more than once, things get a bit more complicated. Let's say our callback has been invoked, and we've reacted by resuming a suspended coroutine. While that coroutine is still running, the button is clicked again, and the callback fires a second time. What happens now? The coroutine is busy executing code in response to the first callback, so it's not going to be waiting by the phone for the next call.

Adding a channel was a big step in the right direction, but we still can't use its suspending send() operation to wait for the receiver to be ready because our sender—that's the callback—isn't running in a suspendable coroutine.

If the sender is coming up with new values faster than the receiver can accept them, something has to give. That doesn't necessarily mean we have to block our callback's thread, though—despite what that trySendBlocking() function's name might suggest. Instead, we can change the behavior of the channel itself so that the sender never has to wait at all.

But the callbackFlow() function doesn't have any extra arguments—so how do we modify its channel?

```
pets/v21/src/main/kotlin/com/example/pets/PetPicsApplication.kt
val clicks = callbackFlow {
  button.addActionListener { event ->
    channel.trySendBlocking(event)
  }
}.buffer(capacity = 0, onBufferOverflow = DROP_OLDEST)
```

Thanks to flow-operator fusion, the buffer() operator can set new options for the upstream channel that was created by the callbackFlow() builder.

Default Capacity

Unlike the Channel() constructor function, a callbackFlow() or channelFlow() always comes with some default buffer capacity. Add a downstream buffer() operator to change its capacity and overflow strategy.

With these new settings, the trySendBlocking() function will never block its thread because it'll never bother waiting for anything. If we click on the button while the previous click is still being dealt with, our new input will be ignored. That's thanks to the onBufferOverflow argument, which tells the channel to simply start discarding extra items when it doesn't have space for them.

As a handy shortcut for this particular buffer configuration, you can also write conflate().

Buffers and Backpressure

Our conflated-channel strategy works great for something like a button click, where every event is basically the same. The event itself doesn't contain any important information, so it doesn't matter too much if we drop some extra clicks.

However, plenty of other asynchronous events use this same multishot callback approach, and not all of them can be dropped. You might be dealing with incoming notifications that each need unique handling or time-sensitive readings from a hardware sensor. By varying the arguments to the buffer() operator and the code you use to send and receive values, you can decide how your consumer will react when the producer gets too far ahead.

If you've worked with Reactive Streams, this all might sound familiar. Adding a buffer() to a Flow is essentially the same thing as configuring backpressure for a Publisher or Flowable. Some of the tools we're learning here are also used internally by Kotlin when you use asFlow() to convert a subscriber-based stream into a suspending Flow.

Prevent a Leaked Callback

Have you tried running the code yet? We've missed an important step, and our program is failing with an informative error message:

```
Exception in thread "main" java.lang.IllegalStateException:
  'awaitClose { yourCallbackOrListener.cancel() }' should be used in the end
  of callbackFlow block. Otherwise, a callback/listener may leak in case of
  external cancellation.
```

When we start collecting our new flow, it's going to add itself to the button's list of registered click listeners. But when the flow ends, the listener is never removed from that list. That's a task leak, even if only a small one. The button will continue to run that callback on each click, even after the flow's consumer has gone away. If the callback is holding references to other objects, those objects won't be eligible for garbage collection while the listener is still registered.

To fix it, we need to follow the instructions in that error message and include an awaitClose() block that unregisters our callback. While we're at it, let's also move our flow into a separate function since we'll be adding a few more lines of code to it:

pets/v22/src/main/kotlin/com/example/pets/PetPicsApplication.kt

```
fun JButton.clickEvents(): Flow<ActionEvent> = callbackFlow {
  val listener = ActionListener { channel.trySendBlocking(it) }
  addActionListener(listener)
  awaitClose {
    removeActionListener(listener)
  }
}.conflate()
```

The awaitClose() function lives at the end of our flow-builder code block, and it does two helpful things. First, it keeps the flow producer running, even when there aren't any value-producing child coroutines running inside the flow's own scope. That's important for callback-powered flows like this one, where the values come from a callback rather than a coroutine. Second, it gives us a place to run cleanup code, which will be invoked when its waiting is canceled.

Encapsulate Your Resources

Great! Our new flow is working perfectly, and it encapsulates the full resource lifecycle—from adding the event listener all the way to removing it after use. Kotlin's flow API enables you to guarantee that if a flow's resources have been initialized by a call to collect(), they'll also be properly cleaned up when the caller goes away.

Use this recipe to integrate any multishot callback into your coroutine-based applications, whether you're dealing with user inputs, message queues, sensor data, or something else altogether. Upgrading your callbacks to suspending flows not only makes them safer and easier to use but also gives you a powerful set of built-in tools to customize, control, and consume the resulting stream of values.

For flows that don't manage an external callback, you can swap callbackFlow() for channelFlow(). Both builders come with a coroutine scope and a channel, but the channelFlow() doesn't force you to use awaitClose() and is designed to be kept active by its own child coroutines instead:

- Use channelFlow() when you want to multitask within a flow, producing values from one or more background coroutines. The flow collector only continues running while it has active child jobs.

- Use callbackFlow() when you want to produce values from an outside callback. If your API has an extra callback to signal completion or failure, that's where you should call the channel's explicit close() function—with or without an error as its argument.

Zip Two Flows Together

With everything in place, it's time to start using our button-click events to control our slideshow.

First, we need a version of our displaySlideshow() function that doesn't include the delay(), since we'll be advancing the slideshow manually instead of on a timer:

```
pets/v22/src/main/kotlin/com/example/pets/PetPicsApplication.kt
suspend fun Flow<Image>.displaySlideshow() {
  createWindow("Slideshow") { window ->
    collect { image ->
      window.contentPane.removeAll()
      window.add(JLabel(ImageIcon(image)))
      window.pack()
    }
  }
}
```

Next, let's think about how we need to wire things up. Each time we receive a click event, we want to advance the slideshow and collect the next value from our getImages() flow. Once again, that means we need both flows to be running at the same time, each in their own coroutine.

If you think back over what you've learned in this chapter, you can probably figure out how we could write this out. The first step would be to launch a background coroutine to start collecting the images into a zero-capacity buffer. Next, we'd need to use our foreground coroutine to collect the button input events. On each event, we'd retrieve and display the latest image from our buffer, allowing the background coroutine to start preparing the next one.

Luckily for us, there's an operator for this, too. It's called zip() since it steps through two flows in a pairwise pattern like the interlocking teeth of a zipper:

```
pets/v22/src/main/kotlin/com/example/pets/PetPicsApplication.kt
suspend fun main() = createWindow("Control Panel") { controlWindow ->
  val button = controlWindow.add(JButton("Click me!")) as JButton
```

```
val images = button.clickEvents().zip(getImages()) { _, image -> image }
images.displaySlideshow()
}
```

Run the program, and use the button to step through the images!

You might notice that we don't need the buffer() operator anymore. The zip() operator needs to collect the images in a background coroutine just to get its job done, and if you look at its documentation, you'll see that it already provides the same functionality as a zero-capacity buffer.

Now with Added Concurrency

 Concurrency adds a new dimension to seemingly simple transformations such as zip() and flatMap(). You might have used zip() before with lists, but with flows, it's more complicated. We have to interleave not just the values but the code that produces them!

You'll notice that the slideshow doesn't start until after the first click. For extra credit, can you change the program to load the first image right away? You might need to rethink the way we're emitting those click events.

Share Once, Observe Everywhere

Using channels, you've learned how to send data and events from one component to another. You've got a reusable recipe that will let you take a repeating callback and consume it as a suspending Flow.

In the last section of this chapter, we'll talk about how you can share your flows with more than one consumer. We'll add a second display screen to our slideshow, and we'll use a single producer coroutine to provide the same data to both windows.

Seeing Double

Let's say we're opening a pet store, and we want to use our image viewer app to provide some background visuals. The store has several display screens, so we want to mirror our slideshow across more than one window.

Calling displaySlideshow() from two separate coroutines could work. Each call will create its own window.

Let's try that—but we'll also add a println() statement so we can see what's happening inside our image flow:

```
pets/v23/src/main/kotlin/com/example/pets/PetPicsApplication.kt
suspend fun main() = createWindow("Control Panel") { controlWindow ->
  controlWindow.size = Dimension(250, 100)
  val button = controlWindow.add(JButton("Click me!")) as JButton

  val images: Flow<Image> = getImages().withIndex().map { (index, value) ->
    value.also { println("Downloaded image $index") }
  }
  val slides = button.clickEvents().zip(images) { _, image -> image }

  launch { slides.displaySlideshow() }
  launch { slides.displaySlideshow() }
}
```

Windows in Windows

 Notice how the slideshow exits automatically if you close the control panel window. Remember, we linked each window to the lifetime of its createWindow() function. Since one window is created by the other, they're joined by structured concurrency. Neat!

Click through the slideshow, and you'll start to see pairs of output like this in the console:

```
Downloaded image 0
Downloaded image 0
Downloaded image 1
Downloaded image 1
...
```

Yes, we're downloading every image twice. Each slideshow has its own collect() operator that runs its own copy of the upstream flow, just like calling the same function from two different places.

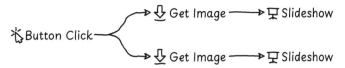

Channel Limitations

Both our slideshows are stepping through the same list of image URLs, and since they're responsible for their own image downloads, they'll both end up doing the same work. Downloading the same image in two different places feels like a waste of time. How can we fix our program so that both slideshow windows share the same source of data?

Your first thought might be to launch a single coroutine and have it send all the images to a Channel. But if we try out a simple example, you'll see why that approach doesn't give us what we need:

channels/v3/src/main/kotlin/com/example/channels/ChannelsApplication.kt
```
suspend fun main() = coroutineScope {
  val channel = Channel<Char>()

  for (name in listOf('A', 'B')) launch { // receiver x2
    for (message in channel) {
      println("Consumer $name received '$message'")
    }
  }

  for (outgoingChar in "Hi!") { // sender
    println("Sending '$outgoingChar'…")
    channel.send(outgoingChar)
    delay(100)
  }
  channel.close()
  println("Done!")
}
```

Channels are designed for delivery of messages exactly once. Run the code, and you'll see that each message is delivered to either one receiver or the other but not to both:

```
Sending 'H'…
Consumer A received 'H'
Sending 'i'…
Consumer B received 'i'
Sending '!'…
Consumer A received '!'
Done!
```

You can think of each message as a unique physical object—only one person can hold it at once, and once you hand it to someone else, you don't have it anymore. Like a dealer handing out a deck of cards, a channel with multiple receivers will share out its messages so that each consumer gets a different set.

That could be a fun way to set up two different slideshows, but it's not the behavior we were after. Instead, we need a way to broadcast each message so that all consumers can receive it at the same time.

Shared Flows

To get the behavior we want, we need to swap our Channel for a SharedFlow. We can create one that fits our needs using the MutableSharedFlow constructor function:

```
channels/v4/src/main/kotlin/com/example/channels/ChannelsApplication.kt
suspend fun main() = coroutineScope {
  val flow = MutableSharedFlow<Char>()

  for (name in listOf('A', 'B')) launch { // receiver x2
    flow.collect { message ->
      println("Consumer $name received '$message'")
    }
  }

  for (outgoingChar in "Hi!") { // sender
    println("Sending '$outgoingChar'…")
    flow.emit(outgoingChar)
    delay(100)
  }
}
```

Like a Channel, a MutableSharedFlow combines both send and receive functionality. Since it's a Flow, consumers can use its collect() function. Meanwhile, producers can call emit(). Unlike the emit() function inside a regular flow() builder, this one can be called from anywhere you like, including from other coroutines.

This time, when you run the code, you'll see more output:

```
Sending 'H'…
Consumer B received 'H'
Consumer A received 'H'
Sending 'i'…
Consumer A received 'i'
Consumer B received 'i'
Sending '!'…
Consumer A received '!'
Consumer B received '!'
```

Unlike a channel, a shared flow broadcasts its messages, making each one available to every consumer at the same time. That means we can serve the same set of results to an unlimited number of downstream collectors.

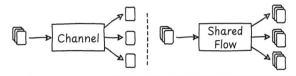

Channel or Shared Flow?

- Use a Channel when your background code wants to hand over each of its output values to a single receiver.

- Use a SharedFlow to broadcast each result to multiple consumers at the same time.

You can think of a MutableSharedFlow as an event hub or message bus. Use it any time you need to share data and events among several producers and consumers.

Ain't No Party Like a Shared Flow Party

You might have noticed one other place where this shared-flow program differs from the version we wrote with channels. What happened to our close() function?

Unlike a channel, a MutableSharedFlow can't be closed. Shared flows never terminate, and it's up to the collector to decide when to stop listening for new values.

But why? One key benefit of this design is simpler error handling. Failures in the upstream flow are always handled in exactly one place—the producer's coroutine scope—no matter how many consumers there are. You can learn more in the design document[1] for shared flows.

So, how do we stop our program from running? We group the consumer tasks into a single Job and cancel it when we're done. Remember, what we need to clean up when we're done isn't the data stream but the coroutines that are interacting with it:

```
channels/v5/src/main/kotlin/com/example/channels/ChannelsApplication.kt
suspend fun main() = coroutineScope {
  val flow = MutableSharedFlow<Char>()

  val receiver = launch {
    for (name in listOf('A', 'B')) launch { // receiver x2
      flow.collect { message ->
        println("Consumer $name received '$message'")
      }
    }
  }

  for (outgoingChar in "Hi!") { // sender
    println("Sending '$outgoingChar'…")
    flow.emit(outgoingChar)
    delay(100)
  }
  receiver.cancel()
  println("Done!")
}
```

In practice, shared flows often turn out to represent event streams that don't terminate on their own anyway. Even if all of its event producers and consumers go away, a shared event bus doesn't stop existing—it just waits for another coroutine to come along.

---

1. https://github.com/Kotlin/kotlinx.coroutines/issues/2034

Materialize Your Errors

Shared flows never end, but that doesn't mean that you can't choose to let consumers know about successes and failures. Just create your own class to represent the events or errors you're interested in, and you can broadcast whatever you like.

Share an Existing Flow

To add a shared flow to our slideshow, we can use the shareIn() operator. Like buffer(), this built-in function will create all the machinery we need, including a coroutine to produce and send our values:

pets/v24/src/main/kotlin/com/example/pets/PetPicsApplication.kt
```kotlin
suspend fun main() = createWindow("Control Panel") { controlWindow ->
  controlWindow.size = Dimension(250, 100)
  val button = controlWindow.add(JButton("Click me!")) as JButton

  val images: Flow<Image> = getImages().withIndex().map { (index, value) ->
    value.also { println("Downloaded image $index") }
  }
  val slides = button.clickEvents().zip(images) { _, image -> image }
    .shareIn(scope = this, started = Lazily)

  launch { slides.displaySlideshow() }
  launch { slides.displaySlideshow() }
}
```

Intermediate or Terminal?

Calling shareIn() returns a Flow, like an intermediate operator. But like a terminal operator, it also executes the upstream code. You could say it splits into two paths—one intermediate, the other terminal. Or maybe it doesn't fit either category!

While you run the code, try saying *slideshow shared flow* 10 times fast.

It works! We still have two windows, each displaying their own copy of the slideshow. But when you look at the output, you'll see that each photo is only being downloaded once:

```
Downloaded image 0
Downloaded image 1
Downloaded image 2
Downloaded image 3
...
```

That's because the two consumers are now using the same shared stream of source data.

Downstream Operators Aren't Affected

 Since a SharedFlow is a type of Flow, you can chain intermediate operators after shareIn(). But don't expect them to join in the sharing! As downstream operators, they'll run their code on-demand in the collector's own coroutine, just like they normally would.

Configure Your Sharing

Look back at the code we just wrote, you'll see that shareIn() has two arguments.

The first is a coroutine scope. With buffer(), we could rely on the downstream collector to create and manage the producer coroutine. But now that we're sharing a single producer coroutine among multiple collectors, that won't work. The shareIn() function needs to create its own coroutine, and that means it needs a scope.

Our second argument is also related to that shared coroutine and controls when it starts running. We chose *lazily*, which will wait to produce values until at least one subscriber starts collecting the flow. Check the documentation to learn about the other options.

Shared flows are sometimes called *hot* streams because they're backed by an active producer that outlives their individual consumers. Channels also represent hot streams, as does any flow that's connected to a channel or other outside data source. Tune in to a hot stream, and you'll join it at its current position. That's in contrast to a *cold* flow like our original image downloader, where each consumer gets a new copy of the stream, starting from the beginning.

Tune in Again Next Time

 You can think of a hot stream like a TV station that's broadcasting live. Tune in late, and you'll miss the start of the show. Cold streams are more like streaming on-demand, where you're in control of the schedule.

Play It Again

Aside from its coroutine configuration, shareIn() also accepts an optional replay argument. It controls the size of the *replay cache*, allowing late-arriving subscribers to receive one or more of the already-emitted values.

Since we didn't pass a value for this argument, it defaults to zero. Let's see what impact that has. Instead of opening two slideshow windows right away, we'll delay the appearance of the second window for a few seconds. When it eventually shows up, what will it display?

```
pets/v25/src/main/kotlin/com/example/pets/PetPicsApplication.kt
suspend fun main() = createWindow("Control Panel") { controlWindow ->
  controlWindow.size = Dimension(250, 100)
  val button = controlWindow.add(JButton("Click me!")) as JButton

  val slides = button.clickEvents().zip(getImages()) { _, image -> image }
    .shareIn(scope = this, started = Lazily)

  launch { slides.displaySlideshow() }
  delay(15.seconds)
  launch { slides.displaySlideshow() }
}
```

Start the code, and click through to the first image. Then, wait until the second slideshow window appears. You'll notice that it starts out blank and stays that way until you click to load a new image. With no replay cache, there's no way for the second window to know about the images that were broadcast before it arrived.

Now, change the shared flow's replay argument from zero to one and watch how the program's behavior changes:

```
pets/v26/src/main/kotlin/com/example/pets/PetPicsApplication.kt
val slides = button.clickEvents().zip(getImages()) { _, image -> image }
  .shareIn(scope = this, started = Lazily, replay = 1)
```

This time, the most recent image is always available in the replay cache. When the new window tunes in to the broadcast, it'll receive that cached value and can start displaying it right away.

State Flows and Observable Data

A shared flow that also tracks its latest value? Sounds a lot like the Observable data holders you might find in some other frameworks or the LiveData class in Android. Pairing a value with a stream of updates is a common pattern in reactive user interfaces, where a view layer watches for changes in an underlying data model.

Kotlin has a dedicated StateFlow class for this use case. It's a subtype of SharedFlow, meaning that you can subscribe to its changes—this time with duplicates automatically filtered out. But it also has a value property that provides instant, non-suspending access to its current contents.

To get started with state flows, swap shareIn() for stateIn(), or replace a MutableSharedFlow() with a MutableStateFlow(). A StateFlow also integrates neatly with Android's LiveData and the State classes in Jetpack Compose. Check the documentation for bridging functions that can convert between all these types.

What Have You Learned?

Now you know how to send data from one coroutine to another, and you understand how to choose and configure the right communication tool for the job. Not only that, but you can suspend a coroutine to wait for any callback, even when it fires more than once.

With communicating coroutines, sending UI events from one screen to another is just the beginning. Using what you have learned, you will be able to design and build applications in new ways. Reactive, event-driven, actor-based—coroutines put it all at your fingertips and keep it all organized with structured concurrency.

We're nearly at our destination, but there's one last thing to do. In our final chapter, you'll learn the coroutine testing tools that will let you ship it all with confidence.

Key Concepts

Channel

This sends data from one coroutine to another—a bit like a Deferred result that can deliver multiple result values over time.

Shared Flow

This broadcasts data to multiple consumers. Use the shareIn() function to launch a coroutine that will collect and broadcast values from an existing upstream flow().

State Flow

This holds a single current value and lets you watch for changes. It's a specialized shared flow that's well-suited for certain kinds of user interface programming, among other things.

CHAPTER 13

Unit Test Without Delay

Like every line of code you write, your coroutines can benefit from thorough test coverage.

You know that suspending functions make your asynchronous code easier to read, write, and run, so it should come as no surprise that they also make it easier to test. However, there are still one or two tips and tricks you'll need to get you started.

By the end of our final chapter, you'll be more than ready to support and maintain your coroutines as they leave the nest and take to the skies. You'll have the tools you need to write comprehensive tests for any suspending function or background task, and you'll know how to track down and fix problems when tests fail or functions go wrong.

Write Quick Tests for Slow Code

Asynchronous antics aside, a suspending function follows the same rules as any other function. Take some inputs, run some code, and return a value. That means your strategy for testing suspending functions is going to be much the same as it is for any other code you write.

But before we start, we need to overcome a familiar obstacle. Most test frameworks don't know about coroutines and can't call suspending functions. How do we write a suspending test?

We'll start this chapter by introducing a new tool to solve that problem. With it, you'll build and test some real code, and you'll learn how to test delays and timeouts without slowing down your builds.

Set Up Your Unit Tests

Ready to get started? The first thing you'll need to do is set up your test framework. We're going to use the multiplatform kotlin.test library, but the techniques you learn in this chapter will work for just about any other test framework you might be using in your own projects.

Here's the dependency you'll need to include:

```
testing/v1/build.gradle.kts
dependencies {
  testImplementation(kotlin("test"))
}
```

To make sure everything's working, we'll start by writing a single passing test:

```
testing/v1/src/test/kotlin/com/example/testing/SimpleTest.kt
import kotlin.test.*

class SimpleTest {
  @Test
  fun alwaysPasses() {
    assertTrue(actual = true, message = "The test should pass")
  }
}
```

If you're working in IntelliJ IDEA, you can run each test directly from the editor using the buttons in the left-hand margin. Or, if you prefer, use Gradle's test task on the command line. When you execute the tests, make sure you see a successful result showing that one test passed:

```
SimpleTest > alwaysPasses PASSED

BUILD SUCCESSFUL in 440ms
```

Test a Suspending Function

Did you get your test class up and running? Great! Now, we need some suspending functions to test.

So, let's start things off with a simple DataProvider interface. We'll apply the suspend modifier to its single fetchData() function since it's designed to represent operations like network calls that fetch data from outside the system:

```
testing/v2/src/main/kotlin/com/example/testing/DataProvider.kt
fun interface DataProvider<out T> {
  suspend fun fetchData(): T
}
```

Nothing to test here, yet. Using this as our starting point, let's add some new functionality.

Say we want to provide some fallback behavior when our application is offline. We'll create a fetchOrDefault() extension function that accepts a default value. When we tell it there's no network connection, we want it to skip calling the data provider, returning the fallback data instead:

testing/v2/src/main/kotlin/com/example/testing/DataProvider.kt

```
var isOffline: Boolean = false

suspend fun <T> DataProvider<T>.fetchOrDefault(default: T): T {
  if (isOffline) return default
  return fetchData()
}
```

This function can behave in two different ways, depending on the value of the isOffline property. Let's write a pair of simple test cases to cover each scenario:

testing/v2/src/test/kotlin/com/example/testing/DataProviderTest.kt

```
class DataProviderTest {
  @Test
  fun useDefaultValueWhenOffline() {
    isOffline = true
    val provider = DataProvider { fail("Should not be called") }
➤   val data = provider.fetchOrDefault("Default value") // error!

    assertEquals("Default value", data)
  }

  @Test
  fun useProvidedValueWhenOnline() {
    isOffline = false
    val provider = DataProvider { "Provided value" }
➤   val data = provider.fetchOrDefault("Default value") // error!

    assertEquals("Provided value", data)
  }
}
```

No Suspending for You

Okay, you probably saw that one coming. Our new tests don't compile because they're attempting to invoke the suspending fetchOrDefault() function from a non-suspending @Test function:

```
> Task :compileTestKotlin FAILED

Suspend function 'fetchOrDefault' should be called only from a coroutine
  or another suspend function.
```

How do we fix it? Adding the suspend modifier to our tests is the obvious thing to try—but it won't work:

```
@Test
suspend fun useDefaultValueWhenOffline() { // error!
```

The kotlin.test library can't run a suspending function as a test, and it'll let us know with an error at compilation time:

```
> Task :compileTestKotlin FAILED

'suspend' functions annotated with '@kotlin.test.Test' are unsupported.
```

The suspend keyword might be part of the core Kotlin language, but that doesn't mean our tests are going to understand it in the same way that our main() function does. If we want to include suspension points in our tests, we're going to need some extra help.

One More Dependency

Kotlin provides a dedicated library for testing coroutines. Let's add it to our build script alongside our existing test dependency:

testing/v3/build.gradle.kts
```
dependencies {
  testImplementation(kotlin("test"))
  testImplementation("org.jetbrains.kotlinx:kotlinx-coroutines-test:1.10.1")
}
```

The core of the coroutine testing library is the runTest() function. It's designed for executing test code, and it'll act as our entry point into the world of suspending functions. All we need to do is wrap each of our tests with this new function:

testing/v3/src/test/kotlin/com/example/testing/DataProviderTest.kt
```
class DataProviderTest {
  @Test
  fun useDefaultValueWhenOffline() = runTest {
    isOffline = true
    val provider = DataProvider { fail("Should not be called") }
    val data = provider.fetchOrDefault("Default value")

    assertEquals("Default value", data)
  }

  @Test
  fun useProvidedValueWhenOnline() = runTest {
    isOffline = false
    val provider = DataProvider { "Provided value" }
    val data = provider.fetchOrDefault("Default value")

    assertEquals("Provided value", data)
  }
}
```

Great! Inside the runTest() block, we're free to call suspending functions. That means we can finally run these tests and see them pass:

```
DataProviderTest > useDefaultValueWhenOffline PASSED
DataProviderTest > useProvidedValueWhenOnline PASSED

BUILD SUCCESSFUL in 965ms
```

You'll use runTest() as your starting point for every test that needs to work with suspending functions or background coroutines, and you'll learn plenty more about its capabilities in the rest of this chapter.

Any Framework, Any Platform

The coroutine testing library isn't tied to any specific test framework, and you can call runTest() from any style of test you like. Use the same functions, annotations, and assertions you normally would, and wrap the whole thing in a runTest() block to add suspending capabilities.

This runTest() function might strike you as similar to the runBlocking() function that we've mentioned briefly before. In fact, on the JVM, it's implemented in a similar way with an event loop that can take charge of the current thread and use it to execute coroutines.

But this function has a couple of other important tricks up its sleeve.

First, it'll change its return type to suit the platform. On JavaScript, runTest() returns the test's success or failure as a Promise, integrating with the asynchronous capabilities of your existing test framework. In our JUnit-style JVM tests, successful tests return Unit, and failures are thrown as exceptions to the caller's waiting thread. By returning the value directly from runTest(), you can write multiplatform tests that work on both platforms.

Second, no matter what platform you're on, this function makes your tests run faster. Let's find out how!

Take Your Time

You have learned how to test a function that has the suspend modifier. But if you check back through the code we've written, you'll see that we haven't done any real suspending. Our dummy DataProvider is always returning its data right away.

In a real app, that data provider is most likely going to be making a network call. That means it'll be communicating with the outside world, spending some time sending the request and waiting for a response.

Let's add the core coroutines library so we can make some more improvements to our fetchOrDefault() function:

```
testing/v4/build.gradle.kts
dependencies {
➤    implementation("org.jetbrains.kotlinx:kotlinx-coroutines-core:1.10.1")
    testImplementation(kotlin("test"))
    testImplementation("org.jetbrains.kotlinx:kotlinx-coroutines-test:1.10.1")
}
```

As well as returning the default value when isOffline is true, we'll also fall back to the default when the data provider takes too long to return a value:

```
testing/v4/src/main/kotlin/com/example/testing/DataProvider.kt
suspend fun <T> DataProvider<T>.fetchOrDefault(default: T): T {
  val timeout = if (isOffline) Duration.ZERO else 30.seconds
  val result = withTimeoutOrNull(timeout) {
    runCatching { fetchData() }
  }
  return if (result == null) default else result.getOrThrow()
}
```

It's a simple enough change. But how are we going to test it?

You can probably think of one easy way—have the tests create a dummy DataProvider that includes a delay() before it returns a value. If the delay exceeds our 30-second limit, we should expect the default value—otherwise, we'll get the value from the provider.

But adding a long delay to a unit test isn't a particularly appealing prospect. Good unit tests run fast. That's important not only to keep your build times down but also to give you the near-instant feedback you need when you're in the process of editing the code.

Still, let's start with the easy approach and see how bad it looks. This is where we'll discover another trick that the runTest() function is hiding up its sleeve.

Skip the Waiting

First, let's add a shorter delay to our data provider—long enough to simulate a real network call but not long enough to trigger our timeout:

```
testing/v4/src/test/kotlin/com/example/testing/DataProviderTimeoutTest.kt
class DataProviderTimeoutTest {
  @Test
  fun useProvidedValueWithDelay() = runTest {
    isOffline = false
    val provider = DataProvider {
➤      delay(15.seconds)
      "Provided value"
```

```
    }
    val data = provider.fetchOrDefault("Default value")
    assertEquals("Provided value", data)
  }
}
```

Run this new test, and you might be in for a surprise. The test passes, but it completes immediately:

```
DataProviderTimeoutTest > useProvidedValueWithDelay PASSED

BUILD SUCCESSFUL in 861ms
```

There's no sign of that 15-second wait. So, how did our code make it past the delay() call and get the correct value to make the test pass?

It's thanks to the runTest() function, which keeps your coroutine tests speedy by skipping unnecessary waiting. If you wrote this code in any other coroutine, you wouldn't be able to get that value without waiting the required time. Remember that because it'll be important later in the chapter.

Instant Timeout

If the runTest() function is ignoring our delay, how can we test that our timeout is working? The timeout is supposed to trigger when the code takes longer than 30 seconds to run. But if all of our delays complete instantly, that'll never happen.

Let's add a test case for the timeout scenario and give it a try:

testing/v5/src/test/kotlin/com/example/testing/DataProviderTimeoutTest.kt
```kotlin
class DataProviderTimeoutTest {
  @Test
  fun useProvidedValueWithDelay() = runTest {
    isOffline = false
    val provider = DataProvider {
      delay(15.seconds)
      "Provided value"
    }

    val data = provider.fetchOrDefault("Default value")
    assertEquals("Provided value", data)
  }

  @Test
  fun useDefaultValueOnTimeout() = runTest {
    isOffline = false
    val provider = DataProvider {
      delay(60.seconds)
      fail("Shouldn't get here")
    }
```

```
    val data = provider.fetchOrDefault("Default value")
    assertEquals("Default value", data)
  }
}
```

Before you run the code, make your best guess about what it's going to do. Will our new test pass?

```
DataProviderTimeoutTest2 > useProvidedValueWithDelay PASSED
DataProviderTimeoutTest2 > useDefaultValueOnTimeout PASSED

BUILD SUCCESSFUL in 828ms
```

Once again, both tests finish nearly instantly, with no sign of those delays. When our delay is shorter than 30 seconds, we get the value from our data provider, and when it's longer, we get the default—just like we wanted.

Virtual Time

How can our timeout be working correctly if our code isn't delaying for the required amount of time?

Here's the secret—the runTest() function isn't ignoring those delays. Each time it encounters a delay() call, it adds the delay amount to an internal counter. By doing that, it can keep track of how much time would have elapsed if the code was running in a real coroutine. When the withTimeoutOrNull() function checks to see how long it's been waiting, the test coroutine gives it the value from that counter. This is *virtual time*—it's counting the seconds like a real clock, but it's not doing any actual waiting.

In large projects with hundreds of tests, those seconds can quickly add up to minutes and hours, so virtual time can be a huge speed boost for your builds. Not only that, but it can let you test code that would otherwise take too long to run. Do you have a scheduled function that's supposed to run once a year? With virtual time, that's no problem—write a test that waits for a virtual year, too.

If you've ever performed in a stage show or concert, you can think of this like the cue-to-cue technical rehearsal. You're still running through the show in the right order, and everyone gets their cue at the right time—but the songs and scenes that take up most of the time are all skipped, and the whole thing is done much quicker than it would be in a real performance.

One important thing to note is that we didn't change any of our non-test code to make this work. You can write the same code with the same delays and timeouts in the same places and have it run in two different ways, depending on whether it's running in a real coroutine or a test.

How Do I Turn This Thing Off?

 Depending on your platform, you might need to use runTest() for tests that wait for real I/O, where you don't want instant timeouts. Virtual time is part of the test's dispatcher. To switch back to a dispatcher with a real clock, use a withContext() block inside runTest().

Expand Your Testing Toolkit

You've learned how to call suspending functions from any test framework and how to speed up your coroutine tests with a time-saving virtual clock.

In the final section of this chapter, you'll use the open source Turbine library to inspect more than the final output of a suspending function. Along the way, you'll discover how to test a component that uses its own coroutine scope to launch background tasks.

Test a Flow

Now that you know how to wrap any test in a runTest() block, testing a suspending function is a lot like testing any other code.

However, as you've learned in the last few chapters of this book, suspension points don't enable suspending functions. They also unlock some important new ways to write code. Using Kotlin's flow() builder, you've written code blocks that produce multiple values over time. When it comes to unit testing, that's going to make things interesting!

Let's start with a Flow that returns a simple series of values, with a short delay() between each one:

```
testing/v6/src/main/kotlin/com/example/testing/DelayedFlow.kt
val myFlow = flow {
  repeat(5) { i ->
    delay(10.seconds)
    emit(i)
  }
}
```

This code will produce five values, and one obvious way to test it is to check that they're all present and correct. We could do that with a terminal operator such as toList():

```
testing/v6/src/test/kotlin/com/example/testing/DelayedFlowTest.kt
class DelayedFlowTest {
  @Test
  fun emitNumbers() = runTest {
    val result = myFlow.toList()
    assertEquals(result, listOf(0, 1, 2, 3, 4))
  }
}
```

Great—that works:

```
DelayedFlowListTest > emitNumbers PASSED

BUILD SUCCESSFUL in 912ms
```

But are we really checking all of our flow's important behavior? We've ensured that it returns the correct values, but we haven't covered those delays. Even if you remove the source flow's delay() step entirely, the test still passes. Can we improve this test so that it will only pass when the delay is working correctly?

Power Up with a Turbine

Instead of collecting all the flow's items at once and then running all our assertions after the fact, we need a way to interleave the two pieces of code. Each time the flow produces a value, we want to switch our attention to the test, check what's changed, and then switch back to execute some more of the flow.

You know what that means, right? Yes, we need to add concurrency and run our flow in its own separate coroutine.

Now, you already know exactly how to do that by using a Channel to pass the items from a background producer coroutine to the foreground consumer. But that's a lot of machinery for a test where we want to keep things simple and easy to read.

To make things easier, we're going to use the open source Turbine library. It simplifies the process of launching a Flow and observing its output while stepping through its code as part of a unit test.

We'll start by adding the Turbine package to our dependencies:

```
testing/v7/build.gradle.kts
dependencies {
  implementation("org.jetbrains.kotlinx:kotlinx-coroutines-core:1.10.1")
  testImplementation(kotlin("test"))
  testImplementation("org.jetbrains.kotlinx:kotlinx-coroutines-test:1.10.1")
➤ testImplementation("app.cash.turbine:turbine:1.2.0")
}
```

With the dependency in place, we've got access to a new test() extension function that we can call on any Flow. Let's put it to use testing the simple code we've just written:

```
testing/v7/src/test/kotlin/com/example/testing/DelayedFlowTest.kt
class DelayedFlowTest {
  @Test
  fun emitNumbersWithDelay() = runTest {
    myFlow.test {
      for (expected in 0..2) {
        expectNoEvents()
        delay(10.seconds)
        assertEquals(expected, expectMostRecentItem())
      }
    }
  }
}
```

Turbine's test() function accepts a block of code where we can make assertions about what's going on. But more importantly, while that's happening, it also launches an additional background coroutine that collects our flow. When we call functions such as expectMostRecentItem(), we receive the values produced by that background coroutine.

With our flow running in Turbine's separate background coroutine, we can observe its execution and output at different points in time. Each time our test() block waits for 10 seconds, we know the flow will have completed 10 seconds of its own execution—so it should have emitted exactly one value. An extra call to expectNoEvents() makes sure we don't see any more values until we've waited another 10 seconds.

Thanks to the runTest() function's virtual clock, all that waiting happens instantly. But the results and the order of operations are the same as they would be if we were dealing with real delays.

Watch Out for Side Effects

With Turbine in your testing toolkit, you can test the output of any asynchronous operation, whether it returns one value or several.

A function's direct outputs aren't the only thing you might want to test. Plenty of functions produce some or all of their outcomes via *side effects*, sending data and signals to other components and systems. Testing a function's side effects can be just as important as making assertions about the data it produces. Turbine can help us out here, too.

For our side-acting function, let's add a simple Observer to the DataProvider we've already written. We'll publish two events—one to announce when the download has started and one to signal that it's finished. As we write the code and its tests, think about what other events you might publish in a real system—such as progress indications during the ongoing download—and how you'd test those.

Here's the code we'll be testing:

```
testing/v7/src/main/kotlin/com/example/testing/DataProvider.kt
fun interface Observer {
  fun notify(event: Event)
  enum class Event { DownloadStarted, DownloadComplete }
}

fun <T> DataProvider<T>.withObserver(observer: Observer) = DataProvider {
  observer.notify(DownloadStarted)
  fetchData().also {
    observer.notify(DownloadComplete)
  }
}
```

In our test, let's start with a DataProvider that includes another short delay. With our Observer in place, we should see the DownloadStarted event as soon as we call our fetchOrDefault() function. Then, after two seconds of virtual delay, we'll see the DownloadComplete event:

```
testing/v7/src/test/kotlin/com/example/testing/DataProviderEventsTest.kt
class DataProviderEventsTest {
  @Test
  fun publishDownloadEvents() = runTest {
    DataProvider { delay(2.seconds) }
      .withObserver { /* TODO: check for events */ }
      .fetchOrDefault(null)
  }
}
```

But what do we put inside our Observer, and how do we check that it's receiving the correct events?

Add Your Own Data

Once again, we want to run our assertions concurrently with the function we're testing. Since we don't have a Flow, we can't use Turbine's built-in test() extension function to create our coroutine and its output channel all in one go. Instead, we'll use the Turbine() constructor function to create a standalone destination for our values. Then, we'll use launch() to start an ordinary coroutine, using the scope that's already provided by our runTest() block:

```
testing/v8/src/test/kotlin/com/example/testing/DataProviderEventsTest.kt
class DataProviderEventsTest {
  @Test
  fun publishDownloadEvents() = runTest {
    val turbine = Turbine<Event>()

    launch {
      DataProvider { delay(2.seconds) }
        .withObserver { event -> turbine.add(event) }
        .fetchOrDefault(null)
    }

    delay(1.seconds)
    assertEquals(DownloadStarted, turbine.expectMostRecentItem())
    turbine.expectNoEvents()
    delay(1.seconds)
    assertEquals(DownloadComplete, turbine.expectMostRecentItem())
  }
}
```

Switching from the prepackaged test() function to a manually constructed Turbine() is a lot like swapping shareIn() for a standalone MutableSharedFlow(). Now, we've got access to an extra add() function, which we can use to send values to our test from any coroutine.

Of course, Turbine isn't the only way to test this code. For this simple scenario, we could even have the observer capture its most recent event in a local variable. But with Turbine, we get a clear and versatile set of functions to control and inspect the code's progress. Check the library's online documentation[1] to find out even more things it can do.

Testing Concurrency

As you learned in Chapter 4, Split Up to Speed Up, on page 59, concurrency lets you define tasks that don't always have to run in the same order. That creates some interesting testing challenges. Not only do you need to make sure that your code will behave correctly when its steps are executed in any possible sequence, but you also need to write tests that can orchestrate each task's timings to reliably reproduce the same snapshot of the system's state. If you thought callback hell was messy, wait till you have to write unit tests for it!

Good tests start with good code, and coroutines already give you the tools to significantly reduce that complexity. Proper use of coroutine scopes will ensure your tests catch every error and wait for every task to finish. Channels give you well-defined points for coroutines to exchange messages, reducing or even eliminating the need for a mutable shared state that might lead to race conditions elsewhere in your code.

---

1. https://github.com/cashapp/turbine

> But your coroutine testing toolkit is also an important piece of the puzzle. By using a single thread and stepping through its coroutines in a predictable order, the runTest() function makes sure a test will always produce the same outcome—no matter what machine you run it on or how many processor cores you have.

Test a Background Task

With the runTest() function and some help from the Turbine library, you've got everything you need to test the outputs and side effects of any suspending function or flow.

Since suspending functions wait for all their work to finish, it's easy to write tests that do the same. But what about functions that don't wait? Let's take a look at a component that uses its own coroutine scope to create and manage background tasks and see how to write tests for those.

We'll start with a simple Activity interface. Like the code we wrote in Chapter 3, Start It, Scope It, Stop It, on page 39, it's going to have a managed lifecycle with onCreate() and onDestroy() methods. You can imagine that these are being called by some framework outside our code's control:

testing/v9/src/main/kotlin/com/example/testing/Activity.kt
```kotlin
interface Activity {
  fun onCreate()
  fun onDestroy()
}
```

Using this interface as our starting point, we'll create a class that runs a background coroutine. It'll use the DataProvider that we've already been using in this chapter:

testing/v9/src/main/kotlin/com/example/testing/DataProviderActivity.kt
```kotlin
class DataProviderActivity<T>(
  private val provider: DataProvider<T>,
  private val observer: Observer
) : Activity {
  private val activityScope = MainScope()

  override fun onCreate() {
    activityScope.launch {
      provider.withObserver(observer).fetchOrDefault(null)
    }
  }

  override fun onDestroy() = activityScope.cancel()
}
```

We won't include any UI code here, but since we're using MainScope(), we'll need to include the Swing dependency that gives us our main-thread coroutine dispatcher—more on that in a moment.

testing/v9/build.gradle.kts

```
dependencies {
  implementation("org.jetbrains.kotlinx:kotlinx-coroutines-core:1.10.1")
➤ runtimeOnly("org.jetbrains.kotlinx:kotlinx-coroutines-swing:1.10.1")
  testImplementation(kotlin("test"))
  testImplementation("org.jetbrains.kotlinx:kotlinx-coroutines-test:1.10.1")
  testImplementation("app.cash.turbine:turbine:1.2.0")
}
```

Over Too Soon

Our onCreate() function doesn't wait for or return a result. That means we'll need to test it via its side effects like we did in our last example. Once again, we'll use a Turbine() to collect and monitor those events it's publishing:

testing/v9/src/test/kotlin/com/example/testing/DataProviderActivityTest.kt

```
class DataProviderActivityTest {
  @Test
  fun publishDownloadEvents() = runTest {
    val turbine = Turbine<Event>()

➤   val provider = DataProvider { delay(2.seconds) }
➤   val observer = Observer { event -> turbine.add(event) }
➤   DataProviderActivity(provider, observer).onCreate()

    delay(1.seconds)
    assertEquals(DownloadStarted, turbine.expectMostRecentItem())
    turbine.expectNoEvents()
    delay(1.seconds)
    assertEquals(DownloadComplete, turbine.expectMostRecentItem())
  }
}
```

Compare this test to the last one we wrote, and you'll see that the assertions, along with much of the setup code, are identical. All we've done is move that launch() block inside our new activity's onCreate() function.

So, what do you think will happen when we run this new test?

```
DataProviderActivityTest > publishDownloadEvents FAILED

java.lang.AssertionError: No item was found
  at app.cash.turbine.ChannelTurbine.expectMostRecentItem(Turbine.kt:206)
```

The test fails, and a little detective work will show that we didn't receive that DownloadCompleted event.

What Went Wrong?

We didn't change much between those last two tests, but the first one passed while the second one failed. This time, the two-second delay() in our test wasn't enough to let the download complete.

What did we do wrong?

The runTest() block has its own coroutine scope, which keeps track of any coroutines it creates. But when we created our DataProviderActivity, we used the MainScope() function to create a whole new coroutine scope.

With no link between the two scopes, our test has no idea that the activity has launched a coroutine, and the activity's coroutine doesn't know that it's running as part of a unit test. If the test doesn't even know the new coroutine exists, there's no way it can wait for it to finish its execution or tell it to skip its delays.

Inject Your Dispatcher

When we introduced virtual time, we briefly mentioned that you could opt out by switching to a different dispatcher. That's because the virtual clock is part of the dispatcher created by the runTest() function. Each call to runTest() creates a dedicated dispatcher for that test—and any coroutines that run on that dispatcher will be controlled and monitored by that test.

To let our test know about our activity's extra coroutines, all we need to do is have them run on the test's own dispatcher. So, how do we do that?

One simple way is to add a constructor parameter to the class we're testing. The crucial item we'll need to pass in is a CoroutineDispatcher. But let's make our updated constructor a little more versatile. Instead of asking for a dispatcher, we'll accept any CoroutineContext item. This will let us pass in our dispatcher, but it'll also accept other context elements or even none at all:

```kotlin
testing/v10/src/main/kotlin/com/example/testing/DataProviderActivity.kt
class DataProviderActivity<T>(
  private val provider: DataProvider<T>,
  private val observer: Observer,
  coroutineContext: CoroutineContext = EmptyCoroutineContext
) : Activity {
  private val activityScope = MainScope() + coroutineContext

  override fun onCreate() {
    activityScope.launch {
      provider.withObserver(observer).fetchOrDefault(null)
    }
  }
}
```

```
override fun onDestroy() = activityScope.cancel()
}
```

To add our new context to our coroutine scope, we're using the scope's handy *plus* (+) operator. Coroutine context is built up from left to right, so if our new constructor argument contains any items, they'll replace the ones the scope started out with.

Context Overrides

 Each CoroutineContext can contain one element of each type—one Dispatcher, one Job, one CoroutineExceptionHandler, and so on. Add a new element to an existing context, and it'll replace any previous element of the same type.

What about that default EmptyCoroutineContext value? It contains no items, so it won't replace anything from the original scope, and the context will stay the same.

Pass the Context

Inside our test, we can use the runTest() block's coroutineContext property to get hold of its current dispatcher. We'll take that value and pass it to our modified constructor, where it'll replace the MainScope() function's starting choice of Dispatchers.Main:

```
testing/v10/src/test/kotlin/com/example/testing/DataProviderActivityTest.kt
class DataProviderActivityInjectTest {
  @Test
  fun publishDownloadEvents() = runTest {
    val turbine = Turbine<Event>()
    val provider = DataProvider { delay(2.seconds) }
    val observer = Observer { event -> turbine.add(event) }

    val dispatcher = coroutineContext[CoroutineDispatcher]!!
    DataProviderActivity(provider, observer, dispatcher).onCreate()

    delay(1.seconds)
    assertEquals(DownloadStarted, turbine.expectMostRecentItem())
    turbine.expectNoEvents()
    delay(1.seconds)
    assertEquals(DownloadComplete, turbine.expectMostRecentItem())
  }
}
```

Run the test now, and it works as expected. Both the runTest() block and the coroutines it's testing are using the same dispatcher with the same virtual clock. When we delay() the test by two virtual seconds, the coroutine inside our activity sees the time advance by the same amount.

Dependency Injection

 Passing in a dispatcher from outside is often referred to as *injecting* a dispatcher. It's a simple form of dependency injection where a class asks for the other objects it needs instead of creating them.

Any time you launch a new coroutine or switch an existing one to a new dispatcher, think about how you're going to test it. If you can swap out its dispatcher during tests, you'll unlock several important benefits. First, coroutines that call delay() will finish faster, thanks to virtual time. Second, you'll be able to control time from within the test itself, using virtual delays to advance the clock one step at a time. Third, the test gains the ability to monitor the success or failure of coroutines outside its own Job hierarchy.

What Have You Learned?

You know how to test timeouts and delays without slowing down your builds and inspect the outputs and side effects of code that's running in a background task. You've completed your coroutine journey and picked up the testing tools you'll need to ship your asynchronous upgrades with confidence. Congratulations!

No book can hope to cover every concurrency conundrum or anticipate every asynchronous API. But now that you understand the design goals at the heart of Kotlin's suspending functions, you're ready to start inventing your own solutions. Combine your new testing knowledge with all the tools and tips you've learned, and you'll write asynchronous code that you, your teammates, and your customers can trust.

You've got everything you need. Now go launch some coroutines!

Key Concepts

Virtual time

This lets you test all your delays and timeouts without waiting for them to complete in real time. It's always enabled for coroutines dispatched inside a runTest() block.

Dispatcher injection

This brings outside coroutines under the control of your tests, letting them use the test dispatcher's virtual clock. If your component creates a coroutine scope, be sure to give your tests a way to replace its dispatcher.

Index

Thank you!

We hope you enjoyed this book and that you're already thinking about what you want to learn next. To help make that decision easier, we're offering you this gift.

Head on over to https://pragprog.com right now, and use the coupon code BUYANOTHER2025 to save 30% on your next ebook. Offer is void where prohibited or restricted. This offer does not apply to any edition of *The Pragmatic Programmer* ebook.

And if you'd like to share your own expertise with the world, why not propose a writing idea to us? After all, many of our best authors started off as our readers, just like you. With up to a 50% royalty, world-class editorial services, and a name you trust, there's nothing to lose. Visit https://pragprog.com/become-an-author/ today to learn more and to get started.

Thank you for your continued support. We hope to hear from you again soon!

The Pragmatic Bookshelf

SAVE 30%!
Use coupon code
BUYANOTHER2025

Kotlin and Android Development featuring Jetpack

Start building native Android apps the modern way in Kotlin with Jetpack's expansive set of tools, libraries, and best practices. Learn how to create efficient, resilient views with Fragments and share data between the views with ViewModels. Use Room to persist valuable data quickly, and avoid NullPointerExceptions and Java's verbose expressions with Kotlin. You can even handle asynchronous web service calls elegantly with Kotlin coroutines. Achieve all of this and much more while building two full-featured apps, following detailed, step-by-step instructions.

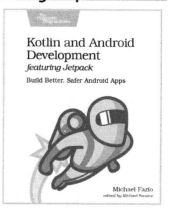

Michael Fazio
(444 pages) ISBN: 9781680508154. $49.95
https://pragprog.com/book/mfjetpack

Programming Kotlin

Programmers don't just use Kotlin, they love it. Even Google has adopted it as a first-class language for Android development. With Kotlin, you can intermix imperative, functional, and object-oriented styles of programming and benefit from the approach that's most suitable for the problem at hand. Learn to use the many features of this highly concise, fluent, elegant, and expressive statically typed language with easy-to-understand examples. Learn to write maintainable, high-performing JVM and Android applications, create DSLs, program asynchronously, and much more.

Venkat Subramaniam
(460 pages) ISBN: 9781680506358. $51.95
https://pragprog.com/book/vskotlin

Agile Web Development with Rails 8

The eighth major release of Rails focuses on the ability to produce production-ready applications. It achieves this while building upon and retaining the ability to produce fantastic user experiences, and achieves all the benefits of single-page applications at a fraction of the complexity. Rails 8 introduces Kamal 2, Thruster, new database adapters, replaces the asset pipeline, and adds a new authentication generator. The result is a toolkit so powerful that it allows a single individual to create modern applications upon which they can build a competitive business—the way it used to be.

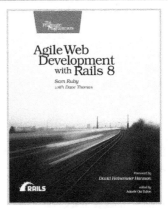

Sam Ruby
(488 pages) ISBN: 9798888651346. $67.95
https://pragprog.com/book/rails8

Next-Level A/B Testing

The better the tools you have in your experimentation toolkit, the better off teams will be shipping and evaluating new features on a product. Learn how to create robust A/B testing strategies that evolve with your product and engineering needs. See how to run experiments quickly, efficiently, and at less cost with the overarching goal of improving your product experience and your company's bottom line.

Leemay Nassery
(226 pages) ISBN: 9798888651308. $53.95
https://pragprog.com/book/abtestprac

The Pragmatic Bookshelf

The Pragmatic Bookshelf features books written by professional developers for professional developers. The titles continue the well-known Pragmatic Programmer style and continue to garner awards and rave reviews. As development gets more and more difficult, the Pragmatic Programmers will be there with more titles and products to help you stay on top of your game.

Visit Us Online

This Book's Home Page
https://pragprog.com/book/sckotlin
Source code from this book, errata, and other resources. Come give us feedback, too!

Keep Up-to-Date
https://pragprog.com
Join our announcement mailing list (low volume) or follow us on Twitter @pragprog for new titles, sales, coupons, hot tips, and more.

New and Noteworthy
https://pragprog.com/news
Check out the latest Pragmatic developments, new titles, and other offerings.

Save on the ebook

Save on the ebook versions of this title. Owning the paper version of this book entitles you to purchase the electronic versions at a terrific discount.

PDFs are great for carrying around on your laptop—they are hyperlinked, have color, and are fully searchable. Most titles are also available for the iPhone and iPod touch, Amazon Kindle, and other popular e-book readers.

Send a copy of your receipt to support@pragprog.com and we'll provide you with a discount coupon.

Contact Us

Online Orders:	*https://pragprog.com/catalog*
Customer Service:	*support@pragprog.com*
International Rights:	*translations@pragprog.com*
Academic Use:	*academic@pragprog.com*
Write for Us:	*http://write-for-us.pragprog.com*

www.ingramcontent.com/pod-product-compliance
Lightning Source LLC
LaVergne TN
LVHW081338050326
832903LV00024B/1194